The Gamemakers

The Gamemakers

By Jack Clary

Illustrations by Dick Oden

A National Football League Book
Follett Publishing Company
Chicago, Illinois

To my wife Pat, who knows
there aren't ever enough words.

Contents

Page

Introduction 8

Paul Brown · Cincinnati Bengals 14

Chuck Knox · Los Angeles Rams 48

Tom Landry · Dallas Cowboys 82

John Madden · Oakland Raiders 108

Chuck Noll · Pittsburgh Steelers 132

O. A. (Bum) Phillips · Houston Oilers 162

John Ralston · Denver Broncos 192

Don Shula · Miami Dolphins 224

Introduction

Vince Lombardi saw a football organization as a microcosm of many things—of society, of business, of free enterprise—and himself as president and chairman of the board.

"Football teams are no different from any other groups," he said. "They are good examples of success and failure, of competence and incompetence, of inspiration and dullness."

Vince Lombardi intrigued America as perhaps no pro football coach before him or after him has ever done. As much as a football coach, he was a philosopher—though not always intentionally. Vince Lombardi would say something to his team—or write it on a blackboard or put it in a playbook—and other people would trip over themselves in a rush to apply it to things other than football.

Consider some of the words of Vince Lombardi:

"The will to excel and the will to win, they endure. They are more important than any events that occasion them."

"I demand a commitment to excellence and to victory and that is what life is all about."

"If we would create something we must be something."

"Some guys play with their heads. That's okay. You've got to be smart to be number one in any business. But more important, you've got to play with your heart—with every fiber of your body. If you're lucky enough to find a guy with a lot of head *and* a lot of heart, he's never going to come off the field second."

"The word 'selflessness' as opposed to 'selfishness' is what I try to teach."

"When you win you get a feeling of exhilaration. When you lose you get a feeling of resolution. You resolve never to lose again."

"Mental toughness is many things. It is humility, because I think it behooves all of us to remember that simplicity is the sign of greatness and meekness is the sign of true strength. Mental toughness is Spartanism with those qualities of sacrifice, self-denial, dedication. It is fearlessness and it is love."

"Contrary to the opinion of many people, leaders are not born. Leaders are made, and they are made by effort and hard work."

"Regardless of what you do put in, every game boils down to doing the things you do best and doing them over and over again."

"Some of us will do our jobs well and some will not, but we will all be judged by only one thing—the result."

"Winning isn't everything, but making the effort to win is."

Lombardi took his messages to the world of business, too. He spoke to business groups; he did a sales motivational film called "Second Effort" that remains one of the biggest successes of its kind; he taped a series of inspirational messages.

In actuality, a coach really is no different than any successful businessman because he has the same responsibilities; only his product is different. The key to the coach's success, like that of anyone in business, is the ability to work with people. Most coaches have the ability to organize and communicate. Some are smarter than others; some are more conscious of details than others; some are more compassionate.

Like the successful business executive, the successful coach is the one who assumes an intelligent approach to his game. He is one who acquires intelligent people to work for him, who is able to teach, who is able to recognize talent, who has the mental and emotional ability to cope with the range of strengths and weaknesses that are on every team and in every organization. Through all of this he builds a human structure, held together by organization and discipline.

The players on a team are no different from the employees in a business. The coach is in charge of the players and how they function under his control; the executive is in charge of the employees. Both jobs require dedication, perseverance, and intelligence.

A coach can be a genius at producing mind-boggling formations and exciting plays but if he cannot relate to the players, it's not likely that he will succeed. A businessman can be a genius with figures or in solving production problems but if he cannot communicate that information to his employees, he will not get results.

Increased interest in pro football in recent years has made Americans more aware of the parallels between the sport and the business world.

In 1967, when he still was at Green Bay, Lombardi was asked to be a keynote speaker at a luncheon session in New York attended by more than a thousand members of the prestigious American Management Association. A snowstorm caused him to be two hours late yet everyone waited to hear him.

When Lombardi arrived he told them, "The strength of a company or a team is in the will of the leaders. If the manager is weak-willed, the company will be poorly directed. A leader in any field must have character and that character is developed through self-discipline.

"A leader must be able to direct people but he also must be able to make people willing to accept direction. Mental toughness is the key to the development of character, the most successful ingredient in leadership. The standards of a team or a company are based on those that are practiced, not only those promulgated, by the management."

The impact was stunning. The businessmen, knowledgeable in the teachings of Harvard's Graduate School of Business and other such institutions around the country, as well as from their own experience, had never heard the fundamental principles of coaching applied so realistically to their own situations. They gave Lombardi a thunderous ovation. Men actually stood on their chairs.

Lombardi later developed a series of taped instructional talks on the overlapping responsibilities and principles shared by professional football coaches and businessmen. The program was tremendously successful.

Lombardi practiced what he preached, as a coach and as an executive. He ran the front office of both the Packers (from 1959-68) and Washington Redskins (in 1969 and until his death in September, 1970). His teams annually turned a business volume in the millions of dollars and he was responsible to the stockholders of each team to prove that his principles were sound and effective.

"Running a football team," he once said, "is no different from running any other kind of organization—an army, a political party, a business. The principles are the same. The objective is to win—to beat the other guy. Maybe that sounds hard or cruel but I don't think it is. It's a reality of life that men are competitive and the most competitive games draw the most competitive men."

He would time and again urge his nonfootball listeners to set an example by leadership. He was only preaching what he practiced. Lombardi appreciated the sacrifices a player's family was forced to make during the season and it was not unusual for him to present the Packers' wives with fur coats or diamond pins after a championship season. He would blast players such as Paul Hornung and Max McGee on the practice field, but he counseled people such as Bart Starr and Ray Nitschke in the privacy of his office.

That was Lombardi the psychologist, the master handler of men. He made his players believe in themselves.

That is the role of the coach, of any leader in sports or outside of sports. Don Shula went to Miami, a team in its fifth season, and brought it home a winner in his first season as coach. He had it in the Super Bowl in his second year and won the NFL championship the next two years. He turned the organization into a first-class football business.

Shula also addresses business meetings and conventions, speaking about the principles that were successful for him. He talks about personnel management, motivation, achievement, pride of accomplishment, and execution.

If there is an area where coach and businessman find different stresses it is in the teaching function. The successful coaches put constant stress on teaching and take pains to hire assistants who are good teachers. The teams that win are those that are most soundly schooled in fundamentals. Those are the things that require work every day, from the time training camp begins until the final practice session of Super Bowl week. Not every head coach is an expert teacher but every one of them believes in its importance. Shula himself admits his first great mistake as a coach was in not insisting on stressing fundamentals in his first coaching season with the Baltimore Colts. He felt that a veteran team like the Colts had such things perfected, but he found to his disappointment that there is no such thing as "having things like fundamentals down pat." Since that year, he has not taken a team through a season without a thorough and constant stress on fundamentals.

This idea was given impetus by Paul Brown when he organized the Cleveland Browns in 1946. He was a teacher by profession, a man who had taught in high school, in prep school, and at Ohio State. He believed that the football field was nothing more than another classroom. It is one reason why he developed the idea of having each player maintain his own playbook so he could study off the field what he had learned at practice. Those who were exposed to Brown and became coaches of their own teams carried his ideas about teaching with them.

Teaching really is a form of motivation, and it is the kind of motivation that is preferred by most coaches. The motivation comes when a team realizes that it can handle any situation or overcome any obstacle. Some coaches—John Ralston and, to some extent, Chuck Knox—advocate more programmed methods of motivation and these also have been successful.

Bud Grant of the Minnesota Vikings is a good example of a rulesmaker. Many coaches allow players to follow their own personal hair styles, but the Vikings have relatively short hair. Most wide receivers "spike" the ball in the end zone after a touchdown, but the Vikings either drop it once the official's signal is made or hand the ball to him. Some team's bench areas are an indistinguishable maze of players wandering back and forth, but Grant has his offensive players on one side, his defensive players on the other. The same subdued manner is evident in the team's dressing room. It's a relatively quiet place. The players reflect the coach who established his principles in his first year and has seen them accepted and passed on by the team's players.

Coaches who have tried to be someone other than themselves also have failed because sooner or later—and particularly in stress situations—they revert back to that real self. Players will not respond to this kind of dishonesty.

When Lombardi was coaching the Packers he heard frequent criticism about his "unimaginative" offense. "I don't give a hoot in hell if they say Lombardi doesn't have any imagination," he said. "I'm winning and that's what I'm getting paid for. The day I start losing they'll say, 'Lombardi has great imagination but he's not coaching at Green Bay any more.'"

Grant has heard the same criticism and so has Shula, George Allen, Chuck Knox, and Chuck Noll. But their style of football reflects their personalities and it has been successful for them.

Some coaches agonize for days after a loss and others vent their emotions in a good crying session. Grant does not dwell on the game just passed. "It is ancient history," he says, "and all you can do is examine the positives and negatives you learned from it and go on to the next opponent." It is hard to tell from looking at Grant whether his team has won or lost a game when it is over. It is also just as impossible to draw out his so-called "football philosophy." Some coaches will talk for hours about the subject, but he abhors all such discussions. He says they lead to a "rigidity of the mind," and adds, "besides, what good is it if situations are constantly changing?

"One precept I've always followed is in getting the big things done first and *then* doing the little things. And it's not a contradiction to say that the more you structure yourself, the more efficient you'll be."

That is Bud Grant. He delegates a great deal of authority to his assistant coaches and allows them to assume all of it. He stands as overseer. So do most coaches, though some—Noll or Knox for examples—will get into a teaching situation and assume that role.

Grant's assistants make up the game plan and then the entire staff goes about the task of "selling" its efficacy to the team. "They are the ones who must execute it so they are the ones who must believe in it," he says. "If there are parts they don't believe in and we can agree with their objections we throw it out. Above all we try to convince them of how it will work by proving what we have devised has the best chance to succeed because of the tendencies of this particular opponent."

Some observers are convinced that all pressure is self-induced, and that those able to cope with it will do so. They maintain that those who can handle pressure will be able to work comfortably at the job and still maintain a life outside. Noll is a good example; so is Grant. Noll leaves his football work in the office, spends as much time as possible with his family, is a patron of the arts, and has unbridled energy for hobbies such as scuba diving, flying, and gardening. Grant is well known for his love of the outdoors. More than just a hunter, he relishes the challenges of nature and its preservation. This does not diminish his capacity for work nor the intensity that he views as necessary to his job. That he has been able to do both is a measure of the way in which he has mastered the pressures of his profession.

Eight coaches are examined in this book and they are as different as they are the same. They share a common desire to control—each of them is an overachiever—and each of them is a literal winner.

But there are differences—some subtle, some obvious—in their modes and methods.

Perhaps you will find yourself in one of them. Perhaps that man will help you organize your life better. Or perhaps he will help you to better understand the game of pro football and the coach's role in it.

Paul Brown

"People think there are great mysteries connected with this game, but there are not. It's just teaching fundamentals."

A late July sun blistered the midlands but not many people in the small Ohio town of Bowling Green paid attention to the large young men who began to arrive at the bus and railroad stations and converge on the modest campus of its small teachers' college in the summer of 1946. The men carried cardboard suitcases, battered leather cases or GI duffle bags that only a few months before had transported home some personal effects from distant lands.

As they trudged up the white steps of the Alpha Xi Delta sorority house, a lean, intent-looking man greeted them.

"Hello," he said, "I'm Paul Brown. Welcome to the Cleveland Browns."

Twenty-two years later, in 1968, a new group of players invaded the Ohio town of Wilmington. As the young men entered a red brick building on the small, tree-shrouded campus of Wilmington College, a still-lean, but now bald man with sharp, alert eyes greeted each of them.

"Hello," he said, "I'm Paul Brown. Welcome to the Cincinnati Bengals."

The men Paul Brown first greeted in 1946 were considered good football players, hand-picked by him because of proven skills. In many cases those skills had been dulled along the hedgerows of France or in the jungle underbrush of a Pacific island. But Paul Brown had the sharpening tool.

But the men Brown greeted in 1968 were different. Their skills were suspect or they would not have been there. They were the castoffs from an expansion draft of the eight other American Football League teams. Or they were eager rookies.

In 1946, few people outside the state of Ohio really knew Paul Brown. He had coached Ohio State University to the national collegiate football championship four years earlier and had been successful as head coach of the Great Lakes Naval Training Center during the war. But he was best known for an incredible 80 victories in eight seasons at Massillon High School, in the eastern part of Ohio.

15

In 1968, there was hardly a football fan who *didn't* know Paul Brown. He had achieved the rare distinction of becoming a "living legend" with the successes he achieved as coach of the Cleveland Browns for 17 years. He had accumulated honors and awards.

Ironically, more was remembered about the alleged shortcomings in his personality than about the principles that resulted in unmatched successes. The critics claimed he was cold, aloof, and tyrannical.

The success that had been forged by tireless work, marvelous innovation, and unwavering trust in his own system was put down as outmoded. The man, they said, had lost touch with the game—a severe indictment for any coach.

But Paul Brown never had lost touch with the game of football. Far from it. From the days when he was founding the Cleveland Browns through his last season as a coach in 1975, there was little variation in the way he approached the game.

Or, for that matter, there was little variation in approach from the time Brown coached at Severn Prep in Annapolis, Maryland, or at Massillon High, Ohio State, or Great Lakes.

That has nothing to do with the Xs and Os. They always are the variables in football. The real strength of the man lies within his spirit. This never has changed. He added his own method of achieving and little changed from the time he left Miami University in Oxford, Ohio, in 1930 and took his first coaching job. In recent years a few concessions crept in, but there were no radical changes.

Every so often there arises a need to set the record straight about who Paul Brown is and exactly what he is like . . . what he did and how he did it.

During pro football's labor-management problems early in 1975, it became popular to add, after noting that the Cincinnati Bengals voted not to strike and to accept management proposals, ". . . of course, they're coached by Paul Brown. . . ."

It was as if Brown had reached down and marked the ballots or had so controlled the minds of his players that they had little recourse than to favor management's view.

"It makes me sick to hear that stuff," said Bob Johnson, center and captain of the Bengals. "I like the man. He's a great coach, but he gets a lot of bum raps for being something that he is not. It's about time people began to look at exactly what he has done and how he's done it before they cast their criticisms."

Who is Paul Brown?

Well, besides being possibly the best coach since the game came from its dark ages, he also is the man who would keep candy in the top drawer of his desk at training camp for the children of his assistant coaches. And he's the man who willingly sought to assume a second family following the death of his first wife, Katie.

"I've got no generation gap problems," he'll tell you proudly of his relationship with his teen-age twin daughters. "We understand each other perfectly. In fact, they keep me young."

Friends in Cincinnati recall seeing Brown at the airport one day a couple of years ago, swinging along with arms around both girls, laughing and talking. He is the Paul Brown who became the first football coach to advance money to his players to help them purchase homes when he coached the Browns; and who insisted that his Cleveland players finish their college educations after they had signed with his first team.

Paul Brown is reflective of his early surroundings, the factories and mills of the upper Ohio River Valley. Even today, in the age of space and computer technology, the work ethic dominates this area and men with arms like locomotive drive shafts are the backbone of its society.

Brown is straightforward, regulates his speech to those words necessary to convey a message, and never leaves a listener in doubt as to what he means.

Yet, with this businesslike attitude, he is a pleasant man who has many friends. He is no backslapper when meeting them in social situations, preferring to maintain a low key, pleasant mien. Bob Trumpy, one of his players, lives in the same suburban area of Cincinnati and in the warmer months often meets his boss when Brown takes the usual nightly stroll that always has been a part of his life.

"He'll stop with his wife and chat for a bit, as friendly and considerate as any other neighbor," Trumpy says. "You'd never know he was the most successful football coach in pro history. He can melt into his environment in a very natural manner and you accept him for it."

Among the wealthiest men in professional football, Brown knows the good things of life and how to appreciate them. He still drives a brown Cadillac.

"Some people say I'm old fashioned," he says without rancor, "but my family doesn't think so. The team must not think so either because many of them spread the word around the clubhouse and it's accepted.

"I really never have cared what people outside my family have thought about my beliefs. I never worry what my friends think because they wouldn't be my friends if they did not embrace most of the things which appeal to us. What is right is right, whether it was at Massillon High School in 1932 or in the National Football League in 1976. Those are the principles which guide my life."

Brown does not moralize about good or evil; he demands that which is good be the standard, period. He once criticized those of the early All-America Football Conference founders who would sign collegians who had not finished their eligibility, but he signed many from his Ohio State teams with eligibility remaining when they returned from the war. The rationale for it being correct was that he demanded in their contract they get their degrees in the off-season; and then pointed out that their only means of economic survival—and the difference between getting and not getting that degree—was playing professional football.

He stood on the sidelines at a game, stoic. On a television screen, where most have seen him, he looks so angry, intense. It was this appearance that gave birth to much of the false impressions during his halcyon days with the Browns.

When a game was finished, he trotted off briskly—a lot brisker than usual for a man in his late 60s—to his team's dressing room. Once inside, he thanked the players for their efforts and, if victory had been achieved, offered his congratulations. There were no victory shouts in this environment. You just didn't approach him that way. But there was no denying the warmth that seemed to abound within the family-style atmosphere he tried to create.

He told his players to "call me Paul." Few did. It was "coach Brown," even for many who had been with him since the beginning of the Bengals' franchise.

There is no question that he was a most demanding coach. There is not a successful coach in pro football's history who wasn't the same way, in his own style. Lombardi's image was that of a driver . . . Tom Landry of a robot . . . George Halas of a tyrant.

Each had qualities that enabled him to survive and excel. All successful coaches have had the respect of their teams—maybe not complete concurrence nor absolute popularity—but the respect that when they laid out a plan, it was the best possible one for the team's good.

That's one of the reasons Brown laughs today when people tell him, "You're not such a bad guy after all."

"All that business about me being cold and aloof was so much press stuff, cranked out mainly by the New York writers when we had our great rivalry between the Giants and Browns," he says. "We were a successful team right from the start in the NFL and to beat us was a real feat. We had some great games with the Giants but always it seemed to be Paul Brown who was coming to town.

"A lot of people seemed to forget I brought along a lot of pretty talented players who went out and did all the work. But it was good for the sport in those days and I really don't mind what people think. It's my players who concern me . . . they always did. Look at the record. That'll tell you more about me and my teams."

Still lean, his stern features punctuated by a sharp nose and piercing eyes melt easily into smiles or laughter as he recalls past days. He's an emotional man to the extent that he has deep feelings for those who played for him and for the sport itself.

People have seen him cry after particularly special moments, like the game in 1970 when his Bengals beat the Browns at Cincinnati and presented him with the game ball. He had left Cleveland seven years before, had become a virtual exile from pro football, then returned to exact what he felt was some measure of overdue satisfaction from the team which had cast him aside.

With the sentimentality, there also is a great pride. In his own way, he covets his successes and takes quiet satisfaction every time he hears of his former assistants referred to as being "a pupil of Paul Brown." Like most coaches, he is as reluctant to heap gushy praise on his successful ex-players-turned-coaches and takes great delight when his own team can beat them.

It was partly his own pride that caused confrontations in Cleveland when Art Modell secured control of the Browns in the early 1960s. There is little doubt that Brown resented a newcomer—and non-football person at that—becoming involved in the day-by-day operation of the team. This was something that had been his domain since the club's founding in 1946 and a position that he was unwilling to share.

It was also the reason that, in dictating the terms of his return to the NFL in Cincinnati, he acquired the only voting stock in the ownership group even though he did not become a majority Bengals' stockholder. The other owners merely have certificates.

"I appoint the board of directors," he says. "I wouldn't have come back unless I was in complete charge. I had it both ways in Cleveland. The players know they cannot bypass me and go to the general manager or the owners. It gives me great advantage over other coaches.

"That is the way it must be. Any other way and in time you'll see the whole structure begin to crumble, and all at once a good team will begin to slide. It's inevitable. Look at the history of great football teams and you'll see all the authority concentrated in the coach."

There is, of course, an oblique reference to his final seasons in Cleveland where he did not have such authority. He always felt the players had easy access to Modell and whenever they did not like his dictums, they would try to undercut his authority with the young owner. Ultimately, the players, notably Jimmy Brown, took credit for forcing the change of coaches with the Browns, toppling what amounted to the Rock of Gibralter of professional football.

Regardless, when Paul Brown plays football, it is his ball and you play and work under his rules or you don't play for him. He has his hand into every facet of the team's operation just as he did in Cleveland. One of the key elements in his success is the people around him—both on and off the football field. It also is one reason for the outstanding success of men who once worked for him and moved on. They were destined for success.

His son, Mike, is assistant general manager; another son, Pete, is director of player personnel. That's not nepotism; both are highly qualified football executives but they also fill key positions in the organization.

Such links are strong evidence of the first commandment of Brown's success—strong organization. He is the first to admit it.

"I believe in being prepared," he says. "Football is war, you know. And wars are won by the army that's fit and ready. That's why I'm such a nut on the subject."

It was that way from the first day he received the coaching job in the All-America Football Conference at Cleveland. A man who never has forgotten a good football player or coach either playing for or against him, he hand-picked that first Browns' team and kept its nucleus intact for 11 seasons during which time he won all four AAFC titles and three of six NFL titles.

He planned out every detail of every day his team was together, beginning with his opening remarks at training camp through the time his team would begin pregame warmups in the championship game. A great many of the innovations with which he has been credited have been the result of this attention to organization—the desire to see that no one better his team. It's one of the reasons he became the first to employ a coaching staff year around; to utilize classroom and teaching techniques usually attributed to non-football learning; to use playbooks and grade players after film study; and to use intelligence tests as a clue to a player's learning potential.

His innovativeness with the Xs and Os has been even more lasting and significant. In addition to being the first to develop detailed pass patterns that opened specific areas of a defense, he also detailed the use of the zone pass defense. All a team needed, he reckoned, was to have one weak link in its man-for-man pass coverage and it was dead.

"You must protect him with a zone coverage," he said. And the elaborate and much-publicized zone defenses of the Baltimore Colts and Miami Dolphins under Don Shula, and those used by Sid Gillman, Chuck Noll, Weeb Ewbank, and Blanton Collier all evolved from this system. In fact, the basic structure of these defenses was built over a quarter century ago on the practice fields of Ohio State, Great Lakes, and the Cleveland Browns.

The combination of his sophisticated pass offense and evenly structured pass defense tore apart the basic elements of what, in 1950 when the Browns entered the NFL, was called the Eagle defense. He had his offensive linemen take wider splits than used then and this forced the defensive linemen to spread with them. The plan of cutting off the running game inside, and of allowing linebackers to help with pass coverage to the outside, and holding up wide receivers was defeated because they were forced to fill the wide gaps in the line.

"A lot of people accepted our zone defense because no one could keep up, man-for-man, with Dante Lavelli, Dub Jones, and Mac Speedie," he said. "Others who played for me got ingrained with our system but they changed some things and added their own thoughts. No one can be like anyone else," he maintains.

"He made it a joke to play some other teams when he was riding high in Cleveland," Ratterman recalls. "He simply outorganized them, and then outcoached them."

Others think he has been so successful because, as Graham puts it, "he just outworks everybody else. His secret is hard work," says Graham. "I don't think that Paul knows any more football or is smarter than the other smart coaches."

There is disagreement there, too. Bobby Mitchell, who once played for Brown in Cleveland, and bridled at his treatment, remembered scouting the Bengals for the Redskins and watching them beat a much more experienced Detroit Lions' team. Someone asked Mitchell how this could happen.

"It sure wasn't a case of Cincinnati having better material," he said. "The man simply outcoached them."

After the Bengals had upset the Kansas City Chiefs in 1969—the year the Chiefs were en route to a Super Bowl IV championship—Curtis McClinton was asked how such a thing could happen. He simply picked up a program, turned to a page where he found a picture of Brown, and then pointed to the picture.

Some of his Cincinnati players see his success in broader terms. Defensive back Tommy Casanova says that Brown surrounded himself with great assistant coaches, dedicated his life to only his team and his family, had unparalleled experience that guided him from pitfalls, and was a master organizer.

"Everything," Casanova says, "worked to complement something else."

Bob Trumpy, tight end on the Bengals, says flatly that it was Brown's attention to detail and the unwavering faith he had in his own system.

"He believed that football is like a golf swing," Trumpy says. "First it is taught, then it is learned, and then it must be groomed. If all else fails, go back to fundamentals."

All of this adds up to credibility and communication in Brown's book. He doesn't single out any one particular strength as being the key to his success.

"Judgment of personnel is a vital factor," he says. "Then you've got to be able to get along with them and have them be at their best. You do this by organizing things well enough so that they believe in what you are doing."

Blanton Collier knows all about that. He joined Brown as an assistant coach at Great Lakes in 1945 and became the first coach to be hired by him at Cleveland. The two coached together at Cleveland until 1954 when Collier left to become head coach at Kentucky, and then succeeded Brown as the Browns' head coach in 1963.

"There was a total positive attitude in everything Paul did," Collier says. "Everything was planned to the most minute detail. For the first four or five years of the eight I was with him in Cleveland, each player and each coach wrote everything that was in the playbook. I mean, we sat there and wrote down what he dictated to us.

"Each coach had to write out what he was going to teach. Then you dictated that to the players and they wrote it in longhand. That meant drawing up every play that went into our system.

"Nothing was left to chance. We even practiced how to practice. We had a complete session of how to go on the field. We had a practice routine whereby every player would be in his classroom seat, in complete uniform at a specific time.

"We'd get the plan for the day and went out on the field together. We'd go through calisthenics, fundamental drills, form type of blocking and tackling. We would practice going out on the field so that each coach would know where his unit would work. And that's where we would work.

"On the day of a game, we'd go out on the field the same way, to the same areas and everything would be as we had practiced it during the week."

In training camp, both at Cleveland and Cincinnati, Brown's team would get one running play in the morning and one passing play in the afternoon. On the previous night, the players would look at movies of the play being run the previous season and discuss its strong and weak points. Then the club would be broken down into units and each unit would be given its particular role in making that play successful.

"The next day," Collier said, "the practice drills were based on a player's particular assignment for that play. Everything would be geared to executing that assignment perfectly. What happened is that drills would become an accumulation of assignments and fundamentals required for each of those plays. Paul was very meticulous and demanding about how they should be carried out."

Mike McCormack was a player and team captain under Brown at Cleveland and later worked as assistant coach under Vince Lombardi and George Allen before becoming head coach of the Philadelphia Eagles. McCormack is now offensive line coach for the Bengals under coach Bill Johnson. He agrees with this approach.

"Paul was completely different than Allen and Lombardi in that he believed in basic fundamentals all the way through," McCormack says. "There was no room for error;

everyone knew his job and he was going to execute. Each man was trained to build confidence in the football team, so much so that everyone on the team firmly believed that it was so much better in certain areas than anyone we would play.

"With Paul Brown, you had confidence in the man on either side of you, that every man around you was going to do his job perfectly so you could not lose."

Lombardi and Allen were radically different. The former bullied his players to be physically better than an opponent and he put them through such a rigorous camp that they eventually were. He preached constantly that he wanted his team strong enough so that it never lost in the fourth quarter.

Allen spends most of his training camp time in building up the veteran players and weeding out the rookies. It's his announced theory that for every rookie in the starting lineup, there will be a lost game through the season. He works on his veterans and preaches that they have something to prove and pays them well to prove it. There is very little time spent teaching, something in which both Brown and Lombardi firmly believed.

"The one common strain between all three," McCormack says, echoing Trumpy's appraisal, "is that they firmly believed their system is the only way to do it. And they never deviated from it."

Brown was the first coach to put so much stress on the mental part of football. Probably no coach ever has demanded less of his players physically on the practice field, nor asked for more in the precision with which they carry out their assignments. That meant that linemen must space themselves to the exact inch between each other so that there be as little margin for error as possible.

"It's a fact of life," Brown says in looking to the strong emphasis he puts on classroom work. "A pro football coach is a teacher, no matter what. The players must learn. No matter what you teach you must get people to want to learn. It was the basic tenet of my coaching at Massillon, Ohio State, Great Lakes, Cleveland, and Cincinnati. People think there are great mysteries attached to this game but there are not. It comes down to fundamentals and they must be taught."

Those who know him well attest to the fact. They'll even tell you that a lot of the Xs and Os being used today are pretty well put in place the way they first were placed back on the blackboards in Cleveland a couple of decades ago. Brown himself chuckles when asked sometimes to trace the origin of a player or coach. Ultimately, it leads back to Cleveland, where it almost seems everything in football today had its beginning.

And if a "beginning" can have a beginning, then all the success that was achieved by Paul Brown started on the barren playing field of Massillon, Ohio, where Dave Stewart coached high school football back in the 1920s. As Paul Brown has been to such as Ewbank, Collier, Shula, and Noll, so Stewart was to Paul Brown.

"Dave Stewart had a way of doing things that impressed me even as a high school kid," Brown says. "He first of all put great emphasis on teaching, on stressing fundamentals. Our high school practices more than fifty years ago were nothing more than extensions of our classroom work. Only the subject matter was different.

"He put coaching on a high level with this approach and it is one that I adopted from the first moment I stepped onto that field in Annapolis. For me, teaching became an obsession as it related to my coaching. And as a coach, I had no other interest outside of my family."

Stewart was a math teacher at Massillon, a member of the school's faculty who also had the job of coaching football. But in the eyes of the lean teen-ager, it didn't seem to be a job.

"I saw him work and never really thought it was work at all," Brown says. "He taught me to enjoy coaching football because he did it in such a way that it became a good time. It was everything to me, the most important thing in my life at that time. I got totally wrapped up in it then and all my coaching life I've never looked upon what I do as a job. It has been a pleasure."

More than that, Stewart gave his young pupil a meaning to the game, that it could be fun, that it was much more fun if you won and that you won only if you had a system. So Paul Brown, who later played quarterback and graduated from Miami University in Oxford, Ohio, began working on a system that would win.

It wasn't until he fulfilled his most ardent wish—to return to Massillon as head coach —that he had a chance to make it work to any degree. While Stewart was subject to non-football curricula as a teacher and was required to teach three classes a day, Brown directed his energies toward athletics. He became director of physical education at Massillon, director of athletics, and coach of all sports.

He kept control of every sweatsock and sneaker as well as every young athlete. All were subject to him regardless of whether they played football or basketball. All the conflicts between the two sports which existed before he came were eliminated.

In essence, it was no different than his method of operation at Cleveland and Cincinnati. It is why he admits that he's at his best when he can control all the factors that make or break a team. It became a belief early in his career and one that has been the driving force in forging his success.

From that, he began to develop the other elements for building his particular football world. Watching him conduct a practice, the leadership-without-fear qualities were the first elements to become apparent.

He commanded respect from those around him. His communications were crisp and direct as they are off the field. His speech is marked by good English, rarely punctuated by expletives, but, when needed, it has a cutting edge.

Even now he does not raise his voice or shout. The thing that impressed players who met him for the first time was his soft voice. If they could not hear him, he'd move closer rather than raise his voice.

The Browns' players of an earlier era respected their coach's toughness and the quickness of his mind even as they were awed by them. Little has changed in that respect with the Bengals of today. Both groups have high praise for his organizational skills particularly those coming from other teams. They were amazed at the split-second timing of the practices, the unvarying routines of the training camps.

What they got was pure Paul Brown. What players on other teams often got was part

Paul Brown, part their own coach's variations, and supplements to that basic system. The man himself was not too proud to listen and observe what others were doing. While he said that "football has to be fundamentally your own thinking," he didn't hesitate to draw on the experience of each of his assistant coaches.

"We sat down and formed a composite plan," he says.

The plan has the prime ingredient for success because it makes sense. For instance, Brown has based his early selection process on four absolutes—intelligence tests, speed, agility, and the ability to learn football. Those, plus size, can determine a player's future without any scrimmage work. The ones who don't meet a composite standard are sent home.

"There is no point in scrimmaging a boy you know is not going to make your team," Brown says. "There is no need to bruise him and no need for you to waste your time on him. I would rather concentrate my time on the players who will be with me during the season."

It was always that way. Blanton Collier says he had the two key characteristics which are necessary to be a head coach: He had a knowledge of which things were important and then he refused to tolerate an exception to any of them.

"I wanted people who worked for the Browns to be high grade, just as I do for the Bengals," Brown says. "I wanted to have trust in them and I wanted them to always trust me. We always found the best places to stay when we were away from home because they had pride in themselves and we felt they had it coming.

"When I came into football one of the things I insisted upon was that I would have a free hand in selecting my players. I was determined that I wanted them to be high class and I picked them on the basis of personality as well as ability. I had always lived by the rule that you don't win with dogs. It's a rule that never has changed.

"We're talking about a five- or ten-year career that can give a young man a quick start in life. He can use that and go on and be a success. I know it can happen because so many of my guys are executives of big corporations all over the country. Even some of my Bengals' players have begun important career work away from football."

Brown places much of the blame for the so-called "dogs" who come into pro football on their exposure to teaching. He laments the college professors he labels "wage earners," those, he says, who don't earn the respect they once did. The result, he claims, is that the same high quality people who once came into professional football aren't any longer —or at least in the same numbers. He does admit that the players of the mid-seventies are better as a group in their outlooks than those of the late sixties and early seventies.

"Part of the problem," he says, "is that people are getting into college and universities who really don't qualify. We've established a lot of these great programs to make people who don't really have the qualifications into something they simply cannot be. The result has been that they wind up leading all the insurrections.

"It makes you feel that being of the 'square school' is okay," he adds, chuckling. "I'll never forget something the dean of women at Miami [Ohio] once told me: 'The eternal verities always prevail, you'll never lick them.' That is honesty, discipline, truth . . .

all the things which are worthwhile. They can never be licked, they'll always be with us."

And he makes it a point to see that his players fit that mold wherever possible. It only makes sense, he says, to have players who share your beliefs, principles, and ideas.

"These are the principles of Middle America and Cincinnati is Middle America," he says flatly.

Again, there is a constant to this thinking. Throughout his coaching career he leaned toward players who were of the midlands, "good, old Ohio boys," he once described them. The mainstays of his great Browns' team—Graham, Groza, Lavelli, the Houstons, Motley—all came from Ohio. So did some of his coaches such as Fritz Heisler, Howard Brinker, and Weeb Ewbank. Others were from areas adjoining Ohio where the thinking did not vary much.

It meant that Paul Brown did not have to change his thinking to suit his players; they did not have to change their basic outlooks to suit him. Everyone fit together comfortably.

Brown admits that he has little respect for some NFL teams when it comes to personnel. He just won't deal with them because of their personnel policies. "I know what they'll offer me and I'm not looking for anyone's problem children," he says. "We try to weed out players like that. Whenever a player gets moved around people all over the NFL want to know why. That's how a guy can get a reputation."

Brown sought first-class players and then he treated them that way, too.

"You can't ask a guy to be something special if you didn't treat him that way," he says. "We started by buying the best possible uniforms and equipment at Cleveland. When players came to us from other teams they were amazed. A lot of those teams made them buy their own equipment back then.

"It was the same thing in traveling and lodging. When we went to San Francisco to play the 49ers back in the AAFC, we stayed at the Fairmont Hotel because my guys were special.

"We checked how they dressed, where they lived, and we still check on the bachelors to see they are living in a high-grade situation. If they're not, we tell them to move. And we want their telephone numbers no matter where they are living.

"We didn't serve beer on our chartered flights like a lot of teams do. I know the ones who didn't drink it would pass it to the ones who did and that's how people got out of line. When we got back home, I made it a point to have the wives, when possible, meet that plane. I was very lopsided in favor of the wife. When I had my early meetings with a new player, I wanted his wife present so she'd know the role I expected of them both. Yet I've never asked any player to do anything I would not have asked any of my three boys to do."

Of course, much more goes into it but there is the basic agreement on lifestyle and philosophy. Next on his list of requirements came the basic teaching elements that Brown found so important during his high school association with Dave Stewart. His ideas in this regard were as basic as the one-room schoolhouse. So were the teachings he dispensed.

First came "why." The word appears more frequently than any other in his playbook . . . "why we [Bengals] run" . . . "why we stress it" . . . "why we take calisthenics" . . . "why we practice." In days past, the players wrote the answers to those questions in their playbooks and even today most can repeat a question and answer verbatim as it was dictated two decades ago.

"If we tell them why—and I've always insisted on telling my players why, why we do everything we do, whether it's on or off the field—they are more apt to accept it and get in the spirit," Brown says. "Good football requires the spirit of the occasion."

That's the teacher in him. It is why he made his coaches and players write everything. The learning process, he firmly believes, goes on while a player writes. And you can believe that he checked to see that it was done as he wanted it.

He had other tricks for learning off the field, too. His players got tested on charter flights to out-of-town games. Mainly, the tests covered their assignments in the upcoming game.

"No one ever failed," a former player says. "If you didn't know the answer you certainly knew where to get it. But in getting it, you also learned something. He checked all the tests but as much as that, it had the purpose of getting us together and concentrating on what was going to happen the next day. We didn't have time for a lot of fooling around and we didn't lose the fine edge we'd gained during our practice week."

Brown carried that practice on away from the classroom, too. Whether at home or on the road, his teams ate together on the night before a game, attended a movie together, and were checked into their rooms together.

"I've got two young children and we always have company on weekends we're playing at home," says Bob Johnson. "There's just no way I can concentrate on a game the next day with so much distraction so I don't mind being with the team the night before a game."

Even in the so-called "new-era," there is conformity to what may seem like outmoded, old-fashioned principles. But, coming from Paul Brown, it's something else. Players know who he is, what he's done, and there is a great measure of respect from the beginning of the relationship. In fact, many of the Bengals' players remember being totally in awe at their early meetings with him.

Casanova recalls that being in his presence the first time was even "awe-inspiring." "It was intimidating just to sit in his office," the Bengals' defensive back says.

That is why Brown could order his players to a Saturday night movie en masse. Such an idea stems from the way college coaches used to spend the night before a game. Brown had declared from the start with the Browns that he had every intention of instilling the college rah-rah spirit and that he would follow—and expect his team to follow—every procedure that had been his practice at Ohio State. And that was regardless of age, position on the team, or anything else.

Naturally, not every player relishes the idea of spending the night before a game at a movie. With Cleveland, there were many instances of Brown checking his players into the movie but in the darkness of the theater, never knowing which ones stayed for the entire show. However, even the disenchanted made it a point to be present when the final check was made later. The desired effect had been achieved as it always seemed to be.

There have been occasional violations. The week before his first Browns' team was to play for the AAFC championship in 1946, for example, he fired his team captain, Jim Daniell for getting into a scuffle with police. Daniell, Lou Rymkus, and Mac Speedie all were out celebrating the end of the regular season when they were stopped for running a traffic light.

A loud argument followed and Rymkus and Speedie were charged with being disorderly, Daniell with being intoxicated. The next day, after reading of the incident in the newspapers, Brown called his team together and asked Daniell if the charges were true.

Told they were, Brown sacked him on the spot but warned Speedie and Rymkus. Of course, the latter two were starters and Daniell was only a backup tackle so the rule was not exercised to the detriment of the entire team. But the message got across. And Daniell still got a full winner's share when Cleveland won the title.

Clearly, that could be construed as double-standard but Brown got away with it then. When he tried it again with Jimmy Brown, he could not. After taking the job at Cincinnati, no one saw any evidence of his deviating to please one person.

"You've got to know Paul was like every other coach in that he was prejudiced toward ability," McCormack says.

Brown's treatment of Jimmy Brown, whose talent he also truly appreciated, may have led to his own demise at Cleveland. That is the consensus of many who were members of those teams from 1957 through 1962 when the two Browns were the dominant forces.

"It was an iron-clad rule with Paul that everyone was equal and that's how he treated us—until Jim came along," a former player says. "Paul let him get away with things that he never tolerated from Motley or Otto Graham or Speedie, or any of his players.

"In practice, Jim would run a play and after going two or three yards past the hole, simply drop the ball and trot away. With Paul, you ran out everything and ran it a long way before letting that ball loose. But players saw this happening and that tight control he had began to slip."

Paul Brown told friends he only was following the advice of Jimmy Brown's college coach, Ben Schwartzwalder of Syracuse. Schwartzwalder, he claimed, said that Jim was a bad practice player because he had fatigue and endurance problems during the week. Come the game, though, he would perform to his capability with the easy-go treatment during the week.

Like any player, Jimmy Brown was aware of this special treatment and of his own importance and status with the team. He did everything, it was said, to take advantage of it. When the club no longer won the championships he felt it should be winning, some people said he began undermining his coach's authority because of access to the front office where Brown no longer had control.

Again, there was a domino effect. Paul Brown had relaxed the rigid set of rules he set up for the entire team to the benefit of only one man; the team resented it; and when the championships failed to come, the system began to break down.

The following years were bleak ones for Paul Brown as he sat virtually in exile at his Southern California home in La Jolla, being paid $80,000 per season by the Browns and submitting periodic scouting reports and recommendations for the team's draft. Those, he says, were pretty much followed but that was of little consolation as pro football climbed to new heights without him.

Of course, such a situation never happened in Cincinnati. While he still feels his position in Cleveland justified whatever he did, he speaks no ill of Jim Brown. "Somehow, deep down inside, I think he knows I was right."

There are others who played under this system who bridled and resented the rules but who also said later that Paul Brown was right. One was Graham, who resented having his plays sent in from the sideline. Once after having been passed by in a list of pro football's all-time quarterbacks, he wrote a stinging rejection of Brown's system. Brown fired back and it wasn't too much later that Otto apologized and he had long since retired as a player.

There also was a game in the early 1950s when Graham, under a heavy pass rush most of the afternoon, disregarded a pass play sent into the game and ordered a run instead.

"The next thing I knew," he says, "I was replaced by George Ratterman and I went over to the sidelines and stood next to Paul. He just looked at an assistant coach and said, 'Now we have a quarterback in there who has some guts.' That was one of the hundred times I could have killed him. But when I went back into the game, I was a better player."

He was no different at Cincinnati. A quarterback named Sam Wyche was traded from Cincinnati a few seasons ago and was asked whether he could ever return and play for Paul Brown.

"Would I go back with him?" he mused. "You bet I would. I was a nobody free agent when he gave me a chance to play. In my mind, he was fair. I remember going to him near the end of my first training camp and asking whether I would make it or not.

"If I wasn't going to make it, I told him, I had to go home and find a job. A lot of coaches would have told me to pack it in since I couldn't stay for the whole camp but he asked me to stay another week, and that he would start me in a preseason game and give me an answer. He stuck to his word all the way."

There were times, Wyche agrees, when he both respected him and disliked him.

"His cold stare is worth a thousand words," he said, echoing the sentiments of anyone who ever has played for Brown. "Like every other man who ever played for him, I thought some of his concentrated discipline was crude. I didn't like to be told I had to go to a movie with the rest of the team the night before a game. And I didn't like having a card game on a plane trip broken up because he wanted to give us a written examination on our game plan. Those were exercises for children, I thought.

"But once I got out from under him and took a calmer look at the situation, I came to different conclusions. Going to the movie, for instance, made you realize that something important is going to happen the next day and that it isn't going to be just another

Sunday. And those written exams on the plane take your mind off silly things and make you think about the job ahead.

"Maybe these are old-fashioned, out-of-date methods but I sort of admire the man for having the courage to carry them on."

There is more to Paul Brown's relationship with his players than mandatory movies and written exams on airplanes. Yet, as Paul Wiggin, the Kansas City coach who played for Brown, points out, he had unusual control over a team that combined fear and respect.

"He had a cold way of getting to you but he got your attention," Wiggin recalls.

At the same time, both Wiggin and Bob Johnson remember instances when he showed great compassion and understanding for the efforts both were putting forth for his team.

"He seemed to know when a guy was on the ropes and when he needed a lift," Wiggin said. "He could feel it. I remember a time with the Browns when I was having my problems and getting told about it. I was getting pretty desperate and wondering how much longer my pro football career was going to last.

"Then came a game in which I had three sacks and he walked up to me afterward and said, 'Thank you.' That's all he said and he walked away.

"But it meant a lot to me just as it did one time when he met my dad and said a lot of nice things about me, probably some things I never had heard from him. But it meant a lot to my dad to hear them and it made him happy. It meant a lot to me for the same reason.

"When I think back about my time with him at Cleveland, those are the things that showed his great love for that team," Wiggin added. "It was that certain feeling that he really did appreciate everyone working together and doing all he asked."

While Paul Brown may not have been the locker room motivator that others are, he strived to make his team better in non-football areas. One reason is that he was so confident that the football side of their lives would receive the proper attention, that he felt comfortable stressing other facets of a man's life. In the end, he says, these would do as much for getting a team prepared to play as all the overt motivation you could muster. He firmly believed that you don't *handle* players, you treat them like men.

"You handle horses and dogs," he says. "My players didn't have to be treated like horses and dogs."

Brown didn't allow himself to get personally involved with any player. His reasons were known to all: He didn't want friendship ever to cloud a decision he may have had to make on a player's future.

"He told us that right at the start," the Bengals' Casanova says. "It was like insurance for him to be sure he would make the right decisions."

Yet when he had to trade a player, he seemed to take pains to see that the new team was one that would use and appreciate his talents. In 1975, he dealt away guard Pat Matson to Green Bay but in making the deal, he chose a team that needed guards and where he knew that Matson would play right away. When he fought Bill Bergey's attempts to sign a contract with the World Football League and then traded him for what he considered disloyalty, he made the deal with McCormack, someone he's very close to.

He knew that Mike's team, the Philadelphia Eagles, needed help at middle linebacker and that Bergey would play and be part of a good organization. He also was helping McCormack, one of "my guys."

Brown always has placed stress on "his guys's" success, both in and out of football. That's one of the reasons he wasted no time with rookie players he didn't think would make it.

He's been known to tell them, "If you were my son I'd tell you to get on with your life's work. This [pro football] can become a blind alley for you. The best you can hope for is to hang on for a year on someone's cab squad. You're bright, you have the ability, and you've got a college degree. You've also had the experience of finding out what this is like. You must see some things for yourself."

"Inevitably," he says, "they did."

Brown says he would like to have been closer to his players and their families as once was the case in Cleveland. Back then, squads were smaller and the group was more tightly knit, almost a family. That's one of the reasons he favored the lowering of the squad limit from 47 to 43 players in 1975.

"It's a move in the right direction," he says, indicating that he feels that pro football still could be played with even fewer men per team. "It allows a coach to get more from every player. The more you can get everyone taking part and contributing, to get every guy thinking he's doing some good, the better off you are.

"Then you can have little things like dinner for the wives or a family picnic like we once had on a regular basis in Cleveland. A big day in our preseason was the annual family picnic at training camp. All the families of players and coaches would participate and it brought everyone a little closer. It also was a way of showing that we appreciated the wives and the sacrifices they were making with their husbands away for part of a summer."

Training camp—on a Monday through Saturday basis—is still basically a man's proposition, women's lib not withstanding. The only time wives are involved now is to deliver laundry or some special family business. But Brown makes it a point to let everyone know that once the week's work is done, they are expected to join their families for the weekend. After the first week in camp, there never have been two successive weekends where he's kept his players.

From the outset, he opposed the once-popular notion that a pro football team had to seclude itself in the north woods, rise with the birds, breathe in the deep air, and adhere to a strictly monastic existence. "It's not human nature to take a man away from his family for so long," Brown says. "I never believed in that approach and I never will."

Brown senses a change in attitude among today's players.

"You've got to be doubly careful now," he says. "The game has become so diluted that a lesser type of person or player can make it. A lot of them look at what they can take, not what they can give when they come into this game. With those large squads, you get those fringe players . . . the lawsuit kind who spend time trying to figure out ways in which they can take you.

"It's this kind of thing that has made coaching a little less enjoyable though not any the more difficult.

"I know we are supposed to be in an age of freedom of the individual but we have the right to ask them to abide by rules we feel will be for their own physical well-being after literally investing thousands of dollars. We also have the right to ask they do the best job possible under the means we set down. This is not a moral question, it is getting strictly what I think we're investing in."

The highlight of every Paul Brown camp was his opening lecture, one that he gave year-after-year with hardly a word changed. For many of those years at Cleveland, the players wrote down every word. He didn't change much at Cincinnati. Here is a sample of one of his Browns' lectures and one he gave the Bengals:

"I don't know how you feel about it but I'm willing and ready to go to work. You can get tired of a vacation. At least some of you must think so too because you reported three or four days ahead of schedule.

"Getting into football is a state of heart and mind as well as physical . . . Don't ever get the idea this stuff isn't important. You may have heard many of these remarks before . . . When you get so you don't pay any attention you're over the hump. Last year at this time, one of the old-timers was whispering while I was up here. I traded him at the end of the season.

"We will start over—right from the beginning. It's a new season. We take nothing for granted. The new fellows start with the old. We figure if you start a house with a narrow foundation you can only go so high. We try to build a broad foundation.

"Tomorrow it may be hot and we'll practice. Later there will be snow and we'll practice. It may be raining buckets and we'll practice. Soon you'll accept this as a part of the routine and enjoy it.

"We want you to ask for no quarter and give none—for exactly four months and one week, the length of our season. If it's worth something, it's worth everything. And we want you to give everything.

"My coaches are my partners, not assistant coaches. What they know, I know. They have nothing to do at night but talk about you. And call us by our first names. We all live together on this team. We're all good friends. We're a happy, friendly bunch. We have just one objective—to win. And remember if you're cut from the squad, be a man about it. We can't keep everybody.

"Here are the house rules. Breakfast is at seven-thirty daily, eight-thirty Sunday; lunch is at twelve-thirty and dinner at six. Be there to eat every meal unless sick or excused. For the evening meal, wear a shirt. On the road, dress with coats and ties. There is no card playing of any sort for any money. Also you must be in your dormitories by ten each night, lights out at ten-thirty.

"This all may sound juvenile to you but to us it isn't. It's for your own bodies. We want you to dedicate your span with us to football.

"Now for the training regulations. Beginning now you're in training. We want to be different from any other football team. We want you to be eager, full of 'go' football.

I want you to be nothing more than a glorified collegiate football team.

"One of the most disgusting sights to me last year was to see one of football's big names—not from this team—signing autographs for the kids with a big cigar in his mouth.

"Keep your wives out of football. Don't have your wife talk football with other wives. It breeds trouble. I don't want one wife complaining to the wife of the quarterback that her husband is being overlooked as a pass receiver.

"I don't want dirty players. I'll take my players cold, deadly smart, hard-hitting, and hard-running. When you meet a dirty football player the meanest thing you can do is to beat him. They can call you names, try to insult you. Just beat 'em, that's the best retaliation.

"Keep this one of the great football teams of all time, a team you'll be proud to say, ten years from now, that you played on.

"I don't want you to play for your check. I want you to play for the sheer desire of licking somebody. You must sacrifice something to get to the top. That's why we ask you to train."

When he opened his first Bengals' camp, this is what he told his players after greeting them and introducing his assistant coaches:

"In my heart I think we have the most knowledgeable group of assistant coaches I've ever been associated with. They'll swear at you. You'll be treated high grade. But they're not out there to win a popularity contest either. They're out there to do a job.

"There'll be no sugar-coating or pampering for some spoiled college kid. For the veterans, I don't know how you've been handled before or how big a name you have or how big a car or how big a contract. Here it's meaningless. The only thing that counts is your dedication to the game. You run on your own gas; it comes from within you.

"There's no room for political factions here. I don't care if you're a Republican, Democrat, black, white, Catholic, Jew, what-have-you. If you're good enough to make it, you will. If you're not, you won't. If you want to see me, come and see me personally. Don't come in bunches . . . I suggest you call each other by your first names. I want you to call me Paul . . . We want you to know each other.

"We have no quotas, no nothing. Nothing but the best player. I've waited five blooming years to get to do this and nobody, but nobody, is going to louse it up.

"House rules are made for everybody so we can live together happily. It's a long, hard, war. You have to go to every meal. There'll be a fifty dollar fine for missing a meal without an excuse.

"I ask you to wear a sport shirt to dinner. At the table, keep the meal enjoyable . . . it's no place for pigs . . . Try to avoid cliques. Know all your teammates. Class always shows.

"Watch your language. I don't want to hear careless stuff around the locker rooms. Trips to Columbus, Cincinnati, and Dayton are out of bounds without permission. We'll tell you when you may leave. Write your letters, study your books, and sleep long and hard.

"If you're a high-grade guy, you'll get somewhere; if you aren't, you're in trouble.

Nothing devastates a football team like a selfish football player. It's a cancer. The greatest back I ever had was Marion Motley. You know why? The only statistic he ever knew was whether we won or lost. The man was completely unselfish.

"We're going to have our problems and we know it. I want to see that we do our best from beginning to end. And it's not going to take long to see who's a tramp, a boozer, or a barroom ladies' man. I've seen them all. We might be an expansion team but we're not going to be a foreign legion.

"As for smoking, for your own good, don't do it. Some of you will but, personally, I don't like to see it. Don't come out of a dressing room and light up a cigar or a cigarette. If you must, do it up in your room.

"Don't set up any love nests in Cincinnati. We're going to find out where you live. Here at camp you go to your room at ten-thirty or thereabouts. At eleven, turn out the lights. There'll be nightly bed checks. If you sneak out after bed checks you'll be fined five hundred dollars and you'll read about it in the paper; and I'll be the first to tell your wife.

"If you're late to practice or a conference you'll be subject to disciplinary action—a fifty-dollar fine for the first fifteen minutes, one hundred dollars for the first half hour and two hundred dollars an hour thereafter. There'll be a one-hundred-dollar fine for missing a plane, plus having to pay your own way to a game and a two-hundred dollar fine if you don't come home without permission. It's an automatic five-hundred-dollar fine for anyone who loses his playbook and you're subject to fine or dismissal if you don't know the material in this book.

"Maybe I've given you the wrong impression about these fines. But I think I had to hand out three fines in all the years I was with the Browns. It just didn't happen. I hope I never have to fine a ball player. Eleven times I've taken teams through to the pro championship game and I've got a pretty good idea of the kind of player it takes to get there. That's why I've taken the trouble to explain these things."

The speech was basically the same until he retired. Players admit they were a bit bored by it after the second or third time but they admit they listened. His old Browns' players didn't have it that easy because his opening lecture consumed 90 minutes and every word had to be written.

Brown's teaching techniques actually began that first day in training camp. The players wrote in their own plays, the defenses against them and the various breakdowns that made up each element. And he checked the books to see that everyone was doing the same thing just as he ordered the same conformity to the team's on-the-field practice.

You think all that would get monotonous or useless after a while.

"I'd look across the room and there was Lou Groza and Otto Graham writing down everything and they'd been doing it for almost ten years," McCormack remembers. "I figured if they were doing it then I had better get after it too and I was there only a year or two by this time.

"A lot of people say this is an elementary school approach but it was effective. I can remember writing, 'Why do we take calisthenics? We take calisthenics because night after night it builds.' You write that for ten years and you'll never forget it. The idea was to develop you as a thinking football player."

The ideas carried over to his weekly practices. Blanton Collier was not overemphasizing anything when he mentioned how the Browns "practiced how to practice." That is how Brown set up his weekly sessions, each day pausing to write out the day's schedule in very deliberate longhand on the team's blackboard. As if it was necessary, say his players.

"If it's two-twenty on a Wednesday afternoon, I can tell you what his team will be doing and I haven't played for the man in twenty years," Ratterman says with a laugh. "That his routine never varied and that he still was successful is a tribute to his organizational ability."

"Everything went by the clock," Wiggin remembers. "If the Browns were to practice at one twenty-seven, we'd be on the field and practice would begin at precisely that moment. Nothing else would be done other than what he had on the schedule. He wouldn't let you buy time. If the work was not accomplished within the time he set, then he reorganized the schedule.

"Part of the reason his practices were so effective was that his staff had been together quite a while [as was the case in Cincinnati] and it was grooved, a precision team. Everyone, coaches and players, knew what to do and did it."

His methods stemmed from his teaching background. He believed a man's attention span wanes after 75 minutes on the same subject. If he hasn't absorbed the lesson by that time, Brown says, there is no use hammering on it again.

His teaching often went beyond his own practice field. When Graham went to play for the College All-Stars in 1946, he sent Blanton Collier to the All-Star camp and the two worked on the fundamentals that would be used in Brown's system between practice sessions for that annual game.

He also had some expert assistance, then as now, from those who worked with him. While Brown has been credited with helping to popularize the fullback draw play, the real credit should go to Brown's assistant Fritz Heisler. Motley often would remain behind to pass block for Graham. But Heisler saw the benefits of trap blocking when interior linemen are on a pass rush. He simply allowed Graham to drop back as if to pass, saw the defense try to pour through to get him, and set up trap blocks in the middle of his line to clear them away. Motley delayed for two counts, then came pounding through a gaping hole in the line.

"Everyone of us worked together to come up with new things," Collier says. "One of the biggest innovations was our development of the flare pass to control the movements of linebackers. We were way ahead of other teams in these things and, under Paul's direction, Otto became a great passer utilizing them."

Much emphasis was placed on the fundamentals. Linemen spent a great deal of time attacking the blocking sled, time and again hitting its padded arms at precise angles, steps, and inclinations . . . just as he had indicated in his classroom teaching that it should be done.

34

Time was even spent going out and feeling the ground so a player would know how to fall and roll. Again, he wanted to be certain it was done correctly. Wiggin recalls thinking how "weird" it felt at the time but before long saw its purpose. When a player was hit, it was important that he knew how to fall and roll without being hurt; nor be surprised from the impact as he negotiated the proper elements.

"People say he's a patterned coach and they're right," Wiggin points out. "That's why he was so successful. His players always knew what to expect and they knew he wouldn't deviate from his plan. There is a certain sense of security in that a player can prepare himself each day for something and know that it will happen. Look at the effect in concentration that stems from this."

Even the time of the on-field workouts had purpose—1 o'clock, the time most NFL afternoon games begin, except those few selected for later showing on national television. All of this may sound as if Brown develops a team of automatons when the opposite is true. His players marvel at his insistence on the most minute points and the time he spends achieving perfection. So do the players who work under the system he passed down to Shula and Noll.

"He didn't mind as much our getting beaten physically as he did if a team beats us technique-wise," Trumpy says. "In practice, he would get right into the middle of the instruction if he thought we weren't getting the message. He gets things done his way."

There is little disagreement to the fact that no coach demands less of his players physically in practice, nor probably demands more in the precision with which they carry out their assignments. The entire idea is to eliminate errors.

"Only the people who make too many mistakes can't play for Paul Brown," Ken Avery, one of his former Bengals' linebackers, has said.

There always was a great intensity to Brown's practice sessions, subliminal because he kept it that way. For one thing, his teams didn't have ups and downs during their week's work. Win or lose the previous week, they expected the same things for the next game.

That was his own particular style of motivation. Players, he says, have the sense to know when they're not doing the job and coaches should have the sense to get upset about it and let them know they're not doing it.

"The idea that you can map out some program of motivation isn't there as far as I'm concerned," he says. "You can be optimistic. One of John Ralston's real strengths is that he's so optimistic and bubbly. But that is the way he is. Tom Landry, by contrast, is very quiet but very strong."

Brown's players knew his attitudes on such things because he told them and because they soon learned to see and accept them in practice. In training camp, he stressed the point that the previous Sunday's game is past and forgotten once the films have been shown and criticism dispensed. He demanded that preparation for the next week—physical as well as mental—began the moment the movie projector was flicked off.

"The real pros do this," he says. "They don't have to get wound up or get behind forty to nothing to start to play. A class person can handle this better than a low-grade person."

He acknowledges that not every player is able to motivate himself.

"You don't win with these," he says. "You can use a certain percentage maybe but you'd better have some self-winders. The guys who get it going from within get it going from where it counts."

Brown didn't walk away and leave the subject to his players. He told them that he wanted each to do the job to the best of his ability, that the coaches would prepare them and that when all the pieces fit together, each would get his fame and fortune.

The job of giving players individual lifts fell to assistant coaches. During a game, if things were going badly because the team was playing badly, Brown let the players know. Likewise, as the team began preparation for a game, Brown would tell the players, "We should be able to beat this team."

"There was no phony-baloney about how great a team was when that wasn't really true," Bob Johnson says. "I liked his approach. I could never respect the artificial coach who always was hollering and telling a team things which the players simply knew weren't true. That's the quickest way to turn off your players."

It is not that Brown is totally uninvolved in getting players emotionally prepared. He has his own ways, one of which is to needle a player about shortcomings or errors; another is to keep the player in a constant pressure cooker about the quality of his performance.

He doesn't raise his voice or rip a man apart doing this. It's much subtler than that; "clever" is the way one of his players describes the treatment.

"You're not playing well enough and we may have to replace you," Brown would tell a player. He didn't say he would replace the man but he forced the player to re-examine himself and reach down and play even better. What's more, he said this in front of the entire team so the player was aware of failing in the eyes of his peers.

Brown also kept a keen mental file on everything a player did. Often he used these little vignettes in film critiques when a player was shown repeating a mistake. He'd be reminded of the first instance and the circumstances. And if that mental dossier included some unsavory things in a man's life, he's been known to wait for the right moment and use them as a part of any current criticism.

Brown was at his needling best during the film critiques. Some of his Bengals' players remember a film session early in 1975 when a player on the kickoff team was shown about to reach the ball carrier, then turned his back as if to stem the force of the collision.

"Now that's what I call raw courage," Brown said, the cutting edge of the remark all but gleaming in the glow of the projector's light beam.

Mike McCormack, an all-pro tackle for several years at Cleveland, remembers a game against Baltimore when defensive end Gino Marchetti gave him a good working over. When the films were being run a couple of days later, Brown began to work on him.

"He said, 'Michael, you're our team captain and we expect more from you than you showed on Sunday,'" recalled McCormack. "'We always felt confident that if the opposition had a tough man and he was opposite you, that you were going to do your job . . . that you could handle him . . . we relied on you but you let us down . . . you hurt the team effort and we disappointed our fans' . . . and so on and on.

"I would much rather he had gotten up there and screamed and ranted and called me names. But he didn't. Each slice got deeper. It was nothing vicious, and he never raised his voice. But he really got to you with that needle."

It all helped, McCormack said, in maintaining the "straight line" approach that Brown has always sought for his teams. With the old Browns it was accepted, at least until Jim Brown came on the scene. But until that time, a player had to fit the system or he didn't play for the Browns.

Brown aimed this particular thrust of his coaching style toward the over-all goal of achievement. It was melted down to a team concept where everyone benefited from the efforts of each other. Brown abhors the individualist as much as he does the "barroom cowboys" and the "chasers." They had no place on his team.

"I don't want anyone telling me how many passes he caught," Brown says firmly. Time and again he holds up Marion Motley as the ideal team player.

"Marion was the kind of player who didn't care whether he carried the ball five or fifty times," Brown tells anyone who asks for what he considers the ideal team player. "He did it all . . . run, catch, block, played defense as well as anyone. I tried to explain this kind of guy to my players. This is the kind of guy we're after.

"When I got a guy here who started telling me how many balls a team threw to him each day in practice and kept track of things like that, then I knew we were dealing with a self-centered guy and someone who wasn't going to fit our style."

A wide receiver of some talent who made the rounds with several NFL teams during the seventies had a brief stop in Cincinnati. During practice one day, he began to recite all the ills of his former team, the Chicago Bears, and how they allegedly ran an offense that did not take advantage of his talents. It was only a matter of hours before he was on his way out of Cincinnati.

"You can't have guys like that on a team," Brown says. "They're disruptive. The kind of a player I avoided at all costs was the selfish football player. You never hear Anderson tell how many he threw or how many he completed. And you can't be successful if you are a player who does this. A guy who becomes obstreperous because he doesn't think enough passes are coming his way disrupts a team. It's a matter of putting yourself down and giving way to the team's overall welfare.

"And I don't see any sacrifice there. The guys who give you the most trouble in this respect are not the intelligent players."

Brown doesn't talk of achievement only in the football sense. He often told his players that football was no different than the real world, where success also is accomplished through achievement. He urged them to set personal goals for themselves outside of football and to strive to meet them.

"There is nothing wrong with losing," he said, "unless you learn to like it. Not everyone can be a winner and if you lose, then you must learn what caused you to lose and how to overcome it."

Brown made no apologies for his winning nor did he get carried away with his unparalleled success, even from the vantage point of looking back over nearly a half century.

"It doesn't happen when you've been through all the wringers and tragic little things I have," he says.

Brown is a firm believer in dealing honestly and openly with players. "You never can be dishonest or lie to a player, or try to give him anything less than the squarest deal possible," Brown says with as much emphasis as he puts on any of his coaching credos. "If a guy thinks he's not getting a square deal you've got to bring him in and try to arrive at a point where he can't say that any longer.

"Try to lie and you lose the team. That means saying one thing, then turning around and doing something else. I attached more importance to a team's respect than to any other phase of my relationship with them, including blocking and tackling."

Perhaps the most severe test he faced in gaining respect, staying credible, and maintaining lines of communication was in his first season with the Bengals. He had a diversity of personalities, not all of his personal choosing. Yet he had to get something from them.

"I put it to them this way," he recalls. "A man who's been put in the expansion draft can go in one of two directions. A real pro says, 'I want to play. I want to prove something.' But if someone wants to use us just to take some money from us, then he isn't going to stay. And I told them that after you're cut from an expansion team, there's no place to go."

There were many who thought Paul Brown had no place to go when he decided to re-enter pro football with an expansion team. Still ringing in his ears was "the game has passed him by" charge and there was a great deal of open skepticism about his ability to apply his football theories to what many considered the "new look" of pro football as practiced in the late sixties.

When he began to build the Bengals, he did so as he built the Browns—up the middle. His first draft pick was Bob Johnson, a center from Tennessee. Next he traded a first-round draft choice to obtain quarterback John Stofa from Miami. Then he drafted two superb running backs, Essex Johnson and Paul Robinson. The latter was AFL rookie of the year, gaining over 1,000 yards in his first season.

"You begin by building up the middle because you've got to start an offense with a good ground game," Brown says. "That's why we took Bob Johnson when there were no quarterbacks of any value in that first draft. It wasn't until 1970 that we were able to get the truly big back, the type that keeps things honest."

It was that way at Cleveland with Motley, Curly Morrison, Ed Modzelewski, and Jim Brown. It's also been that way with Don Shula and Larry Csonka . . . Chuck Noll and Franco Harris . . . Weeb Ewbank and Alan Ameche at Baltimore and Matt Snell with the Jets . . . Lou Saban with Cookie Gilchrist at Buffalo and Denver.

To Brown, the quarterback selection is the most important one. He calls Otto Graham "the greatest player I ever had because to me he was the greatest of all the quarterbacks. No other quarterbacks won all the championships that he won. He's also the greatest player because he played the most important position.

"He was a great athlete. You name it and he excelled. On a football field he had the great combination of being able to throw long most accurately and also had a great touch down close. I've never seen anyone who could equal him in that respect."

Brown has been criticized for calling the plays for his quarterback, but he doesn't feel his methods need any defense, pointing to the record of success and the championships he won. When he does discuss his system, it is hard to dispute the reasons, particularly when he says, "As long as I ran my own football team, as long as I was in control, there was no change in my play-calling."

That's what comes with being the boss. You get to do things your way and everyone knows where you stand. He doesn't mind nor does he care what the critics say.

"A lot of coaches don't want to take the responsibility of calling the plays because it puts the heat on the coaching staff when things go wrong," he says. "I'd rather have people blame me than my quarterback. Quarterbacks improve faster and play better when they aren't criticized for everything that goes wrong. But I don't believe a quarterback can prepare for a game as thoroughly as my staff does each week. When a quarterback shows that he can find the time to research the films of an opponent's defense in as much detail as my three offensive coaches, then maybe I'll let him call the plays.

"If a quarterback wants to go home on Sunday night after we've played and watch films until midnight or two A.M.; if he wants to look at them almost every other night in the week; and watch them in the movie rooms when we aren't practicing, then maybe he should call the plays.

"Hardly a team doesn't wig-wag defensive signals but no one pays attention. But if you do something to control the offense, then everyone is interested. That's the way the public looks at the game."

Brown selected guards to be his messengers because they did not handle the ball. The idea was to control not only what his team was doing but to see that it did the right thing as often as possible. The system has nothing to do with a quarterback's mentality, Brown says, and those who use that as a reason for criticism are unaware of the problems.

"I played the position and I know what the quarterback sees," Brown says. "When he hands off the ball, his back is to the action. When he turns to drop back, he sees little more if he just turns half way. What can he possibly know about what the defense is doing with half a vision or none at all?

"There are a lot of times a team will go into a game with a perfectly solid plan of attack and the quarterback will go out there and start changing everything around. I want to keep control of the game and I want my quarterback in control of the game. With all that is going on around him on the field, all that he must think about, he can't give as much thought to our plan as people can do on the sidelines with all the information in front of us at all times."

Brown feels that the criticism of his messenger system was brought on by the media, who first listened to Jim Brown's complaints at Cleveland.

"He wanted to run inside, run outside, and make decisions on what he felt like he wanted to do," Brown said. "But he still was ground-gaining champion nearly every year, picking up one thousand yards or more each season. And he did it under the so-called messenger system.

"A quarterback who operates under this system always seems to be put down, yet Ken Anderson is a leader nonpareil; so is Staubach in Dallas, who has his plays called. As far as the Bengals are concerned, we are a team and if we win, that's all that matters. If we lose, sorry, but we go down together, too.

"Anderson likes this system. If you have a quarterback who doesn't want all the help he can get so he can look good just for himself, then you're in trouble. A quarterback is still a football player, a cog in the team albeit an important one. But he still must have all the help we can give him to be "successful."

Brown has proved the point with Graham and Anderson. In his fifth and sixth NFL seasons, Anderson was ranked the league's top passer; in 1973, he quarterbacked the Bengals to the AFC Central title.

Anderson agrees that the play-calling system does take off much of the pressure and frees him to concentrate on other things.

Nor did the other Bengals' players mind, though Trumpy sees the only drawback being the inability to keep track of the game's tempo from the sidelines.

"In the huddle," Trumpy says, "the quarterback can't talk to the tackle and say, 'Can you whip so and so?' Everything is run in a series of three plays, with each one setting up the next. We've got a check-off system that Ken utilizes but only when he sees particular adjustments by the defense."

When a pass play was called, the pass and the man to whom it was to be thrown both were stipulated.

"Often you would see a Cleveland quarterback complete a pass to a man who was not open by much while the other receivers were wide open," says Blanton Collier. "That was one of the secrets of his success with his passing game. The quarterbacks had a high percentage of completions but never threw a lot of long passes. Milt Plum was a good example of this because he worked so much on the short and medium completions."

Then it is up to the quarterbacks. Brown tried to make them conscious of their percentage of completions on given patterns and situations, not for any personal recognition, but to be aware of where success is most easily achievable. The quarterback must read the defense and though the plays might be called for him, Brown insists that his quarterbacks be able to do this consistently.

"The modern forward pass play requires that if a quarterback sees a defensive play-er go one way, he must go the other," Brown says. "Every one of our passes is designed to go to a primary receiver, or a number two or three receiver, and finally the outlet receiver. The final selection is up to the quarterback."

Anderson consistently did this well for Brown, a tribute, says the coach, to the quarterback's intelligence and talent. Because Anderson understood the system and its reasons, he did not argue with Brown over who should call the plays but has put his efforts into a discipline that works with the system rather than against it.

In this sense, the system was compatible for all concerned. Brown's upstairs spotters—two in the end zone, three along the sidelines—had all possible information before them, including computer readouts on an opponent's tendencies in every possible situation. As the game progressed the relative success or failure of each play was added.

Brown says that a guard who runs back and forth long enough in this system almost can call the plays himself. He knows the tendencies and situations and all it takes is a slight nod of the head to send him on his way. This is not a haphazard procedure. In practice, the guards stand by their coach and trot into and out of the huddle with each play just as they would do during a game.

McCormack remembers Brown needling Bobby Garrett, an All-America quarterback from Stanford who once was a Browns' top draft choice. Garrett had a tendency to stutter, even in practice, as he tried to repeat the play a guard had brought to the huddle.

"Paul would stand there while Bobby tried to get the play out and after a while he'd say, 'The thirty-second clock is ticking . . .' and Garrett would just get worse," McCormack recalled. "Finally someone suggested letting the guard call the play. What difference does it make who calls it?

"But Paul had his procedure and he wouldn't change. Garrett just couldn't stand up under this pressure and he finally was traded to Green Bay. People often wonder why he never made it. It had nothing to do with his arm or his mind."

There are many stories about the player's reaction to Brown's messenger system and Paul himself was not above a light moment or two when he'd send a guard into the game with orders for the quarterback: "Surprise me!"

Brown remembers a game when George Ratterman was at quarterback for the Browns and he got a play from guard Lindell Houston.

"I don't like that play," Ratterman said. "Go tell him I want another one."

Houston looked startled, turned to leave the huddle, then stepped back in.

"Go tell him yourself," he said to Ratterman.

Nor did Brown always send in plays with a guard. Once, during a time out, he sent equipment man Morrie Kono into the huddle ostensibly to check equipment but gave him a play with some complicated terminology.

Over and over Kono repeated the terminology as he trotted onto the field. Ratterman saw him mumbling to himself as he approached the huddle and bellowed, "What the hell do you want?"

In that instant, the play disappeared from Kono's mind. Now terror-stricken, he didn't know what to do.

"I was supposed to give you a play," Kono told Ratterman, "and you made me forget the goddamn thing."

Ratterman laughed and asked Kono to give him the first couple of words of the play's terminology. He managed to get out the first two and Ratterman held up his hand.

"Got it," he said. Ratterman knew the Browns' system so thoroughly that he could work on such meager information.

There was a game in Yankee Stadium in 1959 when the Browns were getting soundly beaten by the Giants. On this cold, December afternoon, some fans poured out of the stands and began to swarm around the Browns' bench. When Brown saw violence begin to flare, he ordered his team to its dressing room with more than two minutes to play.

Police finally restored order and the Browns returned to the field—but without Paul Brown. He knew he would be a target of any further trouble.

"We had the ball at the time and do you know that the guards still ran in and out of the game shuttling plays even though Paul wasn't there?" McCormack remembers, still astounded at the scene.

Not all the plays were correct—but most were. One that was saved occurred in a Browns' game against the New York Yankees of the All-America Football Conference. Collier sent in a flag pattern pass play but as soon as the team broke its huddle saw it was a bad call.

"Dante Lavelli was the receiver," Collier recalls, "and he saw the play wouldn't work, too. So right in the middle, he broke it off, and headed for the goal post. Otto Graham already had started his arm action to throw to the flag and in the middle of bringing his arm around, changed direction and got a touchdown instead."

"Otto ran off the field, grabbed the head phone and said, 'Did you see what that crazy sonuvagun did?' Both of us agree to this day that it is one of the best individual efforts we've ever seen in a game."

Some of Brown's Cincinnati players didn't always agree with the plays that came into the huddle.

"It seems kind of weird sometimes," one of the Bengals says, "until it works."

That happened in the opening game of the 1975 season against the Browns. The Bengals had a third-and-goal at Cleveland's 13-yard line when Brown sent in a draw play in which Anderson must step back and make a forward handoff to the fullback who is standing in front of him.

"I thought, 'No way this will work,' center Bob Johnson remembers. "But I made my block and bam-o, here comes Essex Johnson roaring past me and into the end zone for a touchdown."

Brown had that play at Cleveland as well as one the Browns still use—a double reverse where the quarterback gets the ball back and throws a pass. There have been games when both teams have used the same play against each other.

He also keeps pretty close tabs on exactly what is being sent into a game in the way of strategy. During the 1971 season, the team had been losing games in the final minutes because it was susceptible to swing passes. After one such play had doomed the Bengals again, Brown stepped to the phone and asked his defensive coach in the spotter's booth what the coverage was supposed to have been.

When he heard the reply, he told the coach: "Well, shove that coverage up your rear!"

Very un-Paul Brown-like, to be sure. But it shows that he is no less human than any other coach caught up in the frustrations of a game. He takes pains to tell his players to forget about things said during the heat of a game or to take them with a grain of salt and consider the stress or circumstances under which they were said.

"I may say things to you that I don't really mean and you must understand that at all times and take it just that way," he cautions his players honestly.

Brown has an excellent working relationship with his coaches—his "partners." They do the nuts and bolts work during the week, as was the case in Cleveland and Cincinnati, with Brown as the overseer. He encourages a variety of views during their meetings but when the time comes to make the decision, he shuts off all debate and decides what will be.

Though Brown is more offense-oriented, no coach made a move without first checking with him. Collier, who ran the Browns' defense from the beginning, remembers being invested with total responsibility to organize and run that phase of the game.

"Paul really was not that interested in defense, though he had a basic knowledge of it and I think he was right," Collier says. "But he would take part in it on defense day to let the team know that it had to be right."

Collier, who always outlined his plans to Brown, recalls preparing for a game against the New York Yankees, who at that time had sprinter Buddy Young at halfback. Buddy was not a good pass receiver but his speed had to be respected. In setting up a goal-line defense, Collier approached Brown with two or three choices and asked his opinion.

"Paul thought a moment and then said, 'The first time let's not cover him at all. I don't think they want to throw to him,'" Collier recalled. "'Okay, it's your football team,' I told him but I would not have made that decision.

"The first time they got near our goal line, they sent Young in motion and they didn't throw to him. We didn't have anyone out there covering him, so the next time they were in that spot, they tried to throw to Buddy. This time we were ready but we made them do something they really didn't want to do. It was Paul's decision that actually forced their hand."

Brown's football strength was offense. When he assumed the coaching job at Great Lakes, he succeeded Tony Hinkle, who had been an assistant coach for the Chicago Bears and had installed the Bears' T-formation offense. Brown found the numbering system unworkable and during the off-season, he put down every idea or notion he had about the T-formation and tried each one in preparation for the 1945 season.

He moved the running backs around, flopped wide receivers to different positions, experimented with men in motion, used some of the double-team aspects of his former single-wing offense at Ohio State. In the end, he had evolved an offense that would begin to revolutionize pro football, one that had razzle-dazzle and ultimately forced coaches to become conscious of the role of the defense.

Much has been written about the famed "Umbrella" defense of the New York Giants. The Browns virtually destroyed the Eagle defense in a 35–10 victory on their National Football League debut, with Lavelli, Speedie, and Dub Jones putting Philadelphia's man-for-man pass coverage to flight.

The Giants' Steve Owen came up with a plan in which his two ends, Jim Poole and Jim Duncan, would either rush, drop off deep, or drop to the shallow hook zones. Combining their efforts with the other backs, it provided an umbrella-type pass coverage against Graham & Co. that succeeded in helping to beat the Browns twice during the

1950 season though Collier and Brown both say the effectiveness of the "Umbrella" defense was lessened.

"In that first game, the Giants' defense dictated to us," Collier said. "In the second, Paul changed things around so that we did the dictating. We set up our passing game so that our two backs stayed in to help with the blocking if Duncan and Poole rushed the passer. If they didn't, the backs released out of the backfield and ran flare patterns.

"If the Giants wanted to cover them after that, they had to adjust to their deep coverage of Speedie, Lavelli, and Jones. Steve Owen later said we were lucky because we happened to hit his defense when the ends were laying off.

"We weren't lucky. That's how it was planned."

Paul Brown's offense always has been considered a "pass-and-trap" offense, a tag hung on him by Greasy Neale, coach of the defending NFL champion Eagles when the Browns whipped Philadelphia in 1950.

"All they do is throw a pass and run trap plays," Neal said.

"The next time we played Philadelphia, it was raining and we didn't throw one pass," Brown recalls with some pride. "We beat them thirteen to seven.

"Sometimes we throw more than others but we want to be balanced wherever possible."

While his Bengals' offense had the same Paul Brown trademark, Cincinnati players say he worked to minimize the chances of any computer trying to solve the Bengals' system. They say the opposition couldn't say they knew what Cincinnati was doing or what the object of the game plan really was until after the game.

This approach should answer the critics who said Paul Brown had lost touch with the game between the time he left Cleveland and started the Bengals. Brown had five years in which to reflect on all that had happened to him in the game of football, and to chart a course for the day he knew would inevitably mark his return to the National Football League.

If there was one good thing that happened, it was his ability to spend more time with his first wife, Katie; to do things that had eluded them most of their married life because of his total involvement in the game as coach and administrator.

She died in 1968, a wrenching loss for Brown. Katie had been with him through every coaching job he ever held. Friends say she often would sit in the stands during a game and knit, totally oblivious to all that was happening at her husband's command. Yet she was her husband's staunchest supporter and the bitterness that Brown felt at having to leave Cleveland was as much a sense of humiliation he felt had been inflicted upon his wife and his family as his own personal loss. And he said so on several occasions.

Many of the Bengals' players remember Katie coming to training camp, blind from the disease that would ultimately take her life. But Paul would gently guide her through the cafeteria line during each meal time, allowing her to select her meal and then taking care to see that it was set out for her. Often, he would cut her meat dishes and when she was finished eating, dispose of her tray, and gently guide her out of the dining hall.

"I hear people say that Paul Brown is a cold man and I think about in the summers of training camp," Bob Johnson says. "He left a mark with anyone who ever watched him under those circumstances and that was one of deep and abiding respect."

Brown's non-football life with his wife during his "exile" took them to all parts of the world and it helped him put his own life in a better perspective.

"I tried never to claim anything from my life in football," he says, "but you can't help but reflect on all that happened. You'd also get quite a perspective on exactly what you do in this world.

"I was in Hong Kong, for example, and found out that people there didn't know who I was nor even what football was. That got things into focus in a hurry. I found I was so wrapped up in myself and my job that I didn't even know the rest of the world existed."

While flying out of Hong Kong, a wing on their plane caught fire. Some passengers donned life jackets and inflated them and Brown admitted that "it looked pretty bad, so that Katie and I decided what we would do and got ready to say good-bye." The pilot landed the plane safely and the fire was extinguished.

The moment the plane set down on the runway I said, 'Old Paul, it looks like you're going to get another chance,'" Brown remembers.

He made the most of it. He and Katie traveled to Canada and spent several weeks watching the Canadian Football League, trying to see if there was anything he could take from its style of play.

What he saw might some day be reflected in NFL rules changes, an area he is vitally involved with as a member of the Competition Committee. He particularly liked the CFL's wider playing field and has recommended the NFL look seriously into adopting a similar configuration.

Brown kept up with the NFL, too. Lombardi, his close friend, invited him to Los Angeles each time the Packers played the Rams and the two would spend the evening before discussing the game, and the elements then in vogue. He used to travel the few miles from his La Jolla home to watch Sid Gillman work the San Diego Chargers, a bit of a switch because Gillman often was his guest at the Browns' training camp when Sid was coaching the University of Cincinnati and Miami of Ohio.

"I got a much more detached view of the game this way," Brown says. "The thing that really impressed me was the increased use of so many sophisticated defenses. There might come a time when we'll have to legislate to control the defense, particularly with the number of men they put on the line of scrimmage."

A friend remembers him at the Coliseum in Los Angeles one Sunday before the start of a Packers-Rams game. He had called to Lombardi during the pregame drills and the two stood and talked. As Vince turned to rejoin his team, the friend noticed a faraway look in Brown's eyes, a feeling of hopelessness on his face.

"It hurts that much?" the friend asked softly, nodding in the direction of the playing field.

"You have no idea how bad it is," Brown replied, his voice quivering.

While he worked at whatever he could to keep up with the game, including the filing of his personnel report to the Browns, the rest of his days were spent playing golf, swimming, taking long walks, and reading. He got his golf handicap down to eight and stayed at the same slim, 160 pounds, his weight throughout his coaching career.

"It was like chocolate cake," he says. "I like chocolate cake but not every day for breakfast. It was fine doing those things for a year or so but then my life seemed to become aimless. Putting me on the sidelines was like setting two roosters next to each other. They bounce around a bit then go at it. It's pure instinct."

He had chances to return to coaching, several in fact. But the conditions—absolute control of the entire operation—were not there. Anything else would have been a retake on his final seasons in Cleveland and that was out.

There are some who say: Why come back? Brown was wealthy beyond his needs and collecting $80,000 a year from the Browns in California; he already was enshrined in the Hall of Fame; he was at a point, age-wise, where most men are ready to enjoy retirement.

It was more than just being bored with his day-to-day existence. There is a drive within Paul Brown that will not allow him to quit at someone else's whim, certainly not to step down in abject disgrace. He knew that he had to get back into football . . . for what the game offered to him and what he still could offer the game, to show those who had scoffed that they were wrong.

He guards the reasons that drive his inner spirit but there is no mistaking his enjoyment of the day-to-day football life. He admits having a greater appreciation of what makes players reluctant to leave the sport, though he always had a feeling for the player who did not want to go when it was his time.

He recalls Lin Houston, one of two Houstons to play for the Browns. The most recent was Jim, an all-pro linebacker with Cleveland until his retirement a few years ago. Brown was the only coach Lin Houston had in football—at Massillon, Ohio State, and Cleveland. Houston had announced his retirement after the 1952 season.

"We'd been in camp about a week," Brown recalls, "when I got a call from his wife. She said Lin had trouble adjusting, that their house was in disarray, that he couldn't sleep or eat. 'Could he come back?' she asked me.

"I said okay but for one year, then he's got to leave and go into his life's work. The next morning at six-thirty, there was a knock on my door. When I opened it, Lin was standing there and I said, 'Well, what do you have to say for yourself?'

"'Aw, coach,' he told me, 'I like the life.' He had a great year because he knew it would be his last and went on to become very successful in private business.

"But when people ask me why I came back, I always remember Lin's phrase, 'I like the life.' And I do . . . I enjoy it. I'm still fascinated by it."

Like Lin Houston, Brown knew his destiny. He was assured that he would be granted a franchise in Cincinnati if he chose to return. He then called a family meeting, flying his sons and their families to California to discuss the matter. Everyone slept on it for a night and the next morning it was agreed: on to Cincinnati.

The genius for organization came back into focus quickly. Brown knew at the start that there would not be success; that his own reputation might suffer as his new team went through the throes of growing. A friend once wrote to ask him how he could justify putting his reputation in certain jeopardy by becoming involved in a new franchise.

"I wrote back," says Brown, "and told him, 'I couldn't care less about any records. If people aren't understanding enough to know that when you begin a new franchise you've got to go through a wringer, that's too bad.'"

He found the building process enjoyable. He began by knowing the limitations of the team and what to expect as it grew. He knew there was no great pressure to succeed immediately and fill a huge stadium as were the cases in previous seasons at Miami, Atlanta, and New Orleans. The Bengals would play in a 30,000-seat stadium, get no television revenue for two seasons so there really was no place else to go but up.

Those who visited that first Bengals' training camp were shocked by what they saw, or at least by what they were conditioned to see—Paul Brown was having the time of his life. One visiting newsman remembers a player being excused from the first contact scrimmage so he could be best man at his brother's wedding. A television reporter asked him for an interview during the course of a practice session. Brown granted him the interview on the spot.

"I felt like a man starting a new family at age fifty-nine," he remembers. "I used to get a kick out of these people coming into camp, spending some time, and then telling my coaches or my players, 'Gee, he's not such a bad guy after all.'

"The truth is that I haven't changed a bit since I returned to football. I am today what I was twenty years ago. I am *me*."

When the Bengals played more skillfully than any previous expansion team, a lot of skeptics learned that Paul Brown really hadn't lost touch with football.

Few people knew what it took to bring the team to a playoff in its third season after winning just three games the first year. Brown remembers.

"We got such a poor allocation of players in the expansion draft for one thing," he says. "New Orleans and Atlanta drew from fourteen teams, we got from only eight since Miami was excluded from contributing.

"We wound up with the dregs. It looked like the French Foreign Legion. We were forced to build from our draft and this really pushed us upstairs. That's why we were in the playoffs within three years. It was unprecedented but it was done totally by draftees.

"To me, the draft is the life's blood of my business—and like I tell my players and everyone else—football is my only business.

"I don't believe in picking up a lot of old people. A man's name or reputation isn't going to make a franchise. I watched New Orleans when they were being put together in training camp about fifteen minutes from my home in La Jolla.

"They had a bunch of old veterans like Paul Hornung, Jim Taylor, and Doug Atkins—why he broke in with me in Cleveland back in the early fifties—and had the idea they would help to build interest in the franchise. Our approach was that the only thing that would build interest was a good, solid team.

Paul Brown has come full cycle because his Bengals' team was successful on the field and at the gate, because the organization is staffed and run the way he wants it.

Chuck Knox

"Always have a plan and believe in it.
I tell my coaches not to compromise.
Nothing good happens by accident."

No matter what the Los Angeles Rams' recent record shows, success did not come easily for Chuck Knox.

He was a winner from his beginning with the Rams starting in 1973, capturing a division championship and building a regular season record of 12-2. Two other division championships followed in 1974 and 1975.

But prior to the "instant" success came 10 years as an assistant coach with two National Football League teams and, prior to that, nine more years learning from the bottom up—starting in high school coaching, then advancing to a college assistant.

To call him a "sponge" is a compliment. In terms of football knowledge and experience, he indeed has been that. He seems to have absorbed every scrap of useful information he could relating to football during his long apprenticeship. It was fodder for his mind, which digested and returned it in the form of a solid philosophy, and intensity of purpose, and a belief in himself that has made him a coach of winners from the beginning.

For most of his 44 years, Knox has directed his mental and physical energies toward that end. Yet, he does not come off as a schemer, a conniver, or a calculating individual.

This is hard to achieve by someone who has dreamed of attaining a certain status within a profession for a long time and then worked tirelessly to make it. Often such a person will cut so many corners, shade so many areas of white and black that everything becomes gray . . . standing only for himself and his accomplishments rather than displaying a depth and perception that marks him as truly successful.

Not Chuck Knox. The total belief in what he does, in what he espouses comes across vibrantly. He has allowed few obstacles to stand in the way of his success. But you know, too, that rather than brutally or insidiously do away with them, he has somehow managed to steer past them.

Knox might have found success as an evangelist. He has the zeal of a missionary.

His coaching background is not unlike other successful NFL coaches.

With Knox, the difference is personality projection. It is the manner in which Knox has sold his program to his players, whether they were the offensive linemen of the New York Jets or Detroit Lions, or the entire squad of the Los Angeles Rams.

Knox has programmed the essential elements of his success so that he works within his own carefully defined limits, meticulously planning what he feels must be done each week to achieve victory. Often these elements are spelled out in clichés which, coming from anyone else, would bore a listener. But when Knox says them, they become solid teaching points.

He talks about the elements that constitute successful football coaching invariably when he speaks to coaching clinics. He speaks from a prepared text yet the words and phrasings that he carries on in casual discussion are almost verbatim from that text. That's how convinced he is that his program is correct.

Looking back over Knox's coaching career, it is astounding to see the steps he has taken, almost as though he knew that each would lead from the smoke and grime of the steel mining town of Sewickley, Pennsylvania, to the prominent position any man assumes who becomes a head coach in the NFL.

Chuck Knox traveled a long road to get to the top . . . from the Pennsylvania high school ranks, to assistant coaching jobs at Wake Forest and Kentucky, and then with the New York Jets and Detroit Lions. Total elapsed time: 19 years. Total interest in him as a professional head coach: zero. Yet when it came time for the last, big move, Knox did not instigate it; the Rams came to him. It was the first time any pro team ever had even asked him whether he'd be interested in being a head coach.

When the bidders, Rams' owner Carroll Rosenbloom and his general manager Don Klosterman, did ask, Knox was ready.

During those 19 years he had organized and outlined exactly what it would take for him to become a head coach and when Rosenbloom and Klosterman asked him, he told them . . . for hours on end, during several visits to Los Angeles and in such withering detail that they quietly dismissed all other candidates waiting to be interviewed. Rosenbloom says he asked Knox to outline each day's work for an entire football season and the man did just that, day-by-day, prospective opponent-by-prospective opponent.

Why would a man of such dynamic and magnetic drives be content to wait so long to become an NFL head coach when all around him others were being solicited from the college ranks or from those with much less time as pro assistants.

"As an assistant coach, I was just concerned with doing the best job I could do," he says. "I really wasn't that concerned with a head coaching job. I figured if I worked hard, things would come."

Not very exciting . . . no recriminations, no born-and-raised-in-a-log-cabin sequences. But that is basic Chuck Knox . . . his public face, the one he projects for the media after a game, win or lose.

Nonetheless, that is a true picture. He saves all the dynamics and magnetism for his players, where it will do the most good. They have bought his style, 100 cents to the dollar and have responded with success on the field. Perhaps coming after the diverse personalities of George Allen and Tommy Prothro, Knox was the right man at the right time.

Allen operated within his own rules, building great pressure, day-by-day, toward mistake-free football. He had his motivating techniques and developed loyalties so consuming that they once got him a two-year reprieve from being fired. But peace of mind never was something his players could count on.

Prothro had his own unique style and the players found themselves almost pressure-free. He had his standards but did not drive them to achieve, feeling that as grown men and professionals, they should be interested enough in the job to do it themselves. Some did . . . and many didn't. From a tether that had been so restrictive to one that hardly bound at all, the Rams didn't quite know where they were going or, perhaps worse still, how they would get there.

Knox's style was different, yet similar. Like George Allen, he demands mistake-free football from everyone. But he does not put the burden on one group to lead the way as Allen does with his defense. Like Prothro, he allows the players to be themselves, never fearful that he might lose control, while at the same time exacting a loyalty from them that is genuine and has its own restraining forces.

Some Rams' observers say he is more subtle in his exacting ways than Vince Lombardi, certainly not as bombastic; more sincere than Allen; more even-tempered than Don Shula, who may be unmatched when it comes to explosiveness. Yet Knox professes deep admiration for all three, plus Paul Brown, in trying to follow a successful pattern within the same profession.

"He has the enthusiasm of George Allen and the savvy of Tommy Prothro," Rams' guard Tom Mack says. "I know one of our other players told me that the first time he talked with us, he was so excited afterward that he said he wanted to go out and play football right then."

Carroll Rosenbloom sees many of the same attributes that helped drive Shula to become one of the NFL's best coaches. He admits that he was looking for "another Shula" when he hired Knox. But he also wanted a coach who was more mature than Don when Rosenbloom hired him at age 33 to coach the Colts.

Knox was 41 when he took the job and Rosenbloom said he found what he was looking for. He paints parallel lines in tracing their careers, noting that Shula took the job in Miami because he knew there was the nucleus of good talent with the Dolphins though some said at the time they were the worst team in the NFL.

"Smart coaches don't take on impossible jobs in losing towns, no matter how much money they're offered. Why do you think Knox took the Rams' job?" Rosenbloom asks. "He's smart. He knew he could be a winner in the Rams' organization.

"Chuck also has the flexibility to move with the times. He keeps up with social changes. During the players' strike in 1974, he never downgraded his players. When a lot of people were going around downgrading Ed Garvey, Chuck said he was trying to understand more about Garvey and his motives and ambitions so he would know better how to anticipate the reasons behind anything the players might or might not do."

Rosenbloom, who has been highly critical of Shula in the past, also says that Knox is the only coach (the fifth to work for him in Baltimore and Los Angeles) "who never tried to impress me. He wouldn't think of it. He saves that energy for winning and for his players. It takes a lot of energy to prepare to meet reporters and owners if you're trying to entertain them. Knox chooses to save that for his team."

The Rams' owner also says that Knox has all the things generic to a winner—a dedication, experience, strength. Rosenbloom compares him to Shula and Lombardi in the latter regard.

But Knox does not drive his players as Lombardi did; nor does he blister them verbally, as Shula often does; nor lead them in locker room pep rallies like Allen. He does throw his cap when things go wrong ("the longer the throw, the madder he is," one player says) but his attitude constantly is built on positive things.

Rosenbloom has been known to get almost lyrical when talking about him, once calling him "the greatest coach I ever had," mindful that he also employed Weeb Ewbank and Shula and that both won NFL titles for him. What prompts these rhapsodies is Rosenbloom's almost unbelieving realization that Knox was the same man after his first two very successful seasons that he was the day he was hired.

"A lot of coaches blessed with that kind of sudden success have a hard time differentiating themselves from God," Rosenbloom says. "But that will never happen to Chuck. He lives by a credo that everyone should copy: 'Do as you would be done by.'"

It can be said that management people must show such enthusiasm because he's their man and they must make the move look good; and when it is good, make it look even better. But the Rams' players, including some of the veterans who have been through as many as five head coaches, add credence to the picture.

"The first thing you notice about him is his tremendous enthusiasm," veteran defensive tackle Merlin Olsen says. "When you talk to him about an upcoming game, he lights up. As the season grinds on and you wear down, that becomes even more important.

"I felt when he was hired there would be a period of adjustment but there wasn't. That's a tribute to the way he approaches his job. He works very hard but, unlike some coaches, he doesn't go around telling everybody about it. Some coaches spend as much time talking about the work as they do working."

Knox has a reminder on the bottom of the cup that he uses to drink his morning coffee. "Now go back to work," it says.

His basic philosophy is a product of his association with Blanton Collier. Collier was a long-term assistant of Paul Brown's before he became head coach at the University of Kentucky, where Knox, Shula, Bill Arnsparger, and John North—all future NFL head coaches—were on the same staff. Knox still seeks Collier's advice on football matters.

Collier's great teaching skills and technical knowledge of football impressed Knox. He was a natural outlet for all of Chuck's creative skills and theories as well as a stimulation to develop others.

"Blanton was the finest teacher that I've ever been associated with. I'm not saying he would make an instant All-America but he could pick up a player who had been coached for a year or two by one man and in a very short time he'd have him executing better than ever.

"His technical sense was helped by a great analytical mind. He could break down films better than anyone I've ever seen. More than that, he could look at a film and tell right away whether or not a technique being taught to a player was really effective.

"He'd never kid himself about such things. If the player wasn't getting the job done, Blanton would say it's for one of two reasons. Either he as a coach was doing a poor job of teaching or the technique was wrong.

"During a game, if the player used a different technique from one Blanton was teaching, and he was getting the job done, then he'd say, 'Well, maybe I should start teaching the technique that he's using in the game. Just think how proficient he would become.'

"I've gone to coaching clinics and listened to coaches talk for two hours on how to make the center snap. When someone asked me once about it, I got all involved in the theory of stepping, handing the ball, head, shoulders, everything. It took me an hour to answer the question. Blanton showed me there was a tremendous gap between coaching theory and the practical application—what a coach does and what he thinks he's doing."

You can see this common sense approach in Knox's teaching methods throughout his pro football career, and now in the way he sets up the Rams' overall picture. He got it from spending almost every night in Collier's home in Lexington, Kentucky, during their association. Before going to bed after each visit, Knox recorded everything the two had discussed. He still has those notes and he often refers to them. He also has stacks of stenographers' notebooks, each containing references to every daily coaching routine since he worked at Kentucky. (So does nearly every other coach who ever worked for Collier.)

Whenever a problem arises that he once faced, he opens the bottom drawer of the filing cabinet in his office and refers to the book in question. For each opponent, Knox will go back to previous meetings, refer to his notes for that preparation period and become fully versed again in what he did before . . . good or bad.

"If it was bad, we don't want to repeat it," says Knox. "If it was good, we want to see if we can improve on it."

Another benefit of his time with Collier was the manner in which Blanton challenged his assistant coaches. It is something that Knox does to his own coaches.

"Blanton always gave you food for thought," Knox says. "No matter what idea you presented to him it had to be well thought out because he would challenge it in a very analytical way. But he'd be the first to say to you, 'That's a good idea,' and then he'd tell you why.

"He also had his own little technique for testing his coaches. He never wanted them to be 'yes men.' Many times he'd come in to our office and say, 'I couldn't sleep last night because I got an idea I think would really work . . . would really be something,' and he

53

would tell us what had come into his mind during the night before.

"Now a lot of assistant coaches might be tempted to say, 'That's a heckuva idea, Blanton.' But Blanton might have just given you something that came to him as he came in the office door and he was just checking you out.

"Other times he would have what really was a good idea and then he'd solicit your opinion again. He never wanted you to anticipate what his thoughts were. Your value to his staff was your ability to relate your ideas, to be able to analyze other ideas and come up with your own opinion.

"This is very important to a coaching staff. You never know when a coach who has not had a creative idea in a month might come up with one that is better than anything you have going at the moment. A head coach must create a climate in which ideas can be freely offered without any danger of a sarcastic reply, without any danger of ridicule. He must see that it is freely discussed and be able to come back and offer direction for that idea. I don't want a one-way street on my staff. I encourage a dialogue, both from my coaches and my players."

That's how Collier treated him. Blanton still has a great regard for Knox. He remembers the hours they spent talking football, with Chuck searching out the most minute detail of every discussion point.

"He was similar to Shula in that he had the same type of drive," Collier says. "He had dedicated himself to being a head football coach in the NFL and he acquired as much information as he could from a variety of people.

"Chuck was very detail-conscious. He worked very closely on what is now called 'option blocking' and you see many NFL teams using it. I used it at Cleveland when I became head coach there to take better advantage of Jim Brown's running."

The germ of the idea was planted in Collier's mind by Lombardi during Lombardi's annual swing through the Kentucky area on scouting trips for the New York Giants. The technique of option blocking and Lombardi's "run to daylight" theories, which he installed at Green Bay, are related.

The run to daylight concept tries to find the natural openings that occur during a play along the line of scrimmage even where the play is not designed to go. In the option blocking scheme, the offensive linemen maintain some control over where these openings occur by blocking the defensive man the way he wishes to go. Collier refers to it as "controlled running to daylight," and it was one of the answers the offenses had for the changing defenses.

"It is the principle of isolation," Collier says. "You try to isolate a defensive man and block him the way he wants to go. The running back would watch the defensive man and go where he isn't."

Collier suggested the germ of that idea at Kentucky and Knox grasped it. When Blanton left Kentucky in 1962, the two had pretty well managed to refine the concept. Knox also proved to be an excellent teacher of pass blocking and this helped get him his first pro job with the Jets, on Collier's recommendation.

"I told Weeb Ewbank there was no better coach in college at teaching pass protection," Collier remembers. "Coming into pro football that is a must. You've got to be able to run with the ball, true; but you must teach a boy to protect that passer. Chuck was an artist at it then and became even better with the Jets and Lions."

Collier can look at the Rams now and see much the same passing game approach that he used at Kentucky and Cleveland. Ermal Allen, a special projects coach for Tom Landry at Dallas, can look at the Rams and see things he discussed with Knox while they worked together at Kentucky and later during long conversations they had when the Cowboys were winning consistently and Chuck was looking for new ideas.

That's how Ewbank remembers him too.

"I still see our 'Eighteen and Nineteen Straight,' being run by the Rams," Ewbank says. "That was the play Matt Snell ran so successfully in the Super Bowl, the basic play in our system.

"We used to say that if you gave Chuck Knox the pencil, you'd never get it back," adds Ewbank with a chuckle.

Knox fit in well with the Jets because the basic line play techniques were the same as he taught at Kentucky—the ones Ewbank and Collier had brought from Paul Brown at Cleveland where both had served on his staff. Ewbank also liked Knox's football approach, one that was quiet, that dealt heavily with teaching. He did not see Knox as a driver but as a man who dealt with his players on an even-handed basis and who could bring home the technical aspects of the game.

"You could see a lot of Blanton Collier in his teaching," Ewbank says. "We used that line option blocking and Chuck did a great job of teaching it and pass blocking."

The latter would become most important to the Jets because within a year they would have Joe Namath as their quarterback. Ewbank had learned not only the value of a great passing quarterback but of the need to protect him when he coached John Unitas in Baltimore. The Browns' system of pass protection protected Unitas and it did the same for Namath.

John Schmitt, who became the Jets' starting center under Knox after being signed as a free agent in 1964, remembers him "being in a class of his own. There was something about him which made him different, an air about him, the way he carried himself. All of us knew it would be just a matter of time until he got a head coaching job."

While he was working with the Jets, he also was listening and watching Ewbank bring a team that was bankrupt, both financially and in talent, and raise it to the brink of championship competition when Knox left to become an assistant coach in Detroit in 1967.

"Weeb had a great eye for personnel," Knox says. "He knew the kind of team he had and he tried to come up with the right kind of player for the position he had to fill. He would tell us, 'We don't want to cut anybody unless we are absolutely sure the guy could not play.'

"I learned a lot about personnel and about the passing game from Weeb," Knox adds. It was all filed away as part of an emerging football philosophy.

So were his experiences with Joe Schmidt at Detroit. This was a necessary step for

Knox because he wanted to learn from someone who had played professional football and who had great insights into how players feel.

"I got a good perspective on how a player feels about the coach, the rules, and everything that goes into a team," Knox recalls. "Joe also had a great feeling about communication in the way he ran his staff. He had come there with only one season as an assistant coach and was very willing to sit down and talk with his coaches, drink a beer with them. This was a man who did not feel that as a head coach, he had been deified. He didn't feel that because he wore the head guy's cap that his assistants were on some lower level.

"It was more eyeball-to-eyeball, a very close relationship in which I felt most comfortable. It is the same kind of relationship I've tried to establish with the Rams."

But it was the idea of getting the player's perspective that really interested Knox. We knew that not having played professional football it must come from someone who did. Schmidt supplied much of this during his meetings.

Knox, it is said, replied by building the best offensive line the Lions possessed since their championship years of the fifties. He ultimately developed starters from two free agents, Rocky Freitas and Frank Gallagher, and polished young players such as Ed Flanagan, Chuck Walton, and Bob Kowalkowski, and later Jim Yarbrough, into a cohesive unit that helped the Lions gain the 1970 playoffs. Detroit had a winning record during each of Knox's last four seasons under Schmidt.

The experiences—Collier, Ewbank, and Schmidt—have given Knox his characterization as an intellectual "sponge," one he feels adequately describes his background. He readily admits learning something from each man, but he is quick to point out that "you can borrow from other coaches, but you can't imitate. Players recognize this very quickly. You must be yourself in everything you do."

Knox does not hold up past experiences to his players as examples of either his accomplishments or how they must view their accomplishments. The only references come when he is pressed and then only in terms of his general satisfaction that a veteran tackle such as Sherman Plunkett of the Jets so readily accepted the techniques Knox taught; or that the Lions' young players responded so well to his techniques because they saw them work effectively.

Knox has blended all of that in his Rams' system. The offense subscribes to the basic Paul Brown tenet of taking what the defense gives. At the same time, he reserves the right to attack suddenly and without warning, another Brown tenet that comes as a reward for being patient. As a head coach, Knox has put great responsibility on his offensive and defensive coordinators, as Schmidt did at Detroit, while working with everyone on his staff to produce a consolidated effort.

"I'm not trying to prove anything or rewrite any football history," he says. "For instance, we don't have a play like the old Green Bay sweep that we intend to establish come hell or high water. We aren't going to run the ball down the other guy's throat if he wants to stop us.

"I never have had any preconceived notions about anything. I only ask one thing about a play or about a formation: Will it work?"

That's about as basic as you can get, but then so are all his coaching principles. Here are a few others:

—"We strive for a mistake-free game. We go over bit-by-bit, our assignments and duties so we can react and not think. Before you ever can win a football game, you have to keep from losing it first. Our statistics the first two years with the Rams showed that for every five times we began a drive that didn't produce a score, the defense stopped us only twice. That means that sixty percent of the time we stopped ourselves by a penalty, interception, fumble, or maybe we ran out of time in either half."

—"'Mistake-free football' in no way means we're going to play conservative football. We just want to play what we call percentage football. We want to know where we're throwing the ball, and when we think there's justification for it. For example, it might be third-and-eight and we're just coming out of our own end zone. Our scouting reports show us our opponent's cornerbacks play for the 'out' pattern so this might be a good time for us to go for the long pass."

—"People get the impression that 'mistake-free football' is computer football, which isn't the case at all. It is based on a philosophy that if we can eliminate our own mistakes in practice as much as possible, by constantly reviewing the basic alignments we'll see in each game, then we're going to reduce our chances for error."

—"Repeated actions are stored as habits and if the repeated actions aren't sound, then what comes out in a game can't be sound. What comes out will be bad habits."

—"We emphasize a one-game-at-a-time philosophy. This is more than a cliché to us. We will not talk about anything but our next game and we insist our players concentrate and think about nothing but that game."

—"Games are not won on game plans, which is a term the media has come to see as the be-all and end-all of every game. I don't worry about game plans. If we are fundamentally sound, we can execute any game plan and that means we give our greatest emphasis to the fundamentals, building them gradually through repetition of the plays we want to use in a game."

—"This game never stands still. It takes a great amount of time and study during the off-season to keep up with the changes. I call it research and development. You research what your team did and you develop it in the direction you want it to go."

—"It is important for a coach to give his players as much individual freedom as possible. Players must feel secure in what they are doing, secure in the knowledge that what they are doing is for their own good and the good of the team. This is a very fine line and successful coaches are the ones who can draw it."

—"That is one reason we go for the simplistic approach. We want to be consistent but we don't want our players to lose some of their freedom on the field. You can make players too cautious. If you have a player with a nose for the football, let him go. Too many times we get so carried away about not making a mistake that we destroy the individual's ability to make the big play."

And then there are his basic coaching philosophies:

On winning: "You get the winning edge by outworking people."

On motivation: "It starts with the head coach and the price he is willing to pay. Then it reflects down to everyone else."

On strategy: "You build on skills that exist. If it takes ball control or the big play to win, that's what we'll do."

On discipline: "I believe in treating individuals the same way. You can't have one set of rules for one guy and not for another."

Knox recites these principles as fervently as if he had been summoned to the top of the mountain and given them on tablets of stone. He knows they are correct for him because he has seen them successfully practiced in one form or another by every coach he ever has worked for, and in all imaginable situations. He finds it as much of a personal principle to be as positive as he possibly can in espousing them lest their effectiveness be eroded by the slightest hint of self doubt.

"Anytime you begin to question what you're doing, the people around you sense it," he says. "That means your coaching staff, the trainers, the players, everyone. But if you give a lot of thought about what you want to do regarding fundamentals, practice plan, and so forth and you know those ideas are sound, you know the principles are good, then there is no reason to doubt them.

"The question then is to find a way to get the player to want to do it, to accept it, to want to do it just a little bit better. That, to me, is the crux of making your philosophy work. There must be a plan for everything and the plan will prevent you from overlooking little things. By having that plan, you'll be secure and self-doubts never will become a factor.

"It's when you're not prepared or you have not planned or you haven't spent the time that you begin to falter. There isn't a day I'm on the job that I don't get my plan together and get in touch with myself."

That is experience talking, the experience of having become a line coach with the New York Jets at age 29 without ever having played professional football; of having played tackle at little Juniata College in western Pennsylvania, far from the big-time of major college competition or the smooth execution of the National Football League.

"When I joined the Jets I faced an immediate acceptance factor," Knox says. "Guys like Sherman Plunkett, Sid Fournet, and Mike Hudock had been in the pros for a while; other guys were older than me. And here I was, getting ready to teach these guys offensive line fundamentals. The acceptance factor that would have been the case had some all-pro offensive lineman been coming in to show them what to do certainly wasn't there.

"So what did I have to do? First, there had to be a knowledge of the technical aspects of the game and the ability to communicate with the people involved; the ability to plan how to teach the various fundamentals so they would know their assignments. That's where I saw the benefit of total preparation. I never had one problem with any of those players nor later on with guys like Winston Hill and Dave Herman. Three of the five guys who started on the Jets' Super Bowl champions broke in under me. Two of them were free agents; the other was a redshirt draft pick.

"That's why I see the main function of a head coach and an assistant coach to be the same. He's got to make those he's responsible for be as successful as they can be. And a successful person is one who works up to or near his full potential. The only thing you can ask any man to do is his best."

How to do it is a question each man must answer for himself. Knox has sought the answers from many who were successful in competitive athletics, including Adolph Rupp who won more games than any coach in college basketball history. Knox became friendly with Rupp while serving on Collier's staff at Kentucky, spending hours talking to him and observing his practices.

Rupp had earned his nickname "the Baron" because he staunchly believed in the dictum that every group needs a leader—that he was the leader of Kentucky's basket-ball team, that he knew the way to win, and that his players would do things his way only.

"'We've got to shake up the balls or they won't bounce the way we want them to,'" Knox remembers Rupp saying. "He was very critical of his players in practice because that was his personality and that's how he achieved great success.

"But that's not my personality and I can't be like that. One thing you can't be as a football coach is an actor. You must be yourself, do what fits your personality. You can't take Bear Bryant's operation, put on his hat, his face, and do and say things he does.

"There are many ways to get things done but you've got to decide which is the best way for you and the players you have. Then you've got to be flexible enough not to impose a plan they can't handle on them."

That is the basis of his thought on strategy: "You build on skills that exist."

That's why the Rams showed unusual poise late in the 1974 NFC playoffs against the Washington Redskins when Allen removed quarterback Bill Kilmer for Sonny Jurgensen. Time and again during his long career, Jurgensen had been a cool hand in such pressure situations, quickly fathoming what a defense was trying to do and then finding a way to pick it clean. But on this day, it didn't happen. Instead, the Rams' defense turned on him, intercepted one of his passes and returned it for a game-clinching touchdown. The predictions that the Rams could not beat a team that had beaten them just two weeks before were as empty as the Redskins' own efforts.

Knox says he wasn't worried when Jurgensen trotted onto the field.

"The answer still is execution," Knox says. "We may know that one quarterback likes to throw one type of pass versus another so we compensate by adjusting our defense. We still concentrate on executing team defense rather than worrying about the particular player. We'll make the adjustments."

All of Knox's explanations are laced with a particular jargon of the street—"street talk" some call it. It is colorful, though in Knox's case not always profane. It gives Knox a tougher mien than he really possesses but which is totally natural to him. Some of the Rams' players—guard Joe Scibelli, for example, who was born and raised in western Massachusetts—find that it strikes a respondent chord. It is more earthy, more realistic than some of the more modulated smoother language of the west. It is a little thing but Knox makes total use of whatever built-in advantage it has.

The projection probably comes across stronger than intended because of the earnestness with which Knox covers every subject, punctuated by the certitude and thought-out approach that he has taken to be so sure of all that he believes. It is one reason why he always has been able to instill a sense of pride wherever he has coached. In Los Angeles, he calls it "Ram Pride."

This is not sloganeering or labeling because he consciously works every day to see that his players maintain a keen pride in *all* they do. It is a factor, he says, that makes a player perform consistently well and it follows that if every player performs this way, then so will the team as a whole. So far, it has worked just that way, but those who watch the Rams at the Coliseum or on television don't see the nuts and bolts work at their Long Beach practice facility where Xs and Os are only one facet of a day's work.

"We stress the sense of pride," Knox says, "but I tell my coaches and my players that pride is not like a coat; it's not something that you lay down for two or three days and then decide when you get up some morning that you'll have pride that day and put it on. It must be there every day and it takes constant work to achieve it, to keep it.

"To me, the pride factor involves coming out every day and trying to be a little better football player than you were yesterday. To me, pride is the performance in practice that you give in a game. You don't want to play like you practice; you want to practice like you play. That's pride.

"The greatest feeling a team can have is to be in a locker room on a Sunday morning with each player knowing that everybody else worked as hard as he did that week, that everybody else on that team is ready to play. You know it's true because you saw them in the meeting when coaches asked them a question and they responded correctly. You saw them make a mistake in practice, the mistake was corrected and they didn't make it again. You saw the quarterback take home films. You know that he looked at them because you rode to practice with him and he talked to you about what he saw the previous night.

"Now you can sit in that locker room on a Sunday morning and get a fine focus on what you must do and nothing else will be distracting. What spoils a player's concentration is when he begins to wonder about what the other guy will be doing. That's when you start to worry and stop concentrating. That takes away from the fine focus you need to win. A guy who has pride will never let that happen, so we try to get everybody thinking this way every day."

Knox was tested early to prove this theory. The Rams were winless in their first four preseason games in 1973 and the grumbling that had begun on his appointment as head coach—"Chuck Who?" some people had said—began to increase. But he found that his players had formed a solid belief in his system and obviously knew that what they were being taught was sound.

"There wasn't anything wrong with what they were doing," he remembers. "They just had to do it better. We did it by winning our last two preseason games, then our first six regular season games. We lost two straight by a total of four points, but then we won six more.

"When we came back out to begin work in 1974 and again in 1975 after having been in the playoffs, we stressed the same attitudes. No detail was too small to be covered; there never was a sense of hitting the practice field and going through the motions. We can say we have 'Ram Pride' but to get it on Sunday we have to work at it from the first day of training camp—everyone, from the coaching staff to the trainers, to the players and the equipment men."

Knox's eyes flash when he talks of such things. He has programmed himself to spread the deep-rooted belief in his own principles and his evangelism is high-key. If there are times when he must reinforce his own selling techniques all he does is open a leather brief case, remove a tape recorder and a stack of cassettes conveying the positive thinking techniques espoused by the Dale Carnegie programs. The speaker on the cassette marked number one: John Ralston, coach of the Denver Broncos and himself a registered Dale Carnegie instructor.

The end result is a good line of communication between Knox and his players. Knox stresses that his form of communication does not mean hollering or raving at them during practice or a game. The screamers, he believes, hurt more than they help. If a player makes a mistake in practice, he wants his coaches—or himself—to get to the player on the way back to the huddle and tell him *why* he made it.

"I don't call it dissident opinion," he emphasizes. "We never have gotten to the stage of argument, we just listen to each other's viewpoints. Everyone basically wants to do the same thing, be successful. So there is no pride of authorship with the Rams. I've said many times that when we win, *they* win, my coaches and my players; and if we lose, *I* lose."

Knox's approach to the older players also is different than with the younger ones. He will adjust the content of his remarks depending on a player's experiences. He'll tell the older veterans things about an opponent, for example, that he never would tell a young player because the latter could not handle them. He does this, his veterans say, because he respects the veteran as a player.

"All of us share this respect and do our best for him because we don't want to let him down," says one Ram.

A good example of his overall approach to player relations occurred in the Rams' first visit to New Orleans under Knox in 1973. On the first day the team began preparations, he made it a point to tell the players they would stay downtown and that there would be a carnival atmosphere on Saturday night around the French Quarter, which he knew they would visit.

"Go out and have a couple of drinks but don't throw the ball over the fence," he told his players. "Make this game a stepping-stone to a championship and, when we win it, I'll take you out and help you throw the ball over the fence."

"If that had been George Allen," one veteran noted, "he would have taken the team so far out of town we never could have gotten into the French Quarter, and then he would have scheduled meetings on Saturday night just to be sure no one tried."

Knox also tells his players not to get into any shoving contests during a game. If it would do us any good at all, he says, "I'd be right out there with you, believe me I would."

61

And his veterans know that he means exactly that.

"Chuck is the kind of person I'd like to have as my friend even if he was not my coach," Scibelli says. "If I met the man in business or as a neighbor, I couldn't like him any more than I do now. That's how strongly I feel about him."

Knox never has felt it necessary to get really close to his players off the field to achieve this feeling. For any coach this is the saddest part of the job—that he cannot carry on the great fraternity the player-coach relationship often engenders into social situations. Obviously, Scibelli's feelings about Knox make that a two-way street, but if the relationship does continue off the field, it must wait until the player's career has ended.

One of the restraining factors is that some coaches simply do not, by their nature, invite players to become close. Paul Brown is a classic example. So are Tom Landry, George Allen, and Chuck Fairbanks of the New England Patriots. But Brown, for one, says the chief reason is that he does not want friendship to interfere with the business of football, particularly that facet concerned with trading or releasing players.

Knox treated his players in Detroit the same way. He always made them feel comfortable in his presence, on or off the field, but never allowed his relationship to go beyond that of player-coach. He wanted all such relationships kept on a strictly professional level, never getting too friendly nor too close to any player. No player could ever say they were his real pal, yet no one ever could say that he snubbed them or that he was cold and aloof.

In the off-season, he relaxes that demeanor a bit, sometimes allowing some non-football matters to intrude on any discussions with his players. Somehow, the talk or the meeting always got back to the subject of offensive line play, or, with the Rams, what was best for the football team.

These have been the feelings of many players whom Knox has coached in the NFL.

Jim Yarbrough was shocked and very disappointed when Chuck left Detroit for the Rams' job.

"Funny," he says, "but I never thought of Chuck Knox in terms of becoming a head coach. I really never thought he'd leave Detroit. There was the loyalty thing, something he always taught us and in which we all reciprocated. I know he was stressing that loyalty to each other means loyalty to the team, but I guess our real loyalty was to him.

"He made us feel we all were in this thing together and that we were on the verge of some great things. I wrote him a note and wished him well after he joined the Rams but I still miss him. I owe an awful lot to him for the good things which have happened to me since I came into the NFL. He made me enjoy playing football, considering that I never had played tackle in my life until I came to the Lions.

"When you saw him get on the bus to go to the airport and then on the charter flight to an away game," Yarbrough remembers, "you could see how serious he was about the game. You knew that you were not on any vacation trip but you were traveling for a very serious purpose."

Knox had to engender this same feeling when he came to the Rams. Many felt at the time that the task would be very difficult because so many veterans had played under two different types of coaches (Allen and Prothro) and might just sit back and force their new boss to prove himself before making any commitments.

"I thought if I worked hard, if I was honest and sincere with them and treated them like men, then respect would take care of itself," he says of the approach he took at Los Angeles. "I don't think you need put respect up there as a goal that must be met. I think that if a head coach and his assistants go out and work, the players will see this and know you have established a program with a purpose.

"Then if they see that you and your coaches know what you're talking about; if you treat them like men with no emotional highs and lows; and if they feel they can talk with you and feel comfortable with you, then the respect will come. I don't think a major goal of mine ever has been to work for respect. I've always looked on it as an outgrowth of whatever else I did."

This is not to say there wasn't a pressure to establish it, Knox adds. The pressure to win is always there, and establishing oneself in the eyes of a team is just one step in achieving victory.

This attitude is a good indication of the side effects Knox has brought about by getting his players to achieve on the field. He makes it easy at the start by not asking them to do something they can't do physically or mentally, or something they don't believe in. He considers those steps most important in achieving first individual success, then team success.

At the same time, he will communicate to his players what he feels they must do to be successful within a game. It might be stopping a team's running game, or one of its backs or a receiver. He then tells them how to do it, as a team, with the defense hearing what the offense must do and vice versa. The special teams come in for their contribution. If Knox feels the game might come down to making one big play, he'll outline what he thinks it will be and who must carry it off.

Late in the practice week, he'll sum up all that has been stressed, then check to be sure everyone knows where the key responsibilities lie. If a linebacker must contain a tight end from getting quickly off the line of scrimmage, the entire team will know that is one of the key elements for victory.

"He believes that when everyone knows what must be done, they are with you," says Leeman Bennett, a long-time assistant with Knox at Kentucky, Detroit, and the Rams. It's also obvious that if you don't do your job, your teammates will know, thus adding another pressure on the player to excel.

"Recognition also is essential," says Knox. "It is one of those little things that really is very big. These are key elements in successful human relationships, things like saying, 'thank you,' and 'I love you,' and 'no, ma'am' instead of a cold 'no.' There certainly is enough time in our work day, regardless of how important our preparation might be, to come up with such proprieties.

"I know when people deal with me that way, I appreciate it if they're decent and thoughtful. I treat people the way I want to be treated."

Yarbrough remembered how Knox treated the offensive linemen in Detroit. He gave the veteran players more leeway and greater benefit of the doubt, figuring they had to be doing something right to be in the NFL for as long as they were. They appreciated this treatment and his recognition of their ability. He would criticize them but he took a soft approach, a pattern he still follows in Los Angeles.

He worked the young players much harder, Yarbrough says. Knox didn't want them to adopt any bad habits—certainly none that could be attributed to him.

"He planted the seed in you to want to be the best," Yarbrough adds. "He really created a pressure with the group to help each other, a togetherness concept. Just look at what he did with the talent at Detroit."

Indeed. Knox found such veterans as John Gordy, Charlie Bradshaw, and Daryl Sanders blended with young players such as Roger Shoals, Ed Flanagan, Frank Gallagher, Chuck Walton and Bob Kowalkowski. Onto the roster came Rocky Freitas, obtained as a free agent from the Steelers and who had been a center and defensive tackle at Oregon State. Knox converted him to tackle and he became a starter before the season ended.

Gallagher, who had played a season of minor league football, also became a starter under Knox. Yarbrough was drafted in the second round in 1968 and, despite the shift from tight end, was starting within two seasons.

"The Lions were a patchwork unit until he came along," Yarbrough says. "He worked hard to bring us along. He was sold on techniques and made a player pay attention to every detail [the Collier influence]. He stressed repetitive learning: that you would do something so often it would become second nature."

Freitas remembers Knox as "an inspirational guy but the inspiration came from his knowledge. Players had tremendous respect for him and tried to play as perfectly for him as possible because we didn't want to make a mistake and let him down."

Yarbrough remembers the agonies many of those Detroit linemen faced if they made a mistake such as offside or holding.

"The toughest part was coming back to the bench," he says. "You'd try to hide but coach Knox would find you and he'd just give you a look that said, 'How could you do that to me?' He didn't always chew you out; he really didn't have to. You just didn't want to make a mistake because you felt like you let *him* down."

That could fall into the category of motivation and obviously Knox does a good job in that area. He puts great stress on it, but solely through teaching, pep talks, backslapping, or fear. In fact, he discounts the effectiveness of both fear and reward motivation.

"Both are temporary," he points out. "Remove the reward or the fear and the motivation ceases to exist."

Knox believes teaching engenders self-motivation. He sees motivation itself as the pride and character a coach puts into an individual. It will come only when he can effect a personality change and get players to do the things that he wants them to do, and get them done with consistency.

How can all this come about?

By teaching, which Knox defines as "the ability to relate to your players, to get them to accept all of the many things a football coach wants them to accomplish."

Not through technical knowledge, he says, because anyone can buy countless books filled with plays and diagrams. The only thing that counts is how successful a coach is when he asks a player to do something, or tries to sell him on a particular technique. To Knox, this is what teaching and motivation is all about.

Knox always has approached this phase of his profession by looking first at the types of players he has. He says there are three types: the "can do," the "can't do," and the "question mark." He defines the "can do's" as the "truly great players, like Jim Brown and there are very few of those on any team." The "can't do's" are few also because they are limited in physical ability and simply cannot do the job. They don't last on a team.

The real test is to reach the "question marks," the players who have the physical skills but still are not getting the job done. The reasons could be psychological, lack of motivation, or faulty skills. As he proved in New York and Detroit, Knox has been successful in taking the bulk of his players out of the "question mark" category and getting them closer to "can do." He has done this by what he terms the "basic principles of coaching," a series of steps he espouses. Here is how he breaks them down:

(1) *To inspire learning*. He creates within the player a desire to do what is demanded, regardless of what technique is being taught. Enthusiasm is a must because this is a basic selling job.

(2) *Concentration*. Learning football, Knox says, is not a matter of intelligence. "I don't give a damn what kind of IQ football players have. Football is a question of concentration. Any football player can learn if a coach gets him to concentrate and when a coach finds the secret of how that's done, he'll be a great coach. Everyone has his own method and every method is right with every individual player as long as it works."

(3) *Belief*. Knox always has believed in what he taught, so deeply and so strongly that he teaches with conviction. A player must understand the depth of that conviction.

"I call my brand of football 'Ram football,'" Knox says. "If I say to one of my players, 'What does Ram football mean to you?' I expect he'll tell me it means 'tougher, smarter, and better conditioned.' We stress those three things every day.

"My position coaches, for example, have got to believe strongly in what they teach. Every great moment in the history of mankind occurred because someone had a belief. If a coach believes strongly enough that he will win and in what he is teaching, then he will be tough.

"When you do that you have upgraded the individual performance levels of each player on the team and caused the team to grow and become better collectively."

(5) *Demand it be done*. Knox demands that what he believes in be done his way to make all this happen, "even if it is something as basic as buttoned chinstraps. If that is a rule, then a coach must be consistent with it and chinstraps have to be buttoned all of the time."

(6) *Evaluate*. He not only evaluates what his team achieves but has followed Collier's dictum and attempts to be totally honest with himself in what he sees. Looking at the scoreboard is one way but not enough, he says, "because we may win a game but the

day is going to come when we could meet someone with equal talent and get beat.

"Look beyond that scoreboard and see that all the things the players are taught are being performed in a game that way. If I spent time in practice teaching a certain technique and then looked at the game films and saw the technique not being followed, I must be doing a damn poor job of teaching. Or maybe the technique is wrong and I should stick with what the player is doing in a game. He obviously feels it is best for him and is having more success with it."

Knox recognizes the difference between the theoretical and practical in coaching and the only thing that interests him is "will it work?"

"If we have a running play, it must earn its keep," he says. "It must meet our standards or we're not going to have it in our offense. It's the same with pass patterns. But the only way we find out is by honestly looking at ourselves."

Knox recalls the great amount of time he once spent teaching the technical aspects of line play and how shocked he was when he looked at the game films and saw his players were not doing the things he so painstakingly had taught them in practice.

"That's when I changed as a coach," he says. "I started to get together with them and make them practice the techniques they would use in a game.

"Another thing was the agility drills. I had them lying on their backs and getting up but I have yet to see a football player function lying on his back. We don't do that now. We do only what is functional, what is directly related to what we will do in a game. We do it without sacrificing the fundamentals."

(7) *Never forget the basics*. This is where Knox plays down the importance of the so-called "game plan." That, he says, is only important if his team is fundamentally sound enough to execute it. The basic fundamentals will motivate players because they will execute what must be done and feel secure they can handle any situation.

While coaching at Wake Forest, he remembers seeing Army's "Lonesome End" offense unveiled against South Carolina in the opening game of the 1958 season. The end, Bill Carpenter, an All-America who later won the Medal of Honor in Vietnam, had a field day against South Carolina's secondary that afternoon.

"It didn't make sense to me," Knox recalls. "If we go out and play on the street, and you put a guy out wide, I put one out to cover him. And if my one guy can't do it, I put two out there.

"That's what I mean by not forgetting the basics. It's the same thing in controlling the line of scrimmage on offense. You do it by the entire offensive line going *together* on the snap count. If that doesn't happen, whatever else we do doesn't really matter."

(8) *Sell skill*. Knox sells his players—enthusiastically, he says—on the idea that football is indeed a skill game and all its elements, such as blocking, tackling, catching the ball are skills that can be improved upon. The improvement must come from concentration on the basic fundamentals. Again the individual improvement will have a collective effect.

(9) *Don't demonstrate*. It is scientifically wrong, Knox says, for a coach to demonstrate a technique to a player or on a player. Players resent being made the butt of some

coach's exuberance, particularly when he knows he cannot retaliate as he could against another player.

"Most of the time, the technique you're trying to demonstrate doesn't come out as you picture it in your mind," Knox says. "I remember I once had a group of offensive linemen to whom I wanted to show a good blocking stance. A friend took a picture while I was in that stance and if those linemen ever had copied it, we'd really have been in trouble.

"After that, anytime I wanted to demonstrate something, I would use a player and be sure that he did everything the way I wanted it done. Then everyone could follow a perfect model."

(10) *Teach, don't holler.* Enthusiasm is great and should be distinguished from ranting and raving, he says. If mistakes are made, the teaching process is the only answer. A player won't understand what he's being taught if all he gets is hollering.

"Take those factors, add the key element of communication, and that is my idea of how you can improve a player," Knox says. "But communication is the key. You must reduce an action to its simplest components, then hammer at it with repetition.

"I remember we had a guard at Kentucky who was a fine blocker on initial contact but who wouldn't stay with his man after he had hit. So we drummed 'hit and stick' into him for a long time. Then we decided we didn't have to say 'hit' because he would do that anyway. So we made him think 'stick, stick, stick' before every play. He turned into a fine blocker."

Knox uses a golf swing to demonstrate what he calls "inductive reasoning."

"You learn five parts of a golf swing, one at a time," he says, "but you can't think of all five at once. After you have repeated the swing over and over you reach the point where you can get up on the tee and think of one part of the swing and your mind will subconsciously direct your body to put the others into operation."

He follows his own example by simplifying the Rams' technical instruction. Because he spent his career as a line coach, most of his examples deal with line play. He gives another when he talks about the lighter mental burden that came when the Rams established their line blocking techniques.

"Their eyes lead them," Knox begins. "They have a point to block on—right on the numbers, between the numbers, left of the numbers, outside the right knee, outside the left knee, all depending on the kind of block we want. They have a specific point on the man to aim at just as the passer uses a spot on the body of the receiver as his target.

"The range of the receiver's arms around that spot provides the margin of error. You simplify the targets and you build the lessons in with repetition, repetition, repetition. It becomes a part of the subconscious. Then a player can concentrate on what he must do at that moment. That lets him keep his cool under pressure."

Knox also believes in emphasizing the so-called "little things" as well as the big things. He cites the kicking game as an example. When does a team utilize the fair catch? When does it utilize the free kick option?

"You don't have fifteen minutes to think about these things when they happen. I want our players to know how they will respond in a particular situation even though that situation may not happen once all season," he says.

Much of this is done by what Knox terms as "visualization." He wants his players to sit back, close their eyes, and visualize themselves in certain situations dealing with their responsibilities.

"Take a linebacker," he says. "He's got to be thinking off the field about the particular coverages. He must go over and over in his mind and get a visual picture of what he must do. Now when he's on the field or is sitting at a meeting and the coach goes over these things, he will know exactly what he must do. He'll have a greater chance to retain it.

"But if he just goes on the field, goes through the motions, and doesn't do anything off the field, then he's going to make a lot of mistakes. We want our players to have those mental pictures stored in their subconscious so in a moment of crisis in a game, they can be pulled out. But if you don't put them in there, they can't be pulled out."

There is more to do than just taking mental pictures. Knox tests his players on everything the Rams do and he has his coaches examine players' playbooks to see what notes have been written inside. If a player hasn't written much but is not making any mistakes, it's okay; if a player hasn't written too much and isn't doing much right either, then he's told to get the matter down in writing and study off the field.

Knox's players in New York, Detroit, and Los Angeles all agree that he has tried to instill in them the great thirst to find out everything possible about playing their position.

"There are many coaches who know as much about football as he does but they are not able to teach the fundamentals," Yarbrough says. "He taught us through the confidence he showed. He would tell us there would be times when we would get beaten physically because the other guy is paid to play defense just as we were paid to play offense. But he tried to emphasize the idea that if we followed the techniques he taught, then we would minimize the times we'd beat ourselves."

What Knox teaches is a technique called "spear blocking." He has his players target on an opponent's body, as he indicated in naming the various areas where a lineman must aim, and then take the opposing lineman where he wants to go using that technique.

Another strong point in Knox's teaching is technique, the key to successful pass blocking. Knox teaches the three-step drop off the line that puts a player in position to battle a defensive charge and do it immediately. Yarbrough says he never had to pass block as a tight end at Florida but, after working with Knox, he was amazed at the short period of time it took to become effective.

"He took those fundamentals and he showed you what each step meant and why it was meant to be," the Lions' tackle recalls. "As long as you stayed interested, he'd work to help you. When he saw a guy give it half a chance or not really care, then he stopped really caring about the player, too."

Freitas says that Knox's great memory helps him, too. The coach often referred to something that happened three seasons before. And if a player happened to be facing the same man that week as he did three seasons back, he would tell him everything he did, what mistakes he made, what fakes he went for—a total picture without ever putting a game film on the projector.

Knox acknowledges that all of this is true. It is, he repeats, why teaching breeds motivation. And why self-motivation begins with practice, with the coach's attitude toward practice.

"I want my coaches going out there every day with specific objectives in mind," he says. "I want them to be so completely honest with their players that they get in their ear a little bit and get them moving the way we want them. This builds pride and character.

"The really great football coaches—Lombardi, Paul Brown, Don Shula, Blanton Collier—all have been great teachers," he says. "Being great teachers they've been great motivators. They had the capacity to take an individual and take him further, improve him and upgrade his performance level more than any other coach possibly could.

"The real test always comes when it's fourth-and-one and your players aren't thinking about getting a thousand more dollars to do this or that. You look at their teams and when those times came, their players reached back down deep, got that pride, that self-motivation, that great burning desire to want to do the job that very moment. When the moment of truth comes, it must come from within the man himself."

Knox acknowledges that since motivation is an individual matter, each player must be dealt with in that manner. It's up to the coach to know his players and be able to reach them in a deeply personal way. Only then will he be able to draw out of them the full effort that he demands. Like everything else, Knox also breaks down into various elements what the methods he feels are most successful for him in doing this. Some of these elements parallel his principles of coaching, which is why he ties the idea of motivation and teaching so closely together. Here is how he lines them up:

(1) Knowledge of football and belief in what is being taught.

(2) Knowing people, because football coaching is a "people" business. If a coach can't relate to his players, he cannot get them to accept his knowledge.

Knox and his coaches spend a great deal of time discussing what they feel must be done to motivate the team, and what they themselves must do to get this done. Some coaches relate individually to the player, others to the team as a whole.

"I call this the 'winning edge,'" he says. "These are not the Xs and Os or any mysterious technical points. I feel they are common sense things which, if given proper attention, can be the difference in a game. And if you give your players a 'winning edge,' then you are showing them a way to become successful. It is another way of motivating them."

Here is how he breaks down his "winning edge":

(1) To build confidence by playing the percentages. "We want to have thought out ahead of time, for every game, what we are going to do on fourth-and-one, whether or not we want to go for it. We don't want to be down there on the sidelines and have somebody get a vision or an idea of what we might do. We may decide, as a staff, that momen-

tum could decide a game so we might go on fourth-and-one because we need a lift. So playing the percentages is nothing more than doing the things we thought out ahead of time," Knox says.

(2) To be basic in his approach to a game. "A confused player won't play well," Knox says. "And every coach knows more than he can teach so we want to stress only those things that we think are necessary to win the game. If we get in a key situation in the fourth quarter and we've worked on thirty pass coverages in practices, the player knows he might have worked only three plays in that coverage. What do you think he's going to say? I know. He'll stand in that huddle and think, 'Oh boy, I don't know. I just hope they throw it to the other side!'

"We want him to say, 'Okay, here's the cover we're running and I've been through this a hundred times. This is what I have to do.' It's the same on offense. I don't want our offensive lineman getting a play and thinking, 'Where the hell did this play come from?' We want to feel secure; we want our players to feel that the things we are trying to do are simple; we want to be consistent."

(3) Don't coach caution into good players. Knox calls that overcoaching. He never stresses negative things to a good, natural player.

(4) Nothing is accomplished without enthusiasm. (Five minutes with Knox and you know how fervently he believes this.)

(5) Look for and recognize mistakes. This means being honest with yourself, he says, and if there is a doubt in any area, go back and check it.

(6) Little things are done by winners.

(7) Having a good team just gives you a *chance* to win. "I really believe that," Knox says. "It no way insures that you are going to win. It's what you do. It's how consistent you can get the players to be. Players, not coaching, win. But poor coaches lose. When we win, the players and my coaches get the credit. I try to make my coaches feel and know that I consider them the best staff in the NFL, bar none."

(8) A coach must be himself. "Players recognize authority and that must come from me, not from someone else wearing a mask that looks like me. Whatever else I do as a coach I must be sincere, I must be me," he says.

(9) A coach must be alert. He must know the rules, the players, the coaches, and all the possible situations he may face.

(10) A coach also must prepare for the psychological ups and downs. "I always know what I am going to say if we win, or if we lose. I know what I'll do if we win, or if we lose. All of this affects the individual player and the moment you say or do the wrong thing, it is too late to erase it."

(11) A coach must always have a plan and believe in it. "'Don't compromise and lose your guts,' is what I tell my coaches. Everything must be planned; nothing good happens by accident. I know that any plan I draw up will keep me from overlooking the little things," Knox says.

Many coaches lump motivation and all that goes with it under the generic heading of "discipline and dedication." Knox feels there is a distinct difference between the two.

"Discipline precedes morale," he says. "You can't have good morale without discipline. The discipline I'm talking about is that which pertains to carrying out the details of your assignment . . . not to jump offside, to line up correctly, to listen in the huddle, to have great pursuit on defense.

"To a lot of people, discipline is length of hair or whether or not a player has a mustache. That is self-imposed but it doesn't necessarily mean that you'll have discipline. You do the other things right and the rules will take care of themselves. You cannot hassle a player about a couple of thousand different things. You must pick out the things that will be important to you, what you think you must do to win and get on with those things."

This is not to say that the Rams don't have rules of personal conduct. They do, but Knox tells his players that he hopes the penalties accompanying them need not be imposed. He does not want to be a schoolmaster and so far this approach has worked. He's fined few players and then only for being late for meetings or practices. There have been no serious disciplinary breaches.

"There must be rules," he acknowledges. "I don't like the idea of fining anyone, but if it has to be done, I won't hesitate."

Again, he feels that a dedicated player never need worry about such things. To him dedication is not only trying to be the very best but understanding how it can be achieved and why it is sought.

"The 'why' is easy," Knox points out. "A player or coach, or anyone for that matter, wants the self-satisfaction of knowing he will be recognized by his peers as the best. Then there is the probability that it will mean more money, not that money in itself should be an end for any man, but only for what it enables you to do for other people.

"Then a player, or whoever, must map out a program to overcome that which keeps him from achieving all of that and work on that program. For a player, it may be working in the off-season, during the season, keeping that objective in mind when he is playing.

"A player cannot have dedication unless he is in good physical condition. His body simply will not let his mind do what it wants because he can't concentrate if he is tired. Then all his mind is thinking about is survival, and practice or playing a game becomes nothing more than an endurance test."

All of this may sound as if Knox is tightly programmed and all that need happen is for him to push a button. That is not so. Knox simply has accepted the successful ways he has seen in others as long as they fit his own personality; then he built something strong enough around this core of knowledge to support all that he is trying to achieve.

The fact that he has come up with a coaching battle plan so highly refined indicates great organizational ability, which is apparent with his team on the field. Scibelli agrees, but says that Knox is not a goal-setter like George Allen.

Allen has laid out, on charts for all of his players to study any time they wish, a number of specific goals he says they must achieve to win. Some of these include a certain number of quarterback sacks per game, a certain number of interceptions or fumble recoveries, or a percentage of successful third-down conversions. Allen marks on his charts whether or not his team has accomplished these goals and, in most cases where they have not, his teams either have not won or have just missed.

"Chuck doesn't do those kinds of things," Scibelli says. "But he can quote you good and bad statistics about a team and its players and about his own team. He believes in the giveaway-takeaway tables [fumbles and interceptions a team loses versus what it gets]. Early in the '75 season, he found we were giving up too many easy first downs by penalties and he worked hard on that."

At the end of each season, he has his staff undertake a month-long statistical breakdown of the team's offense. The assistants go through every play run that season, look at each play against every defense and check the number of times each was used against a particular defense. They total the yards gained by each play, the average yards per try, the average number of times each was used in a game, and the number of times the play achieved its average.

They look at every play from a position-by-position standpoint. For example, they study how the right tackle lined up to see if he was positioned the best possible way for a play to go smoothly. They discuss any common faults of a play in terms of structure and how these could be overcome. Finally, they make their suggestions on how each play should or should not be changed, if that is the consensus.

That is the manner in which Knox makes his plays "earn their keep." The standards he sets are minimum and maximum. That helps keep his organization functional and uncluttered of too many goals that players might have to meet.

"About the only goal he sets for us is to win the Super Bowl," Scibelli says. "The rest of the time he wants us concentrating on doing what is necessary to win each game. He approaches this differently than George Allen in that he at least talks to everyone about it, whereas George never talked to the offense."

Bennett, who sees Knox's organizational ability from inside the coaches' offices, thinks it is the real reason that Knox is now "one of the great coaches" in the NFL. Bennett cites Knox's thoroughness—"he never leaves one thing undone"—and his ability to get the feel of a situation and make the right decision at the right time.

"I call it 'street sense,'" his assistant coach says. "He can feel the reaction of a group to a particular situation. He does it because he believes a person can help himself along and minimize his dependence upon others. He does it by always thinking about football, not the Xs and Os as much as their execution."

Bennett says Knox's other great quality is his ability to judge people. That means putting the right people in the right place at the right time as well as knowing whether the people around him really are right for him and what he is attempting to accomplish. Paul Brown is a stickler for this, for having what he terms "good people," or at least those he knows will respond to his ways.

Knox was more concerned with putting people into the right positions when he took the Rams' job. Before he made any moves, he not only checked the effectiveness of the player but also decided what, on a technical level, could be done to upgrade the performance of someone who had not been playing regularly. The result was six new starters in what had been a so-so defensive unit and the development of a highly efficient offense.

These were not chance achievements. Knox says he puts much study into any personnel decisions, considering first the position and its requirements—the size, speed, agility, and quickness a player must possess to play at a certain position—and second, the mental qualifications necessary to play it.

"In certain assignments, we line up players in different ways. When we give them responsibilities in these alignments, we want to be sure they will be able to carry them out," Knox says. "We play team defense, eleven guys tied to each other so it's very important to carry out the details of each assignment if it is to function properly.

"We also consider the so-called intangible elements, the character of the player concerned; his competitive spirit; whether he is unselfish; his commitment to the team, regardless of whether we win or not. For example, we prefer an end who might not catch a pass but when we win, is pleased with the contribution he's made in comparison to someone who catches eight passes and still can feel satisfied if we lose."

That plan helped running back Lawrence McCutcheon, a non-contributor (three games, no carries in 1972) to the NFC rushing champion in 1974 with his second consecutive, 1,000-plus season. Many thought Knox caught lightning in a bottle but it was a bit more than that.

"We took a look at McCutcheon in 1973 when we had him in that first spring for two days of preliminary drills," Knox recalls. "We were impressed. We said if we could get him to do other things that running backs must do, he'd be a good one.

"We didn't have any film to go on, so when we got to training camp we were determined we'd find out about him. We ran him and ran him and ran him and what he did told us we were right. It was the same way in the preseason games."

McCutcheon also remembers that preseason.

"Coach Knox asked me why I hadn't played more in 1972 and I told him I didn't know," he recalls. "I said it was none of my doing. The coach said he would give me the ball and see what I could do with it. That's what I wanted."

The turnaround by the Rams' defense vividly illustrates the thinking Knox used in his personnel selection. It was the same system he uses in analyzing each offensive play. In this case, he and his staff determined who the best defensive players were and then put together what they felt would be the strongest 11 players on the field at one time. The aim was consistency—week-in, week-out.

"We decided to change things a bit drastically," Knox remembers. "The players here had been primarily a four-three team and we wanted to go to the odd-man line approach. That meant changes in personnel. Fred Dryer and Jack Youngblood had not been starters for the Rams. They had alternated and we decided both should start, so we switched Jack from right defensive end to the left side.

"A lot of people had said neither of those players could do the job full-time but we felt both had the ability to be super football players. For example, Dryer was supposed to be weak playing the run but we changed some techniques and now he plays the run as well as any defensive end in the NFL. Larry Brooks started six games and we saw enough to realize that with work and experience he could be very good.

"Jack Reynolds, our middle linebacker, was another man we couldn't learn much about from the films. He had sat on the bench for three years because people said he didn't have the mobility to play the run. At first we felt the same way, but I felt you still have to put a guy to the test. So we looked at him in practice, we worked with him, and we saw him in the preseason games. He got confidence in himself and pretty soon he was making plays he hadn't been able to make in the past.

"Take Steve Preece, one of our defensive backs. He had been cut by four other teams but there was something in him that gave us the feeling he could play. He was a fine competitor. He had been a college quarterback and was smart. We felt he could give us something that other people could not. We put him at free safety, Ken Geddes at left linebacker, Eddie McMillan at right cornerback, got Charlie Stukes and put him at left corner, and used Dave Elmendorf at strong safety. From them we got a twelve-two team that first year.

"We still get our guys through the computer process. But the ultimate difference is that the practice field is the real proving ground."

One of the biggest moves Knox made that first season was acquiring quarterback John Hadl from San Diego. Hadl quarterbacked the Rams to the NFC West title, winning the NFC's most valuable player award.

But before the middle of the next season Hadl was benched in favor of James Harris. Hadl then was traded to Green Bay and Harris helped win another division title and took the team within a few inches of the Super Bowl.

"That was a particularly difficult time," Knox says of the Hadl-Harris decision. "John had a great year the previous season and he is such a great person. But we had the feeling that Harris could do it. You never know about such things until you try. We had him for a full season, watched him in quarterback meetings, and saw that he really had learned a lot rooming with Hadl. He certainly had the arm and the talent so, all things combined, we felt the move would be a good one. And it was."

The basic dividend of the offensive and defensive changes was the ability of the Rams to play with poise under pressure and to deliver victory or key plays in critical situations. He removed much of the pressure the team had been subjected to under Allen and the confusion that it felt playing for Prothro. Knox kept a close watch on everything that was happening and had much to say about that which he didn't like.

"We used to kid him about us having two offensive line coaches," Scibelli recalls. "Ray Prochaska had the job but Chuck spent a lot of time around us during that first season. I know that he wanted to be sure we got things down just as he laid them out because much of our offensive success would result in proper line play technique. He came up with the right answer for the three-man fronts and four linebacker set-ups, as well as adopting it to the other types of defenses."

It should not be construed that Knox second-guesses his assistant coaches or constantly peers over their shoulders on the practice field. He gives them complete latitude, with the idea that they are more intimately involved with a particular group of players. Decisions are made in staff meetings following as much discussion as Knox feels is necessary to iron out any details or problems. Ninety percent of the teaching spins off those discussions and takes place on the practice field.

Knox is not a believer in burgeoning staffs with what amounts to individual instruction for each player. For example, he doubled the responsibilities of the special teams and offensive backfield coach.

"Off the field, he can work on special teams planning," Knox explains. "That still leaves four offensive coaches for the offensive game plan. But when you're on the practice field, most NFL special team coaches have little to do. That's when he can handle his offensive backfield duties."

Knox also insists on having at least one coach on his staff who recently coached college football. Jim Wagstaff, from Boise State, was his first appointment.

"You need someone fresh from a college staff," Knox maintains, "because the college game always is changing. You need a man who has been dealing with it lately, communicating with the kids. The right mix is to get a man who has been coaching in the colleges but who also had some pro experience as a player and who is able to maintain a good balance in what each game really requires."

He follows the same philosophy about hiring a coach from another staff, particularly one that has been a winner.

"You first of all get new ideas but most importantly your new assistant may challenge some of the things you already do," says Knox. "When he challenges them, you either reconfirm your own convictions that what you are doing is correct or you change them. The line sometimes can be thin because there is much to be said for staff continuity. If you have the right kind of staff, and you yourself are always going back to the principle of not being afraid to check what you are doing and being honest with what you find, that can be avoided. To have one new man come in now and then is probably pretty good but periodic wholesale changes could be harmful."

Knox appoints an offensive coordinator but he feels the offensive line coach should have the most to say about the running game, which generally is two-thirds of a team's offense in any game. From his own experiences, Knox maintains that the offensive line coach knows the most about the team's blocking patterns and the opposition's defensive tendencies against the run. The offensive line coach must determine whether a play's blocking requirements can work before the play is put into the game plan.

The offensive coordinator then zeroes in on the quarterback and receivers and talks directly to them during a game. After two seasons Knox appointed Ray Malavasi, his defensive line coach, as defensive coordinator. He believes strongly that a defensive backfield coach cannot handle the overall defensive coordination because of the importance of his work with the secondary.

"He's got to concentrate on those four deep backs," Knox says. "That's essential because you can get beaten quicker in the secondary than anywhere else. If the defensive backfield coach is the overall coordinator, he has a tendency to look around for the linebackers and that can be fatal."

Regardless of who is in charge of what area, all ideas must clear Knox's desk. He has adopted Collier's method of making his assistants sell their ideas to him—just as Shula does in Miami—and back them with sound, logical football sense. His coaches say that Knox does not come up with a quick yes or no, preferring to digest the ideas thoroughly. He'll talk to them at greater length if he wants more input and also, like Shula, tells his coaches not to be discouraged if he turns them down. If they still are sold on their plan, he wants them to keep coming back until the alternatives are so clear that the plan is finally either accepted or rejected and the reasons for either decision are just as clear.

Knox puts great responsibilities on himself and on his coaches to continue the smooth functioning of their staff relationship in training camp. He was particularly determined before the Rams opened their 1975 camp, following back-to-back playoff seasons, that his coaches return to page one in their books and begin with the most basic fundamentals. He stressed that because the Rams under him had been together for two years. There often is a tendency to take for granted that the groundwork always is secure.

"The alternative," he says, "is finding out somewhere down the line that your base isn't as solid as you thought and then trying to get a fresh start. It's usually too late then. Our aim is to sell our players that training camp begins a brand new year, that last year is history and has no bearing on what we will go over the next six months.

"I told my players that they can take all the trophies and awards we received, add up all our victories on a big white sheet of paper, put them into a wheelbarrow, wheel it out to the fifty-yard line at the Coliseum, and tell the team we're playing, 'Look at this!' How much impact do you think that will have?"

Instead, Knox lays down four objectives for his team each summer: to develop a winning attitude during the preseason; to come out of camp with a sound base of fundamentals; to be so well-conditioned that the team can play four or more quarters at full speed every week; to finish all experimenting once camp closes.

Experimenting not only entails new plays or other changes but also includes seeing that every player gets a solid opportunity to make the team. Knox insists that every man get a specific number of plays in one or two preseason games where he is the key man so that the coaches can make what they consider an honest decision about whether the player can make the squad.

"Too many times I've seen a player cut from a squad simply because he did not have sufficient opportunity to show what he could do," Knox recalls. "I was determined this would not happen with the Rams. We set up a schedule of playing time and made sure it was not dictated by the game. Maybe we wanted a rookie back to carry the ball fifteen times. He stayed in there until he had run his quota."

"The thing I like the least is telling a player he'll have to go, that we don't have a place for him on our roster. I tell them personally because I was the one who gave them the opportunity so I feel I should be the one to tell them why it didn't work out.

"Believe me, after a man has given an all-out effort it's as hard to tell a free agent as a first-round draft pick. But I try to give the man a true, honest picture. If I think he can help another team, I say so. If he can't, I offer to help get him something else. This isn't easy but I try. It's a small world and we're all in it together. The guy I cut today may be in a position to help me somewhere down the road, or vice versa."

The "honest picture" technique is a keystone for Knox. It ranges from his player relations to his game preparations and in all cases, totally encompasses the team as a way of life. It has proven particularly successful in game preparation because the Rams, under Knox, never have gone into a football game under any delusions about what their opponents can or cannot do.

Knox's teams know exactly what they will do in every conceivable situation. Knox doesn't want what he calls "any sideline fish-eye looks," going back and forth whenever decisions are made that are crucial and could affect the game's outcome. Each week, he and his staff draw up a check list that tells them what kind of game they can plan on. They lay out key elements such as establishing the run, field position, substitutions, communication, when to be conservative and when not to be.

"Each of those things is vitally important in itself," Knox says. "For example, take communication. We've got to know going into the game how we are going to handle all the things we plan to do when each situation arises. With substitutions, we may want to rotate our defensive backs and our running backs. How and when? What situations or chain of events will cause us to change a quarterback? Trying to decide when a guy is not going good is a very important decision because if you must take him out, there is a certain stigma.

"We let everyone know every facet of our offensive, defensive, and special teams plan, things like end-of-the-game offense and defense; two-minute drill; scoring combinations; taking a safety, under what conditions and how. Where we will look to kick a field goal, both from time on the clock and place on the field? Where we will punt, how it should be angled? If we get to their goal line, what is the progression of plays? They are different from six yards out than from four yards out. On defense what would cause us to blitz? What about goal-line defense, or the opposition's play-calling tendencies in certain points of the game?

"We want to go into a game knowing exactly where the teams in our conference and division stand. With the new method of determining playoff home sites, that could affect whether or not we want to take the time to win or go after a tie and play the overtime. Sometimes we've started a game with a big play or we've made a big play, a fourth-and-one, early in the game. But we have to know under what conditions and how.

"This outline keeps us on top of the so-called little things because I firmly believe those are the things which really win for you. Everyone does the big things, a really consistent winner thinks of the little ones. That's why a game plan by itself is not the answer; it's the fundamentals you put into the plan to be executed that are the answer. You can have the greatest plan in the world but it's nothing if your team can't execute it."

Yarbrough can understand how the Rams appreciate this kind of preparation. He said the Lions' offensive line never was surprised by any defense during the time Knox was its coach. He had the ability to see things the opposition did that could be used to his own players' advantage, first by using them to prepare his players, then by using techniques which could defeat them.

"Even if you really couldn't do this," Yarbrough says, "he had you believing that you could. Every player went out, regardless of who he was playing against, and believed he had the ability to beat the man across from him."

Bennett says that Knox tries to anticipate situations by putting himself in the place of the man who must make the call. He does this after thorough study and transmits it to his players through repetition, even to the point of foreseeing possible failure. He'll adjust for that, too, because he constantly puts his players and coaches on guard against underestimating what an opponent can do.

"That is what practices are for," Knox explains. "But the key for us is that practice without improvement is meaningless. Every day we go on the practice field we tell our players that we want them to come off as better football players than they were yesterday. If a guy is having a problem, we want him to concentrate on that one problem throughout the entire practice. That relates to every phase of our team because every man is affected."

That includes himself when he leaves his home shortly after 7 A.M. Driving to his team's practice facility in Long Beach, he tries to concentrate on the tempo he'll set for the day's work. He tries to decide which are the most important things his players and coaches must do that day to prepare for the next game.

When he holds his first team meeting each day at 10:30, he tells everyone what the current lists of "must do's" contain for each unit. They do not come in big batches because he knows the reaction will be, "What did he say?" Still, he'll sit at his desk before the team goes on the field for its afternoon drill and begin to jot down points he'll want to cover the next day.

At the same time, his coaches are conducting meetings with their respective units, outlining the day's work, reviewing films of the previous day's practice. Knox also has been known to join these meetings if he feels his presence is required. He also puts great emphasis on what he terms "pre-practice," a time before the team goes full tilt when it jogs or walks through key plays. Later, they'll go through them at full speed.

Practices each day begin at 1:15, or at about the same time the ball is kicked off each Sunday, when the temperature and slant of the sun will be approximately the same. As on game days, he expects his team to have a full meal at 9 A.M. The practice routines do not allow for lunch until after 4 in the afternoon.

Knox's practices are hard and crisp. They aren't all-out scrimmages, but the players hit hard enough to get hurt. The backs are expected to throw blocks just as they would in a game. Knox says this type of intensity is the best way to tune up a promising offensive play. Later in the day, the coaches will review the films of the practices, decide on any changes and be prepared to give them to the players the next day. He and his staff finish around 10 or 10:30 each night.

Knox gives his special teams a full day's preparation instead of taking scattered sessions of the daily practice routine during the week's work schedule.

He insists that his other coaches join this work with the kicking units. Each is given a specific duty, from timing the punter to checking the coverage. With such in-depth preparation, he then feels full concentration can be given to preparing the offense and defense on the other days.

The results of this work on offense are evident in a rushing game that spins off his option blocking system. Knox says the basic premise is for his offense to stay uncommitted longer than the defense. There are no definite holes in the line for the runner to hit. Instead, he'll look for a point of isolation along the line where one defensive man "is put on an island by cutting off the other defensive people."

"Then we block that one man square up, right in the middle of his face, and whichever side he decides to take, we run the other side," Knox explains. "The important thing is for our blocker to hit his man and then stick to him wherever that man goes. If a defensive player has a blocker stuck to him, all he can do is reach out with an arm. Any good runner should be able to go through that for five or six yards.

"With this type of attack, it's the details, not big changes, that make you successful. Getting the blocker to aim for a specific point on his opponent—getting the runner to hit the line of scrimmage at a ninety-degree angle so he can slip through a narrow hole—those are the details that make a play go."

When Knox installed Harris as his quarterback, Knox also began calling the Rams' offensive plays. The Rams' players say their quarterback has the perfect temperament for this system and became a better quarterback in a much faster time than anyone expected because of it. Harris has great faith in his own ability and has been able, under Knox's direction, to blend all the elements into a high degree of competency.

The defense also is not burdened by too many details. Olsen said it developed so quickly and then continued to improve since Knox became head coach because everything has been made so concise. Every player knows exactly what he must do and he doesn't have to stop and consider all the options that existed under Allen's system.

Success has not lessened the pressures of Knox's job, however. Football is a pressure business, he says flatly, but the great pressures are the ones you bring upon yourself. He has laid awake at night thinking about upcoming games—playoff and non-playoff alike.

"You don't lie awake worrying about what someone said about you," he points out. "You lie awake worrying about something you must get done tomorrow, something that may help you win or help make your players successful."

Knox did not have time to get used to the special pressures that exist in the playoffs—and they are highly pressurized, he emphasizes—but he tried to keep his demeanor the same as through the season. What makes it difficult is that one loss puts a team out, something he thinks is unfair in the resulting judgment of a team's overall performance.

"Everyone says there is only one successful team each season and it's the one that wins the Super Bowl," Knox says. "That is true in the strictest sense because we're all ultimately striving to do just that. But I think it is foolish to say that the Oakland Raiders, for example, have not been successful because they have not yet won a Super Bowl. The most important thing, the real way to measure success, is which team has been the consistent winner through all the games that are played."

Knox's biggest disappointments in Los Angeles have been the losses that eliminated the Rams in the NFC playoffs in 1973, '74, and '75.

Los Angeles was blown out by the Dallas Cowboys in the 1975 championship game, and that was painful. The losses in 1973 and 1974, however, were toughest of all. In the first year the Rams lost in the NFL semifinals to Dallas on an incredible touchdown pass from quarterback Roger Staubach to wide receiver Drew Pearson; in the second year the Rams lost the NFC title game to Minnesota when an offside call against the Rams six inches from the Vikings' end zone cost Los Angeles a touchdown.

"There is a powerful lesson there," says Knox, "and that is that you must grow from losing. You can't dwell on a situation like that; you can't hold a wake. Once they're done, they're done. But unless you learn the lessons you must learn from setbacks —whether they're tough or not tough—you become a real loser.

"Through it all you must maintain your emotional stability. Winning and losing are both very temporary things. Having done one or the other, you move ahead. Gloating over a victory or sulking over a loss is a good way to stand still . . . or worse.

"We go out there to win, it's not the end of the world if we don't. We play to win, get an all-out effort, a total commitment in every game. It's what I think Vince Lombardi meant when he said that winning is the only thing. You must know how to win and winning is the only thing you should be concentrating on in a game."

Vince Lombardi was quoted as saying that football was a game "for madmen . . . obsessed with the winning or else they would not be in the game." Knox doesn't agree winning is an obsession nor does he consider himself "mad" because he strives to win every week.

"I guess it's a different way of saying what I strongly believe," he admits. "I'm not necessarily mad. I love my children. I love to do things for people outside of football. I think I'm a human being.

"I think what Lombardi meant by being mad was taking the *time* to do all that it takes to win, the commitment, the long hours. This is not some glamorous job where you just show up on Sunday, put on the thinking cap, and go out on the football field."

A few years ago Knox sought out social situations with Green Bay coaches who had worked for Lombardi at Green Bay; then he picked their brains for Lombardi's ideas. He did the same at Wake Forest, where he worked for Paul Amen, who had spent 13 years as an assistant to Earl Blaik at West Point. Blaik also gave Lombardi so much of his basic approach to football. Knox, likewise, tried to learn as much as he could about the Blaik approach.

Often the measure of the man is when he is not successful, though Knox was not tested too many times in that regard during his first three seasons with the Rams. At the start, Knox showed he was not misled by the panic button. When his team was winless in its first four preseason games, he never deviated from his predetermined plan to prepare the entire Rams' team to adapt and function under his new system.

His coaches in Los Angeles say he does not carry one of those infrequent losses on his back for a week. His recovery, they claim, is quick, generally after seeing the films to find out what happened and knowing that adjustments will be made. Knox tells his coaches and players that to moan about a lost game for four or five days only takes away from the concentration needed to prepare for the next one.

At Detroit, his linemen said a team loss did not necessarily doom them to brow-beating or general chewing out. If they played well, Knox would not say too much. When the team was eliminated from the playoffs just past midseason in his final year with the Lions, he told his linemen, "No one had better lay down. No one ever has laid down on me before and I won't stand for it now."

Carroll Rosenbloom says Knox is much different than Don Shula at comparable stages of their head coaching careers. "I've never known a steadier guy than Knox," says the Rams' owner. "He's unruffled, even-tempered.

"When Shula became head coach, he was just the opposite. He was volatile and as high-strung as Lombardi. That is Don's nature, just as it is Knox's nature to be low-key, though I don't know what he was like ten years ago at a comparable age as Shula. I'm sure Chuck matured as a person before signing on as a head coach. Shula matured while he was a head coach and that's the hard way."

Shula is renowned for his temper. Knox has one too but, according to his players, he never uses it on them. He never tried to be intimidating but always let a player know that when he got on him, it was for his own good and any criticism was directed in a positive way.

"Players appreciated his ability to teach," Yarbrough recalls "so he never had to intimidate you. He just won you over this way. His enthusiasm won you over."

This same enthusiasm has been translated into positive terms in his first head coaching job with the Rams. Winning championships has a way of doing that.

Tom Landry

"If you are prepared, then you will be
confident and you will do the job.
Emotion gets in the way of performance."

The year was 1960, a year when all that had gone before and had been held sacred and safe began to change.

The music became louder, its expressions more intense and suggestive; the politics became freer and spoke of new frontiers; and dissent became a way of life.

Born into this budding maelstrom were the Dallas Cowboys. To appreciate their beginnings, go back two years to New York's Yankee Stadium when the Baltimore Colts took 8 minutes 15 seconds longer than the required 60 minutes to win the National Football League championship. It wasn't so much the Colts had to work overtime to beat the Giants that December Sunday. It was that they did it on television before an entire nation.

Television grasped this old pastime as if it were new. It dispensed its excitement and color to those tired of spending Sunday afternoons raking leaves, taking long drives, or dreading the next day's return to work, and the day-to-day tedium.

Into this new national craze came a new team with the lone star on its helmets.

This team was from Texas, son. From Dallas. Big D. The Cotton Bowl. The Apache Belles and pretty Rangerettes swinging and dancing and kicking like the Rockettes at Radio City Music Hall.

And with the birth of the Cowboys came a team to match the turbulence of the new decade. This team of movement, going from this formation to that, shifting here, shifting there, sending players in what seemed like every conceivable direction. This was something new. It wasn't what Johnny Unitas did. It's what you had tried to do in those touch games at the beach or in the backyard.

The Dallas Cowboys were different, like the new culture. Forget that they managed only one tie in their first season; or that, really, they were a rag-tag outfit composed largely of the unwanted of 12 NFL teams.

There were a couple of other things about the original Cowboys. One was a little quarterback with a bag full of tricks in handing off the ball. You could follow the action when Johnny Unitas handed off but not with this kid.

That "kid" was Eddie LeBaron, a 31-year-old quarterback who stood 5 feet 7 inches. LeBaron performed his deception with the Redskins before he got shot up in the Korean war. And he did it after he came back. But in those days no one paid much notice to the hapless Redskins.

The other thing about the Cowboys was the quiet, unwavering man who always wore a hat and stood almost still as his team blundered about its business on the field. He never seemed to get upset; he never waved his arms or stomped around when things went bad as they most often did.

Tom Landry also was a product of that dark Sunday in 1958 . . . the day pro football had leaped to the attention of the entire country. The game already had its disciples, like the thousands who, for six Sundays a year, would stream into Yankee Stadium and yell: "D-E-E-E-E-FENSE!"

Never had that part of the game been so exalted. Time and again, 11 blue-jerseyed Giants trotted onto the field and three plays later trotted off again amid a torrent of cheers, leaving the opposition in the same place it had found it.

Television began showing these new stars to the nation. Their exploits were legend, not only around Yankee Stadium, but any place newspapers were printed and television signals received in the U. S.

Tom Landry was responsible for much of the success, yet he took little of the credit. He once played for the Giants, directing the "Umbrella" defense that Steve Owen devised to beat the Cleveland Browns in the early fifties. But few really got to know about him until he helped build the Dallas Cowboys. Standing on the sidelines, he was not at all the way you imagined a Texan. He didn't swagger. He didn't wear a 10-gallon hat or cowboy boots. He didn't chew or cuss and he wasn't 6 feet 6 inches tall.

Landry doesn't look much different today than he did in 1960. He doesn't laugh; he doesn't shout. He isn't like Vince Lombardi, urging players, beseeching, cajoling, and threatening. You can't tell whether his team is winning or losing; whether a player has performed magnificently or is so bad he'll be gone the next day. You can't tell a thing from watching Tom Landry.

Landry smiles now when he hears such things. He doesn't consider himself mysterious or imperturbable. If anything, he holds himself quite human. He is chastened by frustration, tempered by hard work, and humanized by a strong belief and trust in God.

More than that, he is an excellent football coach. No one has done more to upgrade defense in pro football than he has; nor has anyone done more to give offensive football a different look.

While playing defensive back with the Giants, he took some general defensive ideas from Steve Owen and others and helped establish the 4-3 alignment as the principle defense in pro football. He refined its parts and coordinated its elements into something people began calling the Doomsday Defense in Dallas.

When he left the Giants to become head coach of the Cowboys, he knew that 4-3 defense so well that he could devise a multiple offense to counter it, to throw off the very elements that had made it so successful.

Landry put all of this football know-how together to win one Super Bowl, came within five seconds of perhaps winning another and of bringing his team to an unprecedented eight straight NFL playoffs. If Green Bay ruled the NFL as a dynasty through the first eight seasons of the sixties with its 82-24-4 record, then Dallas was in the same class through the next six with its 64-19-1 mark. And it competed on a par with Lombardi's mighty Packers during the last two seasons of his tenure at Green Bay, coming within two yards and 16 seconds of winning consecutive NFL titles from those great Packers' teams.

When the Cowboys lost those two close games to Green Bay, people said they blew it; when they lost two more playoffs to the Browns, people said the Cowboys choked and "couldn't win the big one." When they lost in Super Bowl V in the final five seconds, their very legitimacy was questioned.

So was Landry's coaching. People saw him on television and called him a mechanical man. They heard about the Cowboys' computer system and the image was reinforced. They read of players deprecating him and they believed the distorted picture.

Again Landry smiles. There is a serenity about the man that helped him through those low times and which enables him to listen and coolly evaluate the words of his detractors. He does it with the same calm he shows on the sidelines.

There is no rule in football that says a coach must meet a certain set of human specifications. In the eyes of the public, Landry probably is at one end of whatever line is used to measure this profession. In reality, he's middle-ground if you also consider such as Allen, who is a workaholic and who has little life outside football; or John Ralston who often goes home after his team loses and cries with his family; or Don Coryell, who has been known to sleep in his office for days at a time during the season.

The stoicism that is his game personality gives way to warmth and genuine feeling when Landry is among friends. He and his wife, Alicia, are warm, social people who live in the comfortably fashionable north Dallas area. They have a life together outside football that includes friends both inside and outside the Cowboys' organization. Landry enjoys boating and golf as recreation with friends and family and is not too busy in training camp for some brisk games of tennis or racquetball with his coaches.

During the season, he is as busy as every other NFL coach but he also manages a night out with his wife following the taping of his weekly television show. The two will have a quiet dinner and they consider it "their thing" amidst the pressure of his work.

"People want to know what makes Tom tick and he's too damn smart to tell them," says one of his close friends. "He was born polished. He's such a gentleman it's almost spooky."

But Landry does not walk on water, a talent some ascribed to Lombardi. Throughout his life, there is a solid thread of humanity that leaves him no better or no worse than anyone else.

He grew up in Mission, Texas, in the Rio Grande Valley where his father worked as a mechanic in his own garage. At the University of Texas, he was a teammate of Bobby Layne, a blithe spirit and high-roller whose lifestyle was almost diametrically opposed to Landry's. So were those of other players who shared dormitory life with him. Some of the pranks in that athletic dorm are legendary, but Landry's former college teammates say he didn't participate in the more audacious ones.

"Tom's not a prude," one said. "He didn't frown on us or criticize us and he seemed to enjoy some of the stuff we did. But while he didn't participate, he wouldn't let you upset him and he wouldn't upset you."

The description of Landry as a collegian was that he was mature and dependable. He was what might be called "straight." His wife tells of the time they were dating as college students. "He once told me he wouldn't kiss me if I didn't stop smoking," she recalls.

When Landry played football at Texas he already had been through World War II as a 19-year-old bomber pilot. Perhaps that had a lot to do with his demeanor. He flew 30 missions over German occupied Europe and Germany itself. Once he crashed in Belgium after his B-17 ran out of gas on a long flight back from a mission over Czechoslovakia. He brought the plane down between two trees that sheared off the plane's wings. The entire crew walked away without a scratch.

He doesn't talk about his war experiences. All he will say about the crash-landing other than to note it happened was, "A lot of planes were lost that night . . ."

But there is little doubt that the experiences touched him deeply and helped forge an order to his priorities and to his own makeup. Winning and losing football games have a tendency to pale when reflected against such other events.

Yet, after years of war, college, and tenures as a player and coach in professional football, there still is a naivete in his nature.

A friend remembers once discussing a story by former Boston College basketball coach Bob Cousy that detailed his reasons for leaving the collegiate game to become a professional coach. One of the foremost was recruiting, which also included promises by some recruiters to provide "a social life" for a prospect. Cousy had demurred.

"You mean they would get them dates?" Landry asked, eyebrows raised. A "date" to him meant a movie or dinner and dancing.

"Not dates," the man replied. "That means sex."

Landry was outraged. "Do you mean that kind of thing goes on to get kids to come to a school?" he asked incredulously. Told that it did, he slumped back in his chair and slowly shook his head.

"I think I really shocked Tom with that story," said the friend. "I honestly don't think he had any idea that such things were happening. It's his nature to think that people play by rules, as he does."

All of this reflects an inner serenity that is genuine. It is locked tightly into his deep Christian beliefs. It is as much a part of his life as the Xs and Os of football. But he is not pushy with it.

"I'd hate to say my faith's a rock but it's true," he says. "A lot of people say, 'Well, he's a Christian because that's the only thing he can hang on to, the only thing he can fall back on.' That's not true. It is my strength; it gives me inner peace. Without my faith, I'd be in real bad shape. Faith gives a man hope and hope is what life is all about."

Being a head coach, he says, is God's plan for the fulfillment of his life. He is sincere in that feeling.

"That's why won-lost records, championships, and all that has gone on in the past really have so little meaning for me," Landry says with conviction. "I'm not saying that because I'm so non-human that I don't appreciate success and praise. All of us do.

"But when it's all over I don't know that I'll reflect back on how they remember me. My own purpose is to serve God in whatever capacity He wants me to serve Him. That's my only measurement.

"If I lose, I'm going to lose; if I win, I'm going to win. That doesn't mean that I don't work as hard as anyone else or that I don't try to win as hard as anyone else. I do because God expects us to be the best we can."

He sees no contradiction in his Christian beliefs and the organized violence of professional football. They are, he says, very compatible and discernible by intent.

"If you're vicious and want to hurt people, that's bad," he says. "But you don't often find that feeling among athletes. We're tough because we've got to be tough to play pro football. But if we see a man hurt, we don't kick him. We pick him up.

"God gave us talent and expects us to use it. That talent can include being a very good football player like a fast running back, a talented kicker, or an aggressive lineman. As long as Christ is the center of your life and you're doing the things with your talent that are acceptable to him, it's fine. There are many outstanding Christian people in pro football."

Though active in the Fellowship of Christian Athletes and the Billy Graham Crusade, Landry never finds any cynicism among his players about his deep religious convictions.

Few changes have occurred in Landry's football life in Dallas, though players say he has become more communicative.

"When I first came to Dallas," former linebacker Chuck Howley recalled, "I walked into Tom's office one day and saw him looking out the window, apparently preoccupied. I bet I was there five minutes before he even knew it.

"In my last couple of years with the Cowboys, he loosened up. He was friendlier. He even would speak to you when you passed him in the hall."

Not speaking to people was not an intended snub nor was it a reflection of his personality. Most often it would happen early in the week when plans for an upcoming game were being formulated.

"Come Thursday or Friday," former assistant general manager Al Ward remembers, "and he'd see you, give you a warm hello, a big smile. The previous three days he was so engrossed in his thinking that I don't think he even remembered passing anyone in the hall."

No one around the Cowboys really seems to mind those moments because they understand what makes him tick. They've come to appreciate that the silence, the introspection, and deep thought have spelled out many happy Sunday afternoons.

"Tom is not an easy man to read," club president Tex Schramm admits. "You'd never really know it but he is a very emotional person. But the way he conducts himself, he doesn't allow it to show.

"He's also a very confident person and that went a long way toward sustaining us when things weren't always going the way we thought they should. Remember, too, that he is a very honest, straightforward person. He is not a con artist. He treats players like adults. There are some coaches who sell their players a bill of goods. Tom can't do that."

From all of this comes Tom Landry, the coach. He uses the straightforward approach, the distinctive personality and the quiet introspection to forge a detailed plan of attack that bases its success on absolute preparation. That is the real secret for his coaching success, in both New York and Dallas.

"If you are prepared, then you will be confident and you will do the job," Landry says. "Emotion can cover up a lot of inadequacies but in the end it also gets in the way of performance. An emotional team cannot stay that way consistently over a full season or even over a few games."

He does not rule out the people factor, however.

"I like football because of the satisfaction of accomplishment, the general excitement of being involved in this game . . . of new goals and new faces that make life right," he says. "Football is brand new every year because you're dealing with people, with individuals.

"I understand people much better than I ever did before. I'm sure there are some players who say they can't reach me but that's not true. They're reluctant to meet me. They've built a wall around themselves that doesn't hold up when they do come and talk to me."

Landry may not be an overtly emotional man but he recognizes the need for emotion in players, particularly on defense.

"A defensive player is not motivated like an offensive player," says Landry. "An offensive player's motivation may be what he hears, reads, or feels. A defensive player has a certain temperament. He faces a challenge and this motivates him accordingly. If he doesn't have this, then he won't be a good defensive player.

"At the same time, you don't let the emotional factor overrule your style of play. We play a coordinated, disciplined style so we've had more success with less emotional types of players. Our success proves that you don't have to have a guy who tees off every time the ball is snapped. Nor does it mean the type of player we use is any less motivated to succeed.

"For one thing, I don't believe in team motivation. I believe in getting a team prepared so it knows it will have confidence when it steps on a field and be prepared to play a good game. Players can sense this and they respond to it.

"It's a long year and there are a lot of highs and lows. Sometimes it's difficult to get ready to play but if they are not ready, they know it. If you can cause them to be ready, and be prepared for all the situations they'll have to face, they'll be motivated."

In Landry's defense concepts, people are placed in position to control the overall defense rather than to control the other person. Size is not the key factor on the line; speed and coordination are. A lineman needs only to control a designated area. No one can free-lance and, because Landry so understands the habits of the offense, the control points are set to negate the strongest elements of attack.

He teaches his players not to view defense as a matter of having the man nearest the play go for the ball carrier. Landry's concept is based upon shifting groups of players, coordinated within themselves and tightly meshed with everybody else.

Normally, a defensive man tries to go through the blocker to tackle the ball carrier. That's called "hit and react," which also is the instinctive way to make a tackle.

Under Landry's system, the three or four men at the point of attack, working together in tight formation, set up a wall. On a play coming to the right side, for example, the end has responsibility to the outside of the hole, the tackle to the inside, and the linebacker fills the gap between them.

And what if the ball carrier sees the hole shut off and seeks another route? Landry has thought of that, too. It is the job of the others to disregard the movement of the developing play and plug up any other holes that may develop along the line.

"Our defense is designed to stop any play along the line of scrimmage." Landry says. "At least, that's the theory."

It is not an easy style of defense to learn, mostly because it goes against the natural instinct of a defensive player, regardless of his position, to go after the ball carrier.

"If the ball carrier is going inside, it isn't easy for a lineman to learn to go outside," says Cowboys' defensive line coach Ernie Stautner. "They've got to learn that Tom's way is the right way. Once they become accustomed to it, they find it's the easiest way to play the game."

Landry played under Steve Owen, one of the forefathers of modern defensive football in the NFL. After watching the Cleveland Browns offense roll over the NFL champion Philadelphia Eagles in 1950, Owen walked into the Giants' locker room and went to the blackboard. The Giants were to be the next opponents of the Browns, who had come to the NFL from the All-America Football Conference.

"We're going to use a six-one defense and do this," he said, drawing diagrams on the board. "We'll drop the ends off into the hook zones one time, send them to the flare zone another time, and let them rush the passer sometimes. That's how we'll beat Cleveland on Sunday."

And with that, he walked out of the room.

"Steve was not a detail man but he was a great thinker, and innovator," Landry says. "You've got to remember that when he drew up that plan, we hadn't been playing that defense. Someone had to exert leadership at that point so I went up to the blackboard and began explaining to the defense what he meant. That was the first time I ever did anything like that and I was twenty-four or twenty-five at the time. But someone had to do it."

Landry also remembers that 6-1 defense was successful against Cleveland. But instead of trying to repeat it when the teams met later that season, Owen came in with a different plan. It was his famed "Umbrella" defense, a concoction that sent pass defenders fanning out in the manner in which an umbrella is opened. He laid out the idea and that was it.

"I had no more idea of what we were going to do with that than I did in the first game," Landry says. "But we beat them again and no one ever had beaten Cleveland twice in one season."

Owen's influence on Landry was strong because Owen was always willing to try something that he believed in.

"I've carried over the same thinking," he says. "I've worked on game plans with the Cowboys until Friday and then if they still didn't look good to me, I've thrown them out and still tried to get ready by Sunday. That's tough. People tend to get shook up when you do things like that. But I always felt that if you believe enough in what you're doing, then you can do it."

Craig Morton, one of his former quarterbacks, says there have been times when Landry has thrown out the game plan at halftime and come away with a victory. That is because he has such confidence that what he is doing is so absolutely correct, Morton says. "And he usually was right," says Morton.

Landry's big break was being able to run the defensive unit of the Giants with complete authority after Steve Owen left in 1953. No one told him what to do though he would outline his plans in staff meetings with his head coach, Jim Lee Howell.

After that, it was between Landry and his players. Because the Giants had no other defensive assistants, Howell used to sit in on the meetings just so he'd know what was happening in case Landry, for some reason like sickness or accident, might miss the game.

All of this contributed to a significant part of NFL history. In 1958, the Giants tied Cleveland for the division title on the final day of the season when Pat Summerall kicked a last-minute, 49-yard field goal. The next week, in a playoff, Landry's defense shut out the Browns for the Eastern Division championship and advanced to the overtime game against Baltimore.

"One of the greatest times I ever had in football was coaching the Giants' defense," Landry says. When he talks about those years, he has a visible uplift in spirit; he talks about details from those days as if they were last year.

"I felt part of them back then," he says. "Some of the people I feel warmest about were part of that group—Rosey Grier, Sam Huff, Jim Katcavage, Andy Robustelli. We lived through a lot of things together. I really don't get that enjoyment now as a head coach."

The 1975 season came the closest to matching the enjoyment of earlier days. The Cowboys of 1975 had a dozen rookies and few expectations. Yet they advanced all the way to Super Bowl X, where they challenged Pittsburgh down to the wire before losing 21-17. "It was one of the most enjoyable years I've had in sixteen seasons with the Cowboys," says Landry. "Mainly it was because of the quality of the players . . . excellent players, who have excellent character, are good competitors who hit and play football.

When you have those kinds of football players around, it's always a joy to coach."

He didn't always get the execution he desired from his young team, but he knew it would not be consistent.

"Attitude, enthusiasm, people making the big play . . . these can help make up for a lack of great execution," he says. "If you can put all four things together then you're a great team."

Landry's offensive counterpart on the Giants was Vince Lombardi. The defensive players had their own private rivalry with Lombardi's offense. But this never affected the friendship between Landry and Lombardi.

"I knew the players had a rivalry," says Jim Lee Howell, the Giants' head coach then, "but I didn't do anything about it. It was healthy as far as I was concerned, an incentive for each of them to do as well as they could. But I was very careful not to make an issue of the dominance of the defense or even let on that I knew it was so strong and so popular."

Landry and Lombardi rarely discussed offensive philosophies. It was defense—his own and that being used by other teams—that occupied Landry's thinking. He had discovered that as long as teams stayed with the basic pro-set formations with a split back-field or with one of the backs lined up behind the center, then the 4-3 defense would continue to be successful.

As often happens, desperate times dictate desperate measures; and there was an absolute sense of desperation that surrounded Landry when he took the Cowboys' job in 1960. He knew he did not have the talent to operate a defense as successfully as he had with the Giants. He also knew that his team would take its lumps and that it had to have something to appeal to new fans during its growing years.

"I knew those defenses so well that I also had a good idea of what it would take to beat them," Landry says. "That's why I decided to use the multiple offense. No one was using that style.

"Remember, the four-three defenses were based on formation recognition with man-for-man as the basic pass coverage. To be effective, the defense had to have a jump by recognizing first the formation, then knowing what plays could be run from it. I felt that if we used multiple sets, shifting from one formation to another, we could confuse the defense. After all, they had worked all week on perfecting certain keys and if we could destroy or upset those keys, then we had a chance."

The idea was to show a defense one formation and, when it was adjusting its defense to it, shift into another formation and run the play from it before a second defensive adjustment could be made. It was a bit ironic that the man who had perfected the 4-3 defense would become the first to lessen its effectiveness.

Today the Cowboys employ six basic offensive formations, counting their shotgun approach in special situations. They use the I-formation and the four conventional pro sets—each distinguished by the fullback's position. In a "red" formation, two running backs are lined up behind the tackles, the fullback to the strong or tight end's side; they flop in a "green" formation. In a "brown" formation, the fullback lines up behind the center and the quarterback, with the halfback lined up to the weakside of the formation; in a "blue" formation, the halfback is lined up to the formation's strongside.

From these formations, Landry estimates the Cowboys can run scores of variations from the 40 or so basic plays in his offense. Sometimes they'll be run on a quick count, sometimes after one shift, sometimes after a shift in which a flanker or running back goes in motion. The constant movement of the backs and wide receivers before the ball is snapped makes this look distinctive, but when the ball is snapped the final look often will be no different than a team that does none of this.

There is some disagreement about the overall effectiveness of this plan. Robustelli, who assumed defensive coaching duties of the Giants after Landry was at Dallas, thinks the multiple offense was easier to combat in the long run. The secret was a willingness to spend more time in preparation and to understand that the multiple sets limited what an offensive player could do in comparison to his use in the conventional pro-set offense.

"I think," Robustelli says today, "that Tom gave too much credit to the other teams in the league for using the same keys the Giants were using and for knowing his defense as well as we did."

Another problem, of course, is the burden of learning that is placed upon the Dallas players. Calvin Hill, a Yale honor graduate, learned the offense within a year, but others have found it more difficult or haven't learned it at all.

"The offense is something like calculus," says Hill. "If you know why one thing is happening, you can figure out the other things. But then, not everyone catches on to the secrets of calculus right away, either."

Some of which goes to explain why on some days, the Dallas offense has looked so devastating while on other days it breaks down. But if imitation is the sincerest form of flattery, Landry's offensive ideas have proved their merit.

Nearly every team in the NFL uses the multiple sets at one time or other for the same reason that Landry devised the system in 1960—to combat the dominance of the defenses.

The diversified style of attack gave the Cowboys a distinctive look that has lasted to this day.

Most of Landry's early energies with the Cowboys were spent on offense. He did not begin to concentrate on upgrading the defense until the Cowboys were in their fifth year. By that time the Cowboys had Bob Lilly, George Andrie, Chuck Howley, Lee Roy Jordan, Dave Edwards, Cornell Green, and Mel Renfro. Those were the personnel ingredients Landry needed in order to perfect his theories about a complicated defensive system.

"I needed the right people because our style of defense is hard to play," Landry says. "You've got to blend the right talents but once you get the blend, you'll have a good team."

Landry is not one for gimmicks or stop-gap methods. The fact that he began with the multiple offense and still uses it, and that he still utilizes the basic principles of the 4-3 defense is testimony of that fact.

He also knew that defense is the ultimate difference in the making of a champion. Only one NFL team since 1945—the 1960 Philadelphia Eagles—won a title without great defense.

"Defense controls the playoffs and the Super Bowl," Landry says. "You must stay in control of a game to win and that means having a good defense. You can struggle and kick field goals and get by if your defense controls the game."

This phase of football still is his first love, regardless of how many offensive sets he devises.

"The challenge of defense is so much greater," he says. "Offense is predictable. You know what a team will run and the defense must adjust to it. You know when it's coming. On defense, you never know what is coming. You've got to anticipate keys and read formations. That's why the challenge is great."

Landry's first love is defense and he relishes infrequent opportunities to work directly with his defensive players.

In training camp prior to the 1975 season, defensive line coach Ernie Stautner injured his arm and required minor surgery. In stepped Landry.

"Suddenly he was one of the guys," tackle Jethro Pugh recalls. "He got right down there in the pits with us. He showed us techniques and he worked with us. He even laughed and joked with us a little. I've never seen him enjoy coaching so much as he did those couple of days."

Landry doesn't rely solely on personnel to do the job. The Cowboys have not always had the best player at a particular position, but instead had the correct method of attack or defense to complement players' abilities.

For example, with so much emphasis being placed on the three-man defensive line the last couple of years, Landry reached back and resurrected the A-formation or shotgun. This places a quarterback a few yards behind the center, where he takes a direct snap of the ball.

The play gave the Cowboys another distinctive look and it gave quarterback Roger Staubach a good weapon to compensate for an inexperienced running attack. It also helped him overcome a weakness for reading pass coverages.

"We wanted our quarterbacks to get a quicker, broader look at the defense before it converged into all its zones," Landry said. "Our receivers could get the ball quicker this way because we'd start our attack a fraction of a second earlier.

"We kept our running backs positioned with the quarterback so the defense did not know if the play would be a run or pass. This wasn't our primary offense but it gave us an extra weapon whenever we wanted to counteract a defensive strength."

Landry also was the coach who first devised flopping linebackers to take advantage of physical skills. When Chuck Howley and Dave Edwards were his outside linebackers, he used the lighter, quicker Howley—who was much better against the pass—on the weakside, freeing him from the block of the tight end so he could get into a play quicker. Edwards, bigger and stronger, played the run better and was able to mix with the tight end and still be effective.

Landry stayed with basketball player Cornell Green through a couple of seasons of acclimation to the defensive backfield, and came up with an all-pro. The Cowboys also drafted a tight end named Rayfield Wright from tiny Fort Valley State College in Georgia and Landry helped him develop into an all-pro offensive tackle within three years.

"Coach Landry told me the first week I arrived in training camp that I had the ability to play for the Cowboys even though I came from a small school," Wright remembers. "That helped my confidence a lot. Then all the patience that was shown me really made the difference. I was always aggressive but I had a lot to learn and they stayed with me through this learning."

Perhaps Landry's greatest personnel achievement was moving Bob Lilly from defensive end, where he was only so-so for two seasons, to defensive tackle. Landry saw that Lilly could pit his great strength, speed, and reflexes against somewhat lighter guards and centers. Lilly was the only player ever allowed to depart from his assignment in Landry's "flex" defense since his reflexes were so quick that he could make a mistake and still recover.

When Landry was with the Giants, he took an offensive guard named Sam Huff and converted him into the middle linebacker he desperately needed to make his 4-3 defense effective. In fact, Landry and Lombardi talked Huff out of quitting pro football in his rookie training camp, and Landry then worked with Huff at the new position.

"Tom and I both lived at the Concourse Plaza Hotel near Yankee Stadium in those days," Huff recalls. "I'd get home from practice, open a beer, and tell my wife to check the movie schedule. Then the phone would ring and it would be Tom.

"'Sam, got a minute?' he'd say. 'I have some film I'd like you to see.' Well, we only lived a couple of doors apart so I'd go down to his room and three hours later I'd still be there looking at film."

Then as now Landry had the ability to put the right player at the right position. A great deal of credit is given to the Cowboys' scouting system with its computers and "bird dogs," but in the end, the secret has been Landry's ability to recognize talent in training camp and be patient while it is polished into a good football player.

That's why he was content to wait on Green; to watch Bob Hayes, who had minimal college football experience, develop into an excellent wide receiver; and to wait through a five-year Navy commitment by Staubach that paid off when Dallas won a Super Bowl with him at quarterback.

It often is Landry's way to first try a player, who may not fit a particular position, on offense. If he doesn't work out, he'll move him to defense. And if he still doesn't make it but shows enough promise to return the next season, Landry will outline exactly what the man should do—how much weight he should gain or lose, what kind of physical work he should undertake, and what he wants from him in the way of speed and strength.

If the player works at this program, Landry will be patient until the player develops. And even if the player doesn't develop, Landry will voice no regrets at having invested so much time and effort.

The Cowboys place so great a premium on this ability of Landry that he has the final say on all draft picks and trades. Most times, if a selection doesn't work out, it's because the scout's evaluation was not correct or the player did not present the attitude Landry demands of those who play for him.

It is in this area—inter-personal relationships—that the Dallas coach has drawn so much attention, a great deal of it criticism. Many players have left the Cowboys' organization bitter over the treatment they allegedly received; but a lot more have stayed to play well, win championships, and find only the normal venial faults in their coach.

"I don't think I've made enemies," he says. "Players are like people in that they react to the situation they're in . . . they say things on the spur of the moment that many of them usually regret or apologize for later. I have to make decisions affecting players lives. I can't avoid situations where players may dislike me for a decision I had to make. They may dislike me even though that decision might have been a right one.

"Regardless, I still have great faith in people. Being a successful coach often is nothing more than the belief you have in a player—that he can do it. It's most important that he can feel you believe in him."

It also is a two-way street with Landry. He'll believe in a player, but that player still must understand that everything laid down must be done Landry's way. His players say he is not open to many suggestions. They also say he's loosened up over the past decade; he's more outgoing, and he's changed some of his ideas about dress codes, long hair, and beards. But the rules that remain must be adhered to without exception.

Landry has great feeling for the young players who join his team. He says the outside pressures on them are far different today than they were a decade ago. If anything, he is optimistic about the caliber of player coming into pro football. Landry feels the recent collegians are more solid than some who came into the sport in the late sixties and early seventies.

At the same time, he sees "danger areas" that encompass all parts of society. "No one wants any restraints," he says. "But no one is really free unless he has certain boundaries to operate within. A football team can have great freedom of expression if it knows its limits. If it doesn't recognize the boundaries, then there's no freedom. Players are always being challenged and brought back to within those boundaries and it's unfortunate if they don't recognize it."

Pete Gent, a former receiver who wrote a best-selling novel several years ago with pro football as its theme and with Landry thinly disguised as a contemptible sort of head coach, bears no good feelings for his former team. Yet he remembers the day of a game when Landry called him into his office and said he'd decided to bench him in favor of Buddy Dial.

"You've got better hands, better moves, and you know the offense better than Dial," Landry told him. "But you can't make the big play that Dial can."

Gent didn't appreciate being benched or criticized in such a forthright manner and he pointed out all the big plays he had made that season. Landry even agreed with some of his evaluations, but he refused to change his plans.

"I can't explain it," he finally told Gent. "I just know that Dial has it in him to make the big play and you don't."

"And you know something," Gent told friends in relating the story, "I couldn't explain why but I left with the feeling that if Tom Landry said it was so, it was so."

Meredith, for all of the free spirit that possessed him throughout his career and for all the backhanded compliments he may give his former coach as a television commentator, was firmly in Landry's grasp—in season and out.

"I recall getting off the elevator on the eleventh floor of the Cowboys' offices one day in mid-March," Al Ward, now general manager of the Jets, recalls. "The next elevator opened just as I stepped off and there was Meredith, his hair tousled, wearing a pair of loafers, no socks, a wrinkled sweater, and a pair of jeans. He obviously had just gotten out of bed and was going as fast as he could toward the coaches' offices.

"'What are you doing?' I asked him.

"'The man called and said he has some things he wanted me to look at,' Don told me over his shoulder as he sped through the door.

"'How long ago did he call you?' I asked him.

"'About three minutes ago,' Meredith said and he was gone."

It is the same with the Cowboys' off-season conditioning program, something in which Landry places great importance. Every player is expected to follow a stipulated regimen and all the Cowboys are "encouraged" to live in the Dallas area during the off-season so this program can be followed at the team's training site.

"If a guy can't make it on his particular day," Ward says, "he'll call Landry and tell him. Usually, it's for a pretty solid reason like final exams or an urgent business matter. Tom doesn't badger them over it but they'll always let him know what they're doing."

Whether the player is a regular or the fortieth man on the team makes no difference. Landry tries not to treat his players differently, though he readily acknowledges that a coach cannot treat everyone equally, that some players need more attention, motivation, and discipline than others.

"The key is discipline," he says. "Without it there is no morale. Each player knows how the other is treated, particularly if there is a big difference in one over another. So I try to achieve the same treatment for everyone. Lombardi was the best I ever saw in achieving and keeping discipline, but his style of play demanded it."

The only time Landry had a genuine double standard was with Duane Thomas in 1971. Thomas had been a brilliant rookie running back the year before, had helped the team into the Super Bowl, then became enmeshed in contract problem with the Cowboys.

At the same time, the Cowboys were being called the team "that couldn't win the big one." The Cowboys had lost Super Bowl V in the last five seconds when Baltimore's Jim O'Brien kicked a field goal, but they could have put the game out of reach early in the second half had it not been for a questionable fumble by Thomas at the Colts' goal line.

Landry had made up his mind that he would spare no effort to help his team throw off this ignominy. He knew that Thomas was an integral part of any plan and he was willing to put up with Thomas's bitterness to achieve it. He also put up with his not reporting until after the season had begun, and then with Thomas's strange silence.

On plane trips Thomas often would sit with a ski cap pulled down over his face so he would not have to talk to teammates, flight attendants, or anyone else. On lunch breaks, he sometimes would sit alone in his car until it was time for practice to resume. Naturally, tension on the team built because, as one player noted, "It got so that someone would say something and we'd all sneak a look at Duane to see how he was reacting, even though the comment was not directed at him."

Often when Thomas did speak, it was to verbally abuse Landry in front of the other Cowboys. No one ever had tried this before—indeed if anyone had, his name would have been on the waiver wire that night. Landry took it all and even spent hours during that season trying to reach inside Thomas and find out what really was bothering him. Sometimes he felt some progress; more often, he didn't.

"That was a unique case," Landry says in an understatement. "I varied my treatment of the player only because of what the players were thinking. They said, 'Yeah, we'll tolerate something different like that for the best interest of the team.'

"Winning the Super Bowl that year was our only goal. All of us were willing to put up with anything to achieve it. But once we had won the Super Bowl and when the same business started all over again the next season, that was the end. You couldn't expect a team to go through that again."

Landry says the players themselves were responsible for dealing successfully with the Thomas affair.

"There must be a great feeling between players to have a great team, to have good morale," he says. "A team must have the ability to believe in each other. Normally, you eliminate any tension that develops when you have a player who is not being treated the same and who is causing unrest.

"But it took a team like the Cowboys, which had been through so much adversity, which had developed a lot of character—character develops better through adversity than anything else—to get through that. If we didn't have the character, we'd have been four and ten instead of ten and four and Super Bowl champs."

That says something about Landry and his own relations with players. Landry has been the only coach to get two productive seasons from Thomas and Lance Rentzel despite Rentzel's difficulties during his tenure with the Cowboys.

"I believe in people," says Landry. "My job is more than just winning but also dealing, in a way, with people's lives. My main hope in the Duane Thomas case was that I could have found some way to save an individual. I believed strongly in him and that caused a lot of criticism. But I didn't listen to the critics."

It is not unusual for Landry to take a personal interest in a player as he did with Thomas.

"I've always tried to capture a player who is not of my mold and hope he changes his character or personality," Landry says. "This is because of my background as a Christian.

"I guess I haven't been very successful because I don't really believe you change a person's character. But I'm always willing to try because I know the only thing that can change a person's character is Jesus Christ. As coaches, we're really not successful in changing character, just in molding it. Heaven knows, I've tried hard with a lot of players, probably at my own expense as a coach.

"I try to understand. I've spent many long hours of conversation with players, trying to show them why they're moving in the direction they're heading and what they must do to move in the direction they really want to go. Ultimately they want to get where all of us want to go, but they often have a misconception of how to get there.

"I try to get them to think in that direction. I guess my success will come later when they're finished with football and they look back."

That approach does not hold true on the practice field or on game days.

He does not snipe, shout, or threaten, but neither does he pump up, sell, or pat backs.

Landry abhors players who worry about their own performance, their own statistics, and not about what effect their play will have on the team. To Landry, the worst crime a player can commit is being satisfied with being less than the best. As soon as he senses this in a man's makeup and sees it happen on the field, the player is gone. There is a lengthy list of former Cowboys' who prove the point.

"Those kind don't have any place on a football team," he says. "A player must have the ability to divert some of that drive for self-acclaim to team achievement. If he can't, he doesn't stay. That's why you see so many talented players drift from team-to-team.

"Those are the ones who will break the rules to suit themselves. I don't believe in players cheating to win and that's what those kind do."

To understand Landry's philosophy about what players should and should not do on a football field, one must understand what he was like as a football player. Probably, he admits, he could not make his own team today because he did not have enough speed to play cornerback. But if Landry watched himself closely on film, he might take his name off the waiver list.

"He was a smart player," Howell recalls. "A lot of times he'd be outmaneuvered, but he'd never be outsmarted. And if an end didn't watch it, he'd find a stray elbow or two always coming his way. If the guy did catch the ball, Tom would stick him. That's one thing he did pretty good, he really stuck people when he tackled them."

Howell remembers the duels Landry had with Hall of Fame end Pete Pihos whenever the Giants and Eagles would play each other. Pihos ate up other defensive backs in the NFL with five, six, or seven catches a game. But when he came up against Landry, often he'd be shut out or catch just one or two.

"Part of the reason was that Tom knew their offense so well, he'd be breaking to the spot where the ball would be coming even before it was thrown," says Howell. "Then he'd give Pihos a good going over like he did every other receiver. Pete just seemed totally distracted because everywhere he seemed to go, there was Landry knocking down passes, or working him over in that sly way good defensive backs have of handling receivers without getting caught. Or else he'd be hitting him with a solid lick."

Glenn Davis, the former Army All-America who later starred as a wide receiver for the Rams, tells of a game in which Landry gave him a good going over. Finally Davis took off on a pass play and caught the ball six or seven yards over Landry's head. Davis took off and opened up another five yards between himself and Landry by the time he got to the end zone.

"But I could still hear him coming," Davis says, "and I knew he wanted to punish me. When he got to the end zone, I heaved the ball at him.

"'Here,' I told him, 'you've wanted it all afternoon. Now you got it!' And with that, I took off for my own bench. Don't you know, that Landry was right behind me and he chased me right to the bench. He was so mad I'll bet he'd have killed me if he had ever caught me."

"Some players are hitters," says Landry, "and some get motivated just at the thought of going out and tackling or blocking someone. I wasn't that way as a player; I hit because I wanted to achieve. That was my motivation. If I was going to be good, I had to hit. So I did."

Landry shrugs at the suggestion that if there is a weakness in the Cowboys, it is the lack of emotion at the top. The shrug doesn't mean that he agrees; in fact, he does not.

"As the pressure gets greater or if a game is important I'll show more emotion," Landry says. "I've shown emotion in playoff games or when I recognize that something has to happen, either positively or negatively."

Indeed, he's been known to run 40 yards down a sideline, carping with an official over a call. His coaches laugh when they recall a time Landry was so upset with an official that he called him "an s.o.b." For the next couple of minutes Landry said nothing while the game continued. Finally, he turned to one of his assistants and said, "you know, I think I said a four-letter word."

"On the day of a game," says Ward, "you sometimes don't recognize his face. The blood vessels in his cheeks begin to stand out. His eyes, which are deep-set, become even deeper and they are restless. And he can be grouchy and short-tempered."

Before the 1967 NFL title game in minus 13-degree temperatures in Green Bay, the Cowboys' trainers and doctors knew that Landry would be so intense that he wouldn't bother to dress warmly, nor during the game would he leave the sidelines for relief by the special heaters. They all feared frostbite and sure enough, he came out for the pre-game warmup as if he still were in Dallas. The equipment men went over and bodily put the extra warm clothing around him.

After losing to the Packers in the final seconds, the Cowboys' locker room looked like something out of science fiction. The cold had so distorted everyone's faces that they became red and splotchy when entering the heated room. This only magnified the gloom. Landry stood in the middle of the room and looked at his players, most of whom faced their lockers.

"I don't know what to tell you," he began softly. "But you played a great game."

It appeared to bystanders that he really was talking to himself, trying to convince himself that this grotesque scene and the heart-breaking finish to a game played under almost intolerable conditions really was meant to be.

Landry does not deny his own emotions. They can be strong and often are, but rarely in public. During a game he feels it is an integral part of the team's game plan that he remain calm and collected.

"You can't be emotional and concentrate," he says as his standard answer to those who want to know about such things. "A great play might happen on the field but I can't cheer it. I'm a couple of plays ahead, thinking. I have to since the type of offense and defense we play demands it."

Landry claims he always has been able to control his emotions, that it is his makeup to be reserved in situations where people get excited. You are, he says, what you develop yourself to be early in life.

Landry is very conscious of his sideline image, having been reminded of it so often. But, when the ball is kicked off, nothing seems to dent the intense concentration. And the people who then matter most to him—the players—don't mind at all.

"If you know how to read him you can look at him and see the agony and joy in his face," Lee Roy Jordan says. "If we thought he was throwing tantrums and screaming, we might lose control. That's because we've come to appreciate what really is going on behind those eyes.

"He projects poise, confidence, and composure to us. It doesn't bother us that he's not always patting us on the back. His appearance, that almost unflappable look, is really reflecting his unbelieveable knowledge of the game. He's got everything under control in his mind.

"People don't see him during the week when all the work is getting done. He starts by telling us what we must do to win and those guys who've been with him for so long know it's up to us to get ourselves emotionally ready. He'll take care of the preparation."

There are occasional blips on that Landry screen of serenity as the Cowboys go about their work. When he says "damn it," everyone knows something serious has happened. He doesn't berate or chew out his players publicly but everyone knows where they stand within the confines of the locker room.

"The important thing that comes from all of this," Jordan says, "is how we feel about each other, not what other people think we feel for each other."

Landry rejects fear as a prime motivator, preferring praise. But he is judicious with that, something his players have come to expect as the ultimate for achievement. When dispensed, it is merely an acknowledgement by one professional to another.

Many feel that this demeanor, particularly the lack of holding some sort of overt fear over his players' heads, cost him a third straight Super Bowl appearance in 1973. The contention is that Green Bay won back-to-back Super Bowls because Lombardi would not let the Packers acknowledge they had won the first when the next season began. Threats of team complacency were a constant fear to him and much of his bullying and goading was directed at keeping players from losing sight of new goals.

Because he came to prominence at a time when Lombardi ruled pro football, his methods were held up for comparison. Lombardi drove his teams hard. He was vibrant, moving, always emotional—either way up or way down—and his psyche seemed to typify the game itself.

"I remember when Vince and I were with the Giants," says Landry. "We'd lose a game and I couldn't talk to him for two or three days. We always were close friends but I didn't share his feelings about winning and losing."

The failure of the Cowboys as Super Bowl champions after the 1972 season provides another good comparison of the Lombardi method versus the Landry method. Landry admits disappointment in that team's reaction to finally becoming NFL champion. With many of those players now gone, he is now building a team that many feel may surpass the record of the bygone champions.

Fear of failure does not bother Landry.

"In fact, sometimes you have to get into a situation before you recognize what it really is about," he says. "When we lost to St. Louis [38-0] in 1970 and our record was five-four, I told my players, 'nobody loves you, no one is going to be with you. If anything comes out of this season, it will have to be from within, between each other.' It was then that they recognized that if they were going to come off the floor it would have to be done by themselves. When they saw that's how it was, there was a different attitude. No longer did one player criticize another's weak points. They talked about the positive points. The attitude changed completely.

"It didn't come right away. Their first reaction was, 'To heck with it! We'll just go out and play.' In the next game against Washington, the pressure was off and they just played and won and after two games they were solid. [The Cowboys won their last seven games that season and advanced to Super Bowl V, where they lost to Baltimore.]

"It does make a coach's job easier. Sometimes a coach can be so dominant that he can develop the leadership on a team. That is the exception. Leaders still must emerge from each of the units, offense, defense, and special teams.

"Lee Roy Jordan is one. He always wants to win so badly. I don't care who you are, there just was no way you could motivate others to do what he did. Roger Staubach is a leader in his own way. He is a straight line guy who does everything he can to win. Players tend to listen to people who play this way.

"It's hard to find a quarterback who is not a leader. It's hard to find a defensive leader like Jordan without it. A coach cannot do what these players do. He's got to rely on people on the field to do that job.

"There's a misconception about teamwork. Teamwork is the ability to have different thoughts about things; it's the ability to argue and stand up and say loud and strong what you feel. But in the end it's also the ability to adjust to what is best for the team.

"It's not always being together, playing golf, enjoying the pleasurable things. That's the real distinction. So often players will say, 'We don't have any fun get-togethers, we don't go out socially.'

"That has nothing to do with having a successful team. It can be helpful, a byproduct of morale perhaps but when it comes down to the bottom line, people still tend to gravitate to those of similar likes and dislikes."

That suggests cliques and special interest groups within a team. Landry does not dismiss the fact that such do exist; it is the intent of the clique that concerns him most.

"A clique to me is a group that is at odds with another group," he says. "It doesn't mean running around socially together. We're all going to have our own preferences and we're going to gravitate to those who enjoy what we do."

It has been said that pro football is a microcosm of the real world and so it is with the people involved. Some are naturally funny, some droll; some are outgoing, others quiet and introspective. There are grouches and there are blithe spirits. Humor and good-natured kidding are the heaviest byproducts of this relationship and for anyone who enjoys people to any degree, it is not hard to be attracted by it.

Landry is no different. To him, the toughest part of coaching is being forced to remain aloof from the people and personalities. Within the limits of his own personality, he certainly enjoyed that phase of his coaching life while he was an assistant with the Giants.

"Secretly, I guess, I'd love to get close to my players," says Landry. "When Bob Lilly was playing I really would have liked to have had him as my close friend because he was such a great person.

"But you're never able to do things you really love to do. Some of the greatest guys I know are football players and I'd like to be part of things with them because I have such a great feeling for them. But it's still impossible to break down that barrier.

"And yet, it would be great to capture some of what I see and hear around the players because it's such a great feeling. But you can't enjoy that the same way an assistant coach or a player does because it's an injustice to the player to get too close to him. Subconsciously, he'll tend to use that as a crutch."

Another reason it could not happen is that Landry does not make himself totally accessible to his players. It's just not his nature to carry on small talk, though he never has failed to answer completely and sometimes with unflagging patience all questions—from player, press, and public alike.

When those sessions dissolve into chit-chat, Landry simply breaks away. This has given many the impression that he is not a warm person or is trying to maintain a hard veneer around his personality.

"I don't think he's an overly warm person by nature, one who will go out of the way to slap you on the back, and say 'How're the kids? What's your golf score? Did you hear the one about . . . ?'" says writer Steve Perkins, who has followed the Cowboys since their inception. "But I don't think he's afraid to let anyone look inside him to see what makes him tick. He doesn't try to protect anything. What you see is Tom Landry, just the way he is."

People within the Dallas organization will take him just the way he is. The foremost reason is his own unflagging confidence in what he is trying to achieve. That is what held the Cowboys together during the early seasons, through the playoff disappointments, through the loss in Super Bowl V. Landry's own strong belief in his own coaching principles and what he knew to be right sustained everyone.

Frank Clarke, who played with the Cowboys from 1960-67, remembers some players questioning Landry's knowledge of football before they knew much about their coach.

"There were times at the beginning when guys would question his choice of players or the plays he'd select for a game," Clarke remembers. "But after awhile, the doubts began to dwindle. That's when they learned to have confidence in him. The players who really achieved something playing for him are the ones who had the confidence. They're the ones who caused this team to become a winner."

When Landry sets out to achieve something, he wants it to be perfect. The intensity with which he attacks a problem often gives vent to his rare shows of temper and impatience. It was that way even when he was an assistant coach in New York.

"Tom never could understand why players didn't grasp things as quickly as he did, or why they didn't understand immediately what he was talking about," says Jim Lee Howell. "Heck, he could break down a film in five minutes while it would take other coaches a half hour.

"When his players didn't grasp what he was trying to tell them, he'd get up on his toes a bit but he'd never say anything. Instead, he'd just sigh, shrug his shoulders, and begin all over again. But it was plain to see he was impatient at their lack of comprehension."

Landry hasn't changed much at Dallas. Sometimes he becomes so intense that assistant coaches and players alike find him hard to live with. It isn't often but even he is aware of what he calls "my mood."

One day he was asked to appear on a Monday evening radio show. He declined at first, pointing out that was the day he'd be watching films of the team's game.

"I don't know what kind of mood I'll be in," he said, but he later relented and went on the show in apparent good humor.

His desire for perfection spreads to all areas of the team. He does not leave the job of coaching solely to his assistants and if he spots an area—on offense or defense—that he feels needs attention or isn't producing the way he thinks it should, then he'll move in and work with it.

"There isn't an area on that team, except maybe the offensive line, that he hasn't coached at one time or other during a season," says Craig Morton. "He knows how he wants things done and he'll see to it personally they're done that way if he must."

Landry is a product of the old school of coaches' attitudes toward player freedom, but his feelings are flexible—to a point.

"Players talk about individualism," he said, "but I believe they all want to live and work under a single standard. If a player is contributing and performing the way he ought to, he will conform. If he's not performing well or conforming to team standards, he ought not to be around.

"We'll put up with someone who won't conform as long as he gets the job done. But we can't get along with a player who doesn't get the job done or conform, either."

Consider Sam Baker, a kicker who played with several NFL teams during a lengthy career. Always a lover of a good time and a good party—even if he had to throw it for himself—Baker is remembered by some around the Cowboys for once showing up at a Cowboys' game on a freezing day in Pittsburgh sporting a potted orange tree and a broad smile.

On another occasion, the story is told of his missing a team flight, showing up late at the hotel, and heading straight for Landry's room, where he knocked on the door, saluted smartly and barked: "Baker reporting, sir." After which, he executed a perfect about-face and marched off. Landry was surprised, but he definitely was not amused.

Baker was traded at the end of the season.

Billy Parks was a wide receiver who played at Dallas in the early seventies but who had a totally different idea of his role as a member of the Cowboys. He wore white football shoes while other players wore the conventional black; he once took himself out of a game because he said his presence on the field was keeping a black teammate on the bench (Parks is white); and he refused to play one day because another black teammate, Tody Smith, was injured.

Parks also was traded.

Landry is the first to appreciate Christian charity or any other kind of good feeling for his fellowman. But not when it infringes on the workings of his team to a disruptive extent. Nor does he always rely on divine guidance to settle his problems, though he admits that when it gets down to a nitty-gritty decision, he doesn't hesitate to use prayer as an aid to making the correct choice.

"I deliberate, pray for direction, make a decision, and live with it," he says. "In the end, the straightforward course with anyone is the best. If I'm wrong at least the player will feel I was honest and did the best I could. If they recognize you're trying to do the best you can, they usually will respond to it."

Landry is influenced a great deal by what he sees of a player in practice; the guy who gives it all in practice plays in the game.

"One of his great talents is to recognize potential in a player," says Cowboys' owner Clint Murchison. "We have kept players who wouldn't have been kept around on other teams contending. Tom can see something worth keeping in a mass of humanity. Tactics dwindle in importance to that. What a coach can contribute to a team is about ten percent inspiration, ten percent motivation, twenty to thirty percent tactics, and fifty to sixty percent recognition."

Before the 1970 season, Landry announced the benching of Morton and his top wide receiver, Bob Hayes because of their "performance level." Landry was saying nothing more than that his players had to meet certain minimum standards that are taken for granted by every coach. Those included the technical ability to execute, consistency, dedication, and competitiveness. He told his team no one with a starting job could count on keeping it, a radical departure from one who looked upon experience as a key to success.

"There had been a tendency before that for some players to get complacent as starters," he says in explaining this method. "I decided it no longer was time to take chances on waiting for these players to give their best. I was challenging them to prove to me they were good enough to play."

This remains an integral part of Landry's philosophy. He believes in it and makes it known the first day a player comes to the Cowboys. And he makes sure the player understands.

"You've got to have a clear-cut philosophy to be successful and it must be transmitted to your players," Landry says. "They must thoroughly understand everything you are trying to do, so much so that eventually it simply becomes instinctive to them.

"I don't say that my philosophy is the only one. It is the only one for me and the right one for my team. There are many successful philosophies because there are many successful coaches.

"It is the unsuccessful coaches who try to get three or four different ones working at the same time. That's like seeing another team's play on film and trying to adapt it to your system. Then you find it won't work because you don't have the right people but you try to force it on the team. That just has to fail.

"We want everyone on the same path, to know where we are going and what our goals are. That was the first big step we took to becoming a successful team and we did it back in 1965. We said before that season that we wanted an eight-six record or to at least win as many as we'd lose. Then we said, 'This is how we'll do it.'

"Well, we were seven-seven and got to the Playoff Bowl. Then we said, 'This is what we must do from a people standpoint to achieve championship status,' and the next season we were ten-four and had the Eastern Division title. That was one kind of goal— one that was reasonable and attainable.

"But setting a goal is not the main thing. It is deciding how you will go about achieving it and then staying with that plan. That has been the key to any success we've had with the Cowboys."

Many outside the Cowboys' organization picture its success as computerized and cold, with an analytical disregard of the human element, all of which has produced obedient robots of superior speed, strength, and size.

"I think too much attention has been given to the organization and to management instead of to the players," Landry counters. "Something like this tends to get the players feeling differently about their role and they do not feel as important as they should. Football still is a team game, made up of players, and is dependent on how they perform.

"How we get them to perform at the top level is important. We certainly should support them with every bit of advanced technology but we never should reach a point of taking credit as management or putting technological innovations above what the player achieves himself.

"Perhaps if there has been one failing within our organization over the years, it is that we haven't tried to dispel the notion that our success comes out of a computer. It doesn't. It comes out of the sweat glands of our coaches and players."

There are many who may question that conclusion, preferring to look at Dallas's record of playoff futility and the stop-go seasons it so often undergoes compared, perhaps, to the seemingly smooth sailing of such teams as Miami, Oakland, Los Angeles, Minnesota, and Pittsburgh. Yet during the eight consecutive seasons in which it made the playoffs, no NFL team won more games.

What that adds up to is success and what success adds up to in Landry's mind is "when we get the most out of our players. My job seems to be measured in the won-lost column but I don't always think of it that way. The year we went seven-seven [1965] was a very successful year. Our five-eight-one season in 1962 also was a successful one. That really was a tremendous year for all of us, a very satisfying and enjoyable one."

"Of course, knowing what to do with players is very important. We've taken a lot of players who are considered not good enough and they have become good enough. They become good enough because like all the players who've been successful at Dallas, they've been willing to pay the price."

Landry has helped them over that hurdle because he always has preached achievement and has set goals that he demands be met. It is as much a part of his lifestyle as the hat that he wears on the sidelines or the golf game he can only enjoy in the spring when things quiet down. When you talk about achieving goals with Landry, you reach into his soul.

"Achieving goals, which really means winning in some form, is the ultimate in a man's life," he says. "Being the best at whatever you do stimulates life. God gave us a talent to do it and He expects us to do the best we can. Once we win we must give glory to God. As long as I maintain that approach, I'll keep a level head in winning and losing. It won't become the be-all but it's a crime not to be the best you can be within the rules you operate under."

To Landry, there is no suitable alternative to wanting to achieve, to win. If you don't believe in it, he says, you don't believe in free enterprise, capitalism, the American way of life.

"Achievement builds character," says Landry. "People striving, being knocked down and coming back . . . that's what builds character in a man. And character is the ability of a person to see a positive end to things.

"I agree with the thought that losing seasons build character. I've seen very little character in players who never had to face adversity. This is part of the problem in our society right now. A lot of young people really never had to struggle for anything in their lives. When it finally happens, the character isn't there to get them through. What do they turn to? Alcohol, drugs . . . you name it."

While there are no specific references to himself or to his teams of the past, the inferences are clear. Having lived with a team from its birth, he has seen the occasions where character building might have been the only positive thing that happened.

How did he get through those tough times?

"Nothing like the early years will ever happen again," he says. "We still have the three keys that will maintain success. One is players. Quality is very important. You've got to have the best players but players who will build you a winning tradition.

"The old Packers were a good example. In Vince's last year, they sent six or seven players to the Pro Bowl. The next year, with a losing record, only two or three went. Now, were the wrong players going to the Pro Bowl or were the players as a whole reflecting a winning system and a winning tradition? A lot of winning is tradition.

"Then there is coaching. I go to training camp every year scared to death. That keeps me on edge, it makes me careful about evaluating what has happened in the past. I don't look at past records because they mean nothing. But there's always the temptation and it's one you've continually got to fight.

"During those seasons when we kept going to the playoffs people would tell me the law of averages was going to catch up with me. That scared me, too; it made me work harder and the result is that the players also work harder.

"Then there are such things as good scouting and having a good image for your organization. A winning image is a good image. You get respect from people and from other teams."

Landry and the Cowboys had to fight hard for that respect and, in the end, they have earned it. That's why Landry takes a quiet pride in what his teams finally accomplished in Super Bowl VI, and even with losing efforts in Super Bowls V and X. All the years of hearing about not being able to win "the big one" had a lasting effect on everyone concerned with the team. It is worn like a badge of courage.

"We went out and fought for a championship in 1970 and that's what finally made this team," says Dan Reeves, a former player now an assistant coach. "In other years, we were on top right from the start of the season, reached our peak too soon and fell short.

"No one ever will forget that thirty-eight to nothing loss to the Cardinals in 1970. But it probably was the best thing that ever happened to us. We really found out what a genuine thrill it is to go out and battle and fight for something you want real bad and then get it."

Landry chuckles when he is reminded that the team finally seemed to emerge in 1970, 11 seasons after it was formed.

"I thought it would take us three or four years when I took this job," he says. "I was young then and didn't have all the answers. I also didn't anticipate not being allowed to draft that first season. I guess the first big shock of being a head coach came when I realized what ingredients we finally had to make that first team."

Now he sees the difference in making a Super Bowl team and making one that doesn't make it. The difference is a scant one and a team need not lose much to pass from Super Bowl participant to Super Bowl spectator. In the end, it is being forced to repeat all the effort and agony that went into doing it the first time.

Meredith once made a special visit to Landry's home to urge his former coach to give up the game.

"It's taking too much out of you," he said with genuine feeling. "There's got to be more to life than this."

"I certainly don't put all my life in winning football games," says Landry. "If I ever had to make a choice, Christianity and my family would come first and that's where the guilt comes in. The insecurity of this business makes you feel like you must fight so hard, give up so much.

"I've never been concerned about the future. If I wasn't coaching football next year, it wouldn't be a catastrophe. I'd just enjoy my family or being on a boat or reading Westerns . . . simple things like that. Life doesn't have to be a big deal."

John Madden

"The organization has installed a solid framework. Everyone works together, but on the field of play I'm the general."

John Madden's size alone should make him stand out in any crowd. At 6 feet 4 inches and 260 pounds he is a mountain of a man.

John Madden's record should make him stand out, too. In seven years as the coach of the Oakland Raiders his record is 70-21-7. Only Minnesota's Bud Grant (76) and Miami's Don Shula (75) have won more games over the same period; and *no* coach has lost fewer games.

And yet John Madden doesn't stand out. Or at least not at first glance. A man who directs 70 victories before he has turned 40 should be recognized as some sort of boy wonder but John Madden is only a face in the coaching crowd.

One reason may be that of pro football's most successful coaches, Madden is the only one whose team has not played in a Super Bowl (although the Raiders under Madden have won six AFC West titles and played in the AFC championship game five times, losing on each occasion to the team that went on to win the Super Bowl).

But the most important reason may be that Madden works for an organization—and the operative word is "organization"—that prides itself in an all-for-one, one-for-all attitude, an organization in which "I" is passé and "we" is everything.

John Madden may not wear a gray flannel suit but he is an organization man nevertheless . . . and an organization man who works in the very large (figurative) shadow of Al Davis.

Davis, the Raiders' general manager and managing general partner, was a boy wonder of his own in the sixties, turning a derelict Raiders' team into a winner as coach and becoming commissioner of the American Football League at 36.

A lot of people claim the credit for the Raiders' recent success belongs to Davis. That makes Davis angry. "The only credit I should get," he says, "is for naming John Madden coach. He is one of the best and one of the brightest and he has done it himself."

The Raiders' players say the same thing. The team that is on the field is Madden's team; it is directed by him and is responsible to him for what it does. He has total control during a game and if, during the week, he gets or solicits advice from his boss, so what?

"We have an excellent coaching staff and this organization is tops," says Madden. "When I came to the Raiders in 1967, I felt I knew everything about football. Then I learned how a real organization operates. Nothing is left to chance."

Davis and Madden both believe that organization wins football games. It isn't superstars or publicity or squandering a lot of money. The Raiders' way also is more mysterious, something Davis doesn't mind and that also doesn't seem to bother Madden or his players.

"Once you set up the organization as the operating nerve center," Davis says, "you can't blame the coach when you lose. When you have a number of people working in concert, it's the organization that wins or loses. Obviously some clubs in the NFL don't agree because in the time Madden has been our head coach eighty percent of the clubs have changed coaches, some more than once."

Madden put his mind to becoming a coach long before he joined the Raiders in 1967, deciding as a rookie with the Philadelphia Eagles in 1959 that this would be his life's work. Madden had been selected on the twenty-first round of the 1959 draft by the Eagles after being a good, small college offensive tackle for California Poly at San Luis Obispo.

A knee injury in the Eagles' training camp that summer resulted in surgery and it meant the end of Madden's playing career. Rehabilitation on the injured knee also meant coming to the training room each morning that season before the rest of the Eagles arrived for taping. It may have been the best thing that ever happened to Madden because Norm Van Brocklin, then the Eagles' quarterback, also was there early to study films.

Though Van Brocklin never seemed to mind the company, Madden still doesn't think he was too excited at the idea of having an ill-starred rookie for company. The Dutchman talked about football and his thoughts and theories about it.

"That's when I first started learning football," Madden says. "Primarily, I was a player and I thought like a player. I knew my assignment, but I wasn't paying enough attention to the overall picture as I should have. Norm and I spent a great deal of time talking about what was in those movies.

"A lot of times I didn't even have to ask him a question. He would let that film go back and forth, back and forth, and he'd be talking. Sometimes I never knew whether he was talking directly to me or just talking out loud. But I was listening."

Van Brocklin's philosophy then was that a coach must make maximum use of his best players.

"He would watch an opponent's defense and be thinking all the time how he could get Tommy McDonald to run a post pattern best against it," Madden remembers. "No one ran a better post pattern in the NFL at that time than McDonald but still Dutch wasn't satisfied with just running it. He wanted it run the best way possible by the best man.

"Billy Barnes was his bread-and-butter running back and he wanted to see what kind of straight-ahead game he could get for him. Clarence Peaks was an excellent toss receiver. He'd see how he could get the ball outside to him and get him going with it. Bobby Walston was a good, ball-control receiver and Dutch would try to see if he could run a hook-and-out against a defense to get those twelve- and fifteen-yard passes to him.

"All of this was within the framework of his own philosophy. He'd watch films to see how he could take advantage of everything his players could do well. He wouldn't try to get McDonald to run the short patterns and Walston to run the long ones. He'd tell me that offense was nothing more than getting your people to do the things they could do best and finding a way to get them in that position."

Madden's next stop was Hancock Junior College in Santa Maria, California, where he spent two years as an assistant while he got his Master's degree at nearby San Luis Obispo. He became head coach at Hancock in 1962. He won eight of nine games the following year, attracting the attention of Tom Bass, an assistant to Don Coryell at San Diego State. Bass was leaving that job and he recommended Madden to succeed him.

"By that time [he was 28] I had set a goal of becoming a head coach when I was thirty-five," Madden recalls. "Long before, I was taught you had to have goals in life to make you work harder."

The San Diego State job proved to be the perfect stepping stone. Coryell, now head coach of the St. Louis Cardinals, says Madden brought with him the idea that a wide-tackle-six defense (six man front, two linebackers, three defensive backs) was the best possible defense; Madden had used the defense successfully in his final season at Hancock. Coryell himself preferred the Oklahoma or 3-4 defense that became popular in the NFL in 1974, with all of its variations and linebacking moves.

"I told John he should consider both defenses," Coryell recalls, "and he asked for time to really study them. He came up with his own variations of the two, using overshifting alignments that were well thought out and executed."

Coryell says Madden was an intelligent coach who organized his work and used his players expertly. Madden also was able to delegate authority.

"His great intensity and dedication to succeed was something," Coryell says. "He drove himself and then he drove those who worked and played for him to be successful. It was the only way he knew how to do the job.

"Sometimes our practices got a little heated because John didn't even like to lose a scrimmage. He never let those players give up; he never allowed them to slough off one play just because it was practice."

San Diego State fans began talking about the Aztecs' "kamikaze defense" because it seemed they were motivated, as one observer noted, "to play maniac football." It quickly became a tradition at the school. Each year the defensive unit felt it could not show less intensity than the one the season before and the inevitable happened: Everyone played better.

It wasn't long before Coryell turned over all the defensive chores to Madden and made him in effect, head coach of the defense. People would ask Coryell about that part of his game and he would tell them, "Don't ask me anything about defense. Go talk to John.

He's the coach of our defensive team and he is in complete charge of it."

For three years Madden helped forge the San Diego State defense into a unit the equal of the team's high-powered offense. But he never lost sight of his overall goal to become a head coach and when the 1966 season ended there was widespread speculation that he would get the top job at Utah State.

A visit by Davis changed some of the direction of his thinking. The Oakland executive came down to San Diego to scout Aztecs' quarterback Don Horn and he met Madden. The two discussed a lot of football that day and Madden made a strong impression on Davis.

"I was impressed with Madden's knowledge and by his enthusiasm," Davis recalls. "I sensed then that he had a strong rapport with the athletes and I liked that, too. I believe in perception—call it intuition if you will—and I decided he was something special.

"A year later I was in the process of hiring a couple of assistants for Johnny Rauch, then our head coach, and John came quickly to mind. At that time I wasn't thinking of him as a future head coach of the Raiders. But I knew that if he came with us he would help us."

It was not an easy decision for Madden. In fact, it took him several days to weigh the advantages of becoming an assistant coach in professional football against the possibility of becoming a head coach at a major college.

"I kept wishing there was something wrong with the deal that Al offered," Madden recalls, "so I could have walked away and not even looked back. But no matter how I looked at it, in light of what I had then and what might—and the word *might* kept sneaking into my thinking—happen, the coaching spot with the Raiders was the only move."

Coryell all but told him the same thing.

"I agreed with him that it was a step upward," Don says. "He had a chance to go on to a head coaching job in the pros or one of the major colleges. I could see that and I wasn't ever worried that he'd get stuck in a dead end or not make it. He was ready at that time for a move, for something with more breadth, something that would make him a better-rounded coach."

Looking back at that decision in 1967, Madden is still amazed Davis hired him.

"People ask me, 'Who is the biggest influence in your coaching career?' and I put his name right at the top," says Madden. "It took a lot of guts for him to hire me. I was thirty-one years old with zero years of pro coaching experience and all of a sudden I was coaching his team's linebackers.

"It would have been much easier to do something else, to get someone else with more experience. But I soon found out that he doesn't always do things the easy way. He wants to do them the right way. Without him having the confidence and hiring me, I just don't know what might have happened."

New pro coaches often have a credibility disadvantage, especially ones with limited pro experience. Madden did not have that problem. "Tom Dahms and Charley Sumner had been coaching the defensive line and defensive backs and sort of split the linebackers' responsibility. But there never was any one person the players could point to and say, 'Well, so-and-so used to do it this way. How come you want it differently?' For the first time they could look at me as 'their coach' and that really means something to a player. He likes to have someone he can identify with at all times, someone he can go to with a problem peculiar to his position, lay it out, and expect full and complete understanding."

Madden's linebackers corps was a good one—Dan Conners, Bill Laskey, and Gus Otto—and he quickly earned his players' respect. Laskey says they "had not expected a newcomer to pro football to be so knowledgeable."

Madden didn't bring a new defensive philosophy from the college game. He learned and accepted the one used by the Raiders.

"As a new coach coming in, the only thing you really can implement is the way you get along with people, how you teach," Madden says. "But you don't bring in new ways of doing things. You adjust to your new surroundings. The only new wrinkle you have is their approach to what they do, then comes your way of getting it across and the way you interact."

During the next two years—including one in which the Raiders went to Super Bowl II, the other in which they lost the AFL championship to the New York Jets—Madden grew quickly as a coach and human being. His thoughts of returning to the college game vanished; his goal now was shifted to becoming a head coach in the NFL.

It came a lot quicker than he thought it would. Rauch and Davis did not get along because Rauch resented Davis's intrusion into the coaching area. And Davis was never totally satisfied with Rauch's work, anyway. Though his team just missed returning to the Super Bowl, Rauch abruptly resigned and Madden, only 33 years old and with no record as a pro player, was given the job.

The veteran players on the team were delighted with the choice, however.

"I never had any real daily person-to-person contact with him," says Jim Otto, "but I just couldn't help but notice his dedication and his enthusiasm. Those things get to a player, particularly if he believes, as John does, that professional football is an emotional game. He was raw emotion on the practice field sometimes and that really rubbed off on people.

"I know when I heard about him getting the job I really was excited. I wasn't looking forward to seeing someone else come in from outside the organization and having to break in a new staff and himself. We were a winning team and I didn't want anything to spoil that."

At the time many felt that Madden would be successful because of the pro football theory that winning owners hire winning coaches. The winning aspect in itself is a pressure cooker because there is room for comparison. Rauch had been a winning coach (25 victories in two seasons) but Madden claims he never had any doubts that he could not do the same.

"You must have the confidence and you either do or don't," he says. "You can't manufacture it. I had it from the day I got the job. I just started going forward and never looked back. A lot of people brought up my age but I never questioned it. Others wondered if I would have to prove myself because I never had been a head coach and was taking over a successful group of players.

"I really never thought much about that, either. The only thing I could do was to deal from honesty what I felt had to be done, and tell them that's the way it would be. I never anticipated any problems and since we won twelve games that season [1969] and the divisional title, I don't think there were any."

That is not to say that Madden didn't see the differences in becoming a head coach and being an assistant. He did, because it was one of the things he anticipated during the times he had "played" at being a head coach. Mentally he had prepared himself to at least accept those differences and then cope with them as they arose.

"Coaching at any level never is easy," he says. "The difference in being the linebacker coach of the Oakland Raiders and being its head coach is one of specialization. For two years I concentrated on the role the linebackers would play. When I became head coach, I had to be concerned with all areas. That doesn't mean I worried more or slept less. It's all in what a person wants to put into his job.

"You want to win just as much when you're an assistant coach because you still have the same desire. I worked just as hard when I was an assistant. If I hadn't, then I wouldn't have been a very good assistant coach, would I? And I certainly wouldn't have been picked as head coach."

Madden is Davis's coach but he is his own man and he calls his own shots when it counts. Davis is the overall director of the organization's day-to-day activities, the overseer of all Raiders' business. Several years ago Davis noted that pro football had reached such proportions that to be successful, an organization needed a dictator of sorts. Davis makes final decisions on scouting and has a strong influence on trades. And while both Madden and Davis shun the specifics of their early relationship as managing general partner and head coach, it is easy to believe that Davis watched intently as his young head coach went about his job.

"He okayed and suggested improvements on game plans in those days," says one source close to the Raiders, "but on game day, he left it up to Madden to make all the tough decisions. Now he pretty much leaves him alone all the time."

The turning point probably came halfway through Madden's first season in 1969, when the Raiders soundly thrashed the Buffalo Bills, who were coached by Rauch. The skeptics had been withholding their verdicts on the coaching switch until there could be a direct comparison of the two coaches.

Davis seized the opportunity of the 50-21 victory to call a press conference that amounted to a public knighting of his coach.

"I wanted to say this before," he said, "but I was afraid some people would think I was just sticking John up as a target in case we lost. My role has changed since he's been head coach from giving direction to giving assistance.

"I am no more important than the lowest assistant coach today. Madden is in full control of the troops. Rauch never had such authority here. Madden doesn't need my help or advice; Rauch, on the other hand, did. The pressure doesn't bother Madden."

That still is Davis's philosophy.

"When do I have time to coach?" he asks with a laugh. "I'm just an organization guy who likes to think I've put together a good thing. John Madden is part of that. So are the players. So is everyone else who works here. I don't go to every workout. I don't send plays down from the top of the stadium.

"John and I talk and I tell him some things I know about the team we're going to play. Has he thought of this? Has he thought of that? He usually has.

"I do know this. John Madden doesn't get enough credit for what he has accomplished. I don't really know why. I guess it's an image thing. People know me; they didn't know him. I talk a lot and I've been around a long time. Maybe everyone thought I was too young to quit coaching in 1965 so they can't believe I have. But I have."

Davis admits if he were coaching the Raiders or if he exerted any real overt influence on what the team did it would "have a different personality." He would call for more discipline ("John can laugh with the guys, I probably couldn't as much as he does"). He also says he wouldn't be as conservative in his offense as the Raiders are under Madden.

"I would throw the ball more," says Davis. "I'd go for the big play although John likes the big play, too. But our overall outlooks are a bit different. At the same time we're a good blend. We bounce things back and forth—but he's the coach. Not many people realize it but he's one of the best at staying cool and making the right decisions when the game's in progress. I get the credit for naming him the coach, that's all."

Madden does not deny that Davis was—and is—a strong influence on him.

"You've got to realize that in any job a lot of the ground rules already are set," he says. "Your philosophy is sort of handed down from the top. Part of it, anyway. But I'm still John Madden and I do certain things differently than others do them. My own personality comes across gradually. The Raiders' organization has installed a solid framework. I try to build from there, carefully and gradually. Some things must be done my way or else I'm not John Madden. I can't be a phony. That wouldn't do me or the players or the organization any good. Everyone works together, but on the field of play I'm the general. The decisions are mine."

Those decisions have been made easier by Oakland's ability for coming up with outstanding football players. The Raiders are one of only two NFL teams (the Cincinnati Bengals are the other) that do not belong to any of the scouting combines so their evaluations are their own.

There are no great mysteries involved. Davis is an excellent evaluator of talent and Madden shares his feelings on how players should be used. Thus there is a straight-line approach and the chances of a player being picked with one position in mind, then being shifted around to suit the whim of the coaching staff is avoided. The ratio of bad selections is cut noticeably that way.

"We look for players who can contribute to the organization over a long period of time," Madden says. "We look for long-range solidity, not for the momentary contribution. We want the type of guy who is a solid player and person. He doesn't have to come to us and live or die on whether he'll play full time as a rookie.

"We also pick a man with the idea that he'll be able to play for eight to ten seasons. We don't know that he can but it's a criterion. He may not be able to play in his first season or in the second but we're looking most at his overall contribution.

"In 1968, for example, we got Ken Stabler and he didn't play for five seasons. We got Art Shell the same year and he didn't play for the first two years. By not playing I mean they were not starters. They made their contributions in other ways."

Unlike many teams, notably Dallas, the Raiders do not hold to the "best athlete" concept. Madden says a player can be a great athlete in college but he questions how long those talents stay sharp. He does not want players who come to him in peak talent years and begin to lose the edge after a season or two.

"There is one key point about picking the so-called 'great athlete,'" Madden says. "It doesn't mean a thing if he doesn't perform within the team in mind. There are a lot of guys like that, guys who look great in their underwear, guys who are great in one-on-one in basketball. But in a game, they don't always work out."

It's the same with drafting for a specific need, Madden claims. He does not take a right offensive tackle in the draft simply because he feels he *must* have a right offensive tackle.

"If we were to go into a draft with a preconceived notion of exactly what we must have, there might not be a first-round pick who really is worthy of being a first-round pick. But because you have to fill a position, you take the player on the first round anyhow. The man either is there and worthy of his pick or he's not," Madden says.

What he wants to eliminate is the "need" factor. Tackle John Vella, who was drafted in the second round in 1972, is a good example. At the time, the Raiders had two superb tackles in Art Shell and Bob Brown, an all-pro. Vella did not play regularly with the Raiders for two seasons but when Brown left, there was someone to take his place, someone who knew the system and had gained enough experience to be immediately competent.

When the Raiders drafted Stabler, Daryle Lamonica was most valuable player in the old American Football League. Now Lamonica is gone and Stabler is an acknowledged star. The idea, says Madden, is to always have a backup ready so there's no panic to find an immediate replacement.

Madden's feelings about drafting objectively as opposed to need are so strong that the team will not pick a player with the idea that he will play a particular position or replace a particular player in two or three years. Most of the time a player eventually will play the position for which he is picked but the decision will be made without pressure.

The antecedent to this attitude is getting additional starting players through trades. The Raiders have excelled in this area, too, seeking to maintain a team balance of young to veteran players.

"What happens," says Madden, "is that as your young players come in, regardless of need, your old players retire, and your middle-age players become old. There is a constant flow this way. That's the reason we never draft for a starter, initially, but for a backup.

"But if there is an immediate need for a starting player through injury, we can find that vacancy either by elevating a backup player or by trading for a quality player."

Two good examples are the acquisition of defensive tackle Otis Sistrunk and former defensive end Bubba Smith.

Sistrunk had a tryout in Washington after some success in minor league football at Norfolk, Virginia. But George Allen let him go. A year later he signed with the Rams, but the Rams sent him to Oakland for a third-round draft pick while also giving up a fourth.

"Otis became an amazing story because he came and started for us the first season we had him," Madden says. "But we needed a defensive lineman because we were down to six in training camp. That is an example of where we had a need for a player and were forced to trade for one.

"We put him in there, and he worked right into a starting job. We probably were looking at him with different eyes because of the shortage of players, but he still proved he could do the job.

"We wanted Bubba Smith as a defensive end the next season because of an injury problem. It meant trading a starting tight end, Ray Chester, to get him. A lot of people were surprised we'd trade a good, young tight end like Ray but we had Bob Moore ready and we felt no compunction in making the trade. Bubba played two seasons for us and moved on but Moore has moved in to play very well.

"So we're always in a position to make a trade if we must and not feel a great pinch in having to give up a quality player to get a quality player. There is always a reservoir of talent available—either ours or on other teams. But the main thing is that we don't allow our squad to get so thin that we're suddenly left with no help and are put in a pressure situation to make the replacement."

"Our team never will be too old, nor will it ever be too young. If a team becomes too old at the same time, the next step is that it becomes too young at the same time. It's been proven too often that top clubs that merely stand still soon find themselves slipping back into the middle of the pack. I know that a great reason for the success of this organization is that it never has stood still in its personnel development."

There are other reasons, too. Look at the Raiders' roster and you see players with winning backgrounds in college. That is one of the unwritten rules in personnel selection. Madden and Davis both point to Stabler, who was the quarterback on Alabama's great teams of the mid-sixties. Vella and halfback Clarence Davis both were on champion teams at USC as were tight end Bob Moore at Stanford, defensive backs Neal Colzie and Jack Tatum at Ohio State, tight end Dave Casper at Notre Dame, and linebacker Monte Johnson at Nebraska.

That is not to say that there is a blind spot in picking only players from top 10-ranked schools. Gene Upshaw (Texas A&I), Otis Sistrunk (who never played college football), and Shell (Maryland-Eastern Shore) are some examples. "But you'd have to be an idiot to look at them and not know they're football players," Madden says.

The Raiders do not use computer readouts. They prefer common sense and logic instead. In 1973 they chose punter Ray Guy on the first round and then used him exactly as they had hoped—as a mighty weapon that pins other teams in their territory. "A lot of things can change if we punt the ball from inside our twenty-yard line and the other guy has to put it in play on the other side of the fifty," says Madden. "The defense isn't always fighting for its life and it can make the other quarterback stay honest. It can also scare the hell out of him if he continues to take the snap around his own twenty-yard line because our punter keeps putting the ball down there. Pretty soon the guy is thinking about not making the mistake and he becomes conservative. And pretty soon our offense is getting the ball inside that guy's fifty-yard line. Then it's our kind of ball game."

The key in every player selection is speed. All else can be taught, Madden believes, but a player either has speed or he doesn't. That's not only at the key running back and receiver positions on offense but on defense as well. The Raiders' defensive backs always have been swift and, in some cases, they've sacrificed bulk and power on the defensive line for swift, quick-striking ends.

Their offensive philosophy always has dictated speed in the outside receivers such as Wells and Branch and, when he was younger, Biletnikoff as well. When the zone defenses took away Oakland's "big bomb" attack, Biletnikoff still was effective because of his great catching ability. Mike Siani, who isn't as swift as many wide receivers in the NFL, had the same attribute. The speed factor returned with Branch, who has the capability of simply running through the zone coverage.

Some critics of these personnel selections claim that the Raiders never have been an NFL champion because they do not have great running backs. Madden, who is against overloading his team at one particular area, disagrees.

"You can't oversimplify football success by pointing to one thing," he says. "I coached in the Pro Bowl and thirteen Miami players were picked. They had good people everywhere. That's what it is all about—good players doing a top job consistently over the year. You can't narrow it to a single item. We always try to have the best possible people at every position and we don't want to become a team everyone looks at and says, 'They have this guy and that guy so all they really can do is this.'

"It used to be said that if you took away the bomb you could beat our passing game and thus beat us. If you look at us now, you can't say if you take away the pass, you beat us. If we lose the pass we still feel we can run the ball, play good defense, and win. Likewise, if they take away our run, we can play good defense and make enough with our pass and also be successful. That is how we built this team."

Nearly two dozen personnel scouts from other NFL teams were on hand at a 1975 Raiders preseason game and Davis saw them and noted with a mixture of pride and pleasure (and maybe some consternation), "They're just waiting for us to make a move. We teach 'em [players], train 'em, and somebody else gets 'em. It's like we're running a school for 'em."

All of which is a bit remarkable considering that Oakland never has drafted higher than nineteenth since the common draft began in 1967. But their effectiveness is in the early rounds—33 of its 43 players in 1975 were picked on the first seven rounds of the draft. And 17 of those were chosen on the first two rounds.

"The Raiders do their work with those first seven picks and if you draft well in those positions, then you will be assured of quality coming onto your squad each year," one personnel director said. "Oakland just doesn't seem to make a lot of mistakes with people. That's one reason why you see a lot of scouts following their ball club in the preseason."

One player everyone missed was Marv Hubbard. Hubbard was an eleventh-round draft pick in 1968 from Colgate University in upstate New York. He was waived by Oakland, signed by Denver, and released. He spent a year playing for the Hartford, Connecticut team in a minor league and was re-signed by the Raiders after a strong season.

"We had Hewritt Dixon when we let Marv go the first time, though we felt he was a fine player," Madden remembers. "But it was a matter of numbers. When we scouted him at Hartford—and we kept a good touch on him—we decided we'd like to have him back. We didn't put him there to get any experience. Everyone had a shot at him on two waiver situations."

Madden calls Hubbard a "late bloomer," like Stabler and Sistrunk. Stabler didn't play his first two seasons because of injuries and personal problems. He was on the verge of giving up the game.

"I didn't try to persuade him," says Madden. "I let him make the decision himself. The self-motivation was all his."

Does that mean Madden won't chase a player who has talent?

"Not at all," he says. "You might not know the reason and when you do find out, it could be a very simple thing. It could be something like a feeling a guy has that stems from something someone said. It's happened with us where players *heard* they were cut and had begun packing their bags. And the reports weren't even true.

"We almost lost Hubbard because of such a freaky thing. It was my first year as coach and someone came and said that Marv was packing his bags to leave camp. I went to see what it was all about. He said it was the same date as the year before when he got cut and he had heard it was going to happen again. He had assumed this but I told him it just wasn't true, that he was doing fine and it looked like he was going to make it.

"It's different, though, if a guy comes to me and says, 'I quit, I just don't want to play.' If he doesn't want to play, you can't beg him to stay."

Madden disdains the "great athlete" theory, but he is not afraid to take a chance. When he took the job, he inherited a number one draft pick named Eldridge Dickey. Dickey, a quarterback at Tennessee A&I, was used sparingly as a receiver and kick returner by Rauch in his first season. There was skepticism then about the ability of a black quarterback to be effective in the NFL but Madden pushed all that aside and gave Dickey his shot.

"When he was drafted, we thought he had that potential," Madden says. "We gave him a chance and he also learned something about the other end of the pass. It didn't hurt him either way, though he was unable to make our club. I'm not a guy who is sold on stereotype notions about what a guy can or cannot do. We want everyone to prove themselves out."

That was the case with Monte Johnson, the Raiders' middle linebacker who ousted veteran Dan Conners from a job before the 1975 season began. Johnson had been a reserve defensive lineman at Nebraska, playing behind the likes of Rich Glover and Larry Jacobson, a pair of Outland trophy winners. He never started a game at Nebraska but his duties as a reserve linebacker in 1974, his second pro season, helped prepare him for the assignment.

"We followed Johnson throughout his college career," Madden says. "He had the super size, speed, and strength to be a linebacker. He blossomed when we used the three-four defense in 1974, and in training camp in 1975 he adjusted to the middle position extremely well."

Madden claims the evaluation of college players is a difficult business.

"You've got to be a lot more general scouting the college player than you do evaluating under your own system because you don't know what that player has been told or how he's been motivated by his own coach," Madden says. "You also don't know what his specific role is under that coach. They may want different results or a different type of person for what they are trying to accomplish. So the man's role may be different under his college coach than it would be under you. If we came across a college team doing the same kinds of things we do in every respect, then our judgment could be pretty much absolute before we ever got the kid to camp.

"Regardless of the system, one constant is getting a solid person. Once you get one, then it's the coach's job to get him ready and to motivate him."

To Madden, motivation is both the culmination of an effort he calls "motivational readiness" and the positive benefits that winning experiences bring.

"This whole idea, to me, is a dual responsibility between the player and the coach," he says. "There must be desire, intensity, and a feeling of wanting to be the best on the part of the player. That comes from within him. You can't manufacture pride. You may have to show them sometimes what it is, maybe define intensity for them, but in the end, the players must be ready to do their part. That's what I call motivational readiness. If they're not ready, then the coach must see that it's done. And if that doesn't work because the player won't accept the mandate, then that is the point where you part company.

"The player also must have good experience because it breeds interest in even more good experiences. That's when all that you're trying to accomplish begins to make sense. That's when they begin to believe in the need for the hard work, dedication, pride, intensity, and total involvement."

Madden believes the burden is on the coach to carry the message. To pick out one or two players and say they are prime examples of what he is trying to prove is, to him, saying that none of the other players have the same motivation.

"I honestly don't think that's true," he says. "There may be degrees in that some players are more outgoing and some do it from within. It's like faith; you can't see it but you know it's there because you can feel it."

When he was playing, Otto was a prime example of a man who reflected his coach's attitude. Otto says he never had to be pushed too much because he came into football knowing the intensity of the job. And he says he worked with the same intensity every day in practice that he did in a game.

"I never tried to explain why I was one way and another player was a different way," Otto says. "I never knew why myself because I went out on the field and did everything I had to do to be successful. I never went for fancy frills or for cute or different philosophical approaches. To me, football never was that complex. You either made the block or you didn't. But if you didn't you came back more determined than ever the next time to be successful."

Otto says that Madden makes his players aware of what they must do to be successful in a game through serious and intense preparation. Everyone on the team knows what it will take in the way of individual execution.

If there is a word that describes Madden's method of relating to his players he prefers it to be "honesty." He has the reputation of being hard-nosed; he says he is honest. His players say he tells it like it is; he says he is honest. Those who follow the team's fortune say Madden never minces words; he says he is honest.

"The worst thing that can happen to a coach who intends to stay in one place for a long time is to be called a phony," says Madden. "That's the cardinal sin. The players might not like to hear what you have to say but at least they know it is what you really feel. It must be that way. I tell our players, 'You have to hear things you really don't want to hear; you must look at things you really don't want to see.' That's a tough attribute because honesty isn't always saying things on the plus side; you've got to be able to say the negative things, too.

"I don't think about myself being hard-nosed. If something must be done I go ahead and do it. If there is someone who feels they must be tough and they're not, they're not being honest. And if there is someone who isn't tough and feels he must be, he is not being honest either.

"If there is a time when you're going to be mad, then you're going to be mad. And if you feel that way and let it go by, then you're being a phony. If I get mad, it's for a good reason, either for an action or as a reaction. I don't go around acting mad all the time just to look or sound tough. But when the time comes to be that way, I'll never back down."

There are some who feel a coach's best psychological weapon is to keep his team off balance, to never let it know how he really feels. Some do it by maintaining a very cool exterior, praising only when absolutely necessary. Madden rejects this.

"He gained the respect of every player on the team with his honest approach," Jim Otto says. "It's the only way I've ever known him. He'll slap a guy on the back when one is due and praise a guy after playing well. He'll also criticize a guy who did not play very well."

Madden's attitude toward his players is relaxed and open, but he keeps a personal distance.

"I don't believe players are looking for a friend," he says. "They have a lot of them. I don't try to get on the same level. I don't socialize with my players and I don't do it too much with my assistant coaches, either. The Raiders aren't that type of organization. We pretty much follow our own pursuits and our own friends once we leave the office or practice field."

His players say his relations with them are good because he established a strong rapport from the beginning. If there is a problem his first reaction is to sit and talk with the player about it. He wants to find out the player's side and if it is concerned with football skills, Madden will always check the films before trying to come up with answers. He takes the same approach with non-football problems. His door always is open.

Madden wants players and coaches to have a feeling for each other. During the players' strike, he did not close off the lines of communication to those who chose to honor the picket lines. They always could come to talk to him about either the problems of the strike itself or their status with the team.

"Basically," one said, "they all seemed to be concerned with where the strike was taking them and he tried to explain in a very honest manner what the alternatives and perhaps even the consequences would be. He was very honest. He never tried to brainwash nor coerce a player into thinking a particular way. That was one of the key reasons this club came together so quickly when the strike ended and why it was so successful that 1974 season when a lot of other teams were having problems."

Madden says he takes that approach not only because it is his own nature but because of the kinds of players who are coming into pro football. In addition to honesty, most modern players demand a mature approach to problems.

"The college kids are much more intelligent and sophisticated today," Madden says. "You don't gain a thing by trying to talk down to them or trying to bulldoze them. That's a quick way to lose them. How could I tell a kid coming into my camp that I'm an honest guy, that I abhor a phony and then go out and give him some big line about what is right and what is wrong?

"A coach in the pros today must approach these young men intelligently. He must give reasons for what he wants done and be able to back up those reasons with solid, sound facts. The day is gone when you're going to get some guy to run through the wall for you just because you say it's there and it must be run through.

"And once a college kid becomes a pro, then he is the same person he was before only a few years older. So the responsibility in your personal relationships never really changes."

This is not a stance that Madden adopted once he became the Raiders' head coach. His communication with players was "super" at San Diego State, Coryell says. "John had a great way of making himself understood because he spoke their language. That is a gift you find only in successful teachers. They are able to take everything they must teach and grind it down to a common denominator where it is understood by the most intelligent and the least intelligent," Coryell says.

After the Raiders lost to the Pittsburgh Steelers in the 1974 AFC title game, Madden was stopped by a couple of reporters after leaving the Oakland locker room.

It had to be one of the low points of his life, yet when one of the reporters asked him to preview the upcoming Super Bowl, he didn't growl or tell the man to get lost or to drop dead.

"A helluva defensive struggle," he said of the game that would match Pittsburgh and Minnesota. "If it ever goes into sudden death, you'd better have your lunch along. It might last three days."

Then Madden flashed a trace of a smile and left. "How do you like that?" said the other reporter. "He just lost the biggest game of his life and he can treat you like it was half-past Wednesday afternoon."

That's how he treats everyone. He'll often break up long meetings in the Raiders' offices by walking out of the room and making small talk with other employees. He had regularly attended a football clinic in Allentown, Pennsylvania, where the ranks are heavy with high school and college coaches. Madden wades into this group as if he were teaching on the same level. He speaks their language. He does not come loaded with films of the Oakland Raiders or tales of this great play or that great formation. He comes to learn and to listen and is good at both.

"I enjoy days like those," he says. "It's good to know what's going on in the high schools and colleges. It's good to keep in touch. A lot of the stuff we're using in the pro game now came from college coaches. The more we know what's going on at all levels of football the better off we are."

Madden remembers listening to Bear Bryant lecture for nearly three hours a couple of years ago. He says he didn't learn anything new about football but he enjoyed hearing his personal philosophy about the game.

Some coaches could go from one end of the year to the other and not spend any time with their fellow coaches, and it doesn't bother them a bit. But Madden spends a great deal of time at every opportunity talking and exchanging ideas with the likes of Chuck Noll, Don Shula, Tommy Prothro, and George Allen.

"You can talk to some coaches," he says, "but with others, there's just nothing to say. Fellows like Noll, Shula, and Prothro, if they say something, they give it to you straight. In particular, I have a lot of respect for Chuck Noll. I've learned a lot about defense from him."

Madden does not have an offensive or defensive coordinator, preferring to spread the responsibilities among everyone connected with either unit.

"To designate one guy as the boss of the offense or defense would stifle creativity," Madden says. "What we try to do is to keep everything together. If we have an offensive play, it's not my play, it's ours. That way we get teaching. When we begin to draw up a game plan we get together and we talk about it. It's a collective effort.

"A coach and his staff must be with it. Each personality must come forth. The head coach's forte, in knowledge and personality, must shine through and he must know what is happening to people around him."

Again you get a strong sense of the organization concept in his thinking. That reflects Madden's own relations within the Raiders' staff when he was an assistant coach. He often refers to how well everyone on Rauch's staff got along and says such a relationship is a must.

"That's one of the things that impressed me so much with the organization as Davis set it up," he says. "Everything is so well organized and functions so efficiently because he has the right people working for it. There was no way I ever wanted to change that relationship."

When Madden fills vacancies on the Raiders' staff he solicits the opinions of his assistants.

"The reason is that all of us have to work so closely together and have to spend so much time together throughout the year that there must be harmony," he says. "It does no good to bring in people you think will be good for your operation and find out the other coaches really have no feeling for them, either as coaches or as people."

This method of free discussion is part of a day's work for Madden and his staff. He encourages it in everything the team must do and doesn't mind when the ideas and the reactions flow in a lively manner.

"That's what this job is all about," says Madden. "I don't want to put anyone down where they won't feel free to make a strong contribution. That's the only way you can get teaching. Like motivation, it must come from within.

"If it's something they don't know, they can't teach it. If it's something that's been stuffed down their throats, they really can't teach it either. When you build collectively, what comes out is *ours*. We're all talking the same language and won't have people going in different directions. When one person controls everything, you get some people for and some against—and everyone is not together.

"But when everyone is equal all ideas are treated equal. Everything comes out as one, collective work and you get it taught as one, collective package rather than a bunch of pieces. You don't get someone saying, 'This is good, it's my idea; but *this* is someone else's idea and I don't understand it.'"

On the field, Madden allows autonomy for each coach for his particular unit. He spends most of his time with the quarterbacks, receivers, and running backs, perfecting the passing game. When they are working against a defense, he'll also see the linebackers and defensive backs so he has those elements of his team under scrutiny most of the time, too. But if there is a particular unit he feels has slipped or is not performing as it should, he'll also make sure it shapes up by telling that unit's coach about it.

"Madden is a very curious person by nature," one of his players notes. "He stands out on that practice field and when the quarterbacks are not working—even in the time when players are returning from a pass pattern—he'll be looking over that practice field to see what's happening. He can spot something forty yards away.

"Sometimes that's his own way of letting everyone know he's around and interested. And when you hear him yell, you certainly know he's interested."

The all-consuming interest stems from an equally all-consuming dedication to the job.

"My job is a way of life," he says. "There are no days off. To be successful, a coach must be totally dedicated. He can't own a summer cabin in the mountains or play golf in his spare time because there is no spare time. If I don't give this job one-hundred percent, I'm out in left field and that's how it should be.

"When something is a way of life like this it's bigger than a job or a profession. To say that you have a mixture of football and family isn't true. I couldn't say that. How can you say you have a family life when you come to summer camp in July and stay until September, and then when you do go home, you're never there.

"I have a very independent wife. In the summer she'll go to a tennis camp or take our two boys some place for a vacation. She's a doer and has her own life. She taught for years as a college English teacher and isn't afraid to test her intellect or explore things which interest her. One of her prime qualities is her independence."

Madden says he works 18 hours a day in season and almost as much out of season. "I'm not fishing for credit," he says, "just stating a fact. Other coaches do it, too.

"I want to coach forever. If I were to be fired it would not be a badge of merit but a deep hurt. I hear that baseball managers consider being fired a badge of merit or that every coach or manager is hired to be fired, and some say they'll be rehired before the next season.

"You can't name three pro football coaches in the last twenty-five years who were fired, then after being rehired were successful. I firmly believe that if I ever got fired it would be because I didn't do the job well enough with the Oakland Raiders. Perhaps subconsciously I work every day to keep from being fired . . . but every day I work to do the best job I possibly can. Both mean the same thing to our organization."

That philosophy is as important to him in January as it is in July when the Raiders begin training camp. Actually, the training camp experience really never ends because Madden and his coaches work with their younger players for all but two or three months a year when possible. Sometimes they'll have them together as much as three or four times during the spring—once a month from March through June. The veterans come for one precamp check-out and it used to be more before the Players Association managed to get an agreement for only one mandatory out-of-season training session.

"You don't improve a team only in the draft," says Madden. "That's just a beginning. At one time we made a lot of mistakes about cutting players simply because we couldn't tell the difference between guys who didn't know what they were doing and those who couldn't do it.

"We turned to a system of development camps and got what amounted to almost a year's experience for our rookies even before their first season began. We placed a great deal of stress on getting these players properly oriented toward our system and pro football in general. When we got into training camp and they were thrown into work with the veterans there was a great deal more competence on their part. At least we

125

knew who could and who could not do the work by that time."

The hard work continues through the season. It begins the morning after a game, when all the coaches view the game films together, then break down their own particular segments and grade every play and every player. Dusk is falling over the Bay Area when that task is completed and new cans of film are brought out—those of the upcoming opponent—and another game plan begins to take form.

"We work to midnight or so on Monday and Tuesday nights getting that game plan in order," Madden says. "We show our players the game film on Tuesday morning and begin working with them that day on the upcoming game. We want to give them the beginnings of our thoughts and ideas about what we will do so they'll have something to think about before Wednesday's practice."

Before anything is done on Wednesday, the special teams come in for an early session at 11:30 in the morning and the rest of the squad checks in at noon. The day's practice is filmed and the quarterbacks return for a two-hour session that night so they'll be thoroughly familiar with all offensive plans for the upcoming game.

"We want them in total accord with what we've planned and this gives us a great opportunity to work everything out," Madden says. "We want their input after a day's work with the game plan. We want them to tell us what they like as well as what they don't like. We have a rule not to try to shove something down the quarterback's throat just because it is the result of something we think will go.

"There just is no logical reason to tell a quarterback he must run this sweep or throw that pass if he really doesn't feel it will work. Sometimes we can persuade him it will. Maybe we'll tell him to look at it again in practice, to get the feel of what he must do before any final decision to discard it. The result is that when there is an area of non-agreement, both the quarterbacks and the coaches now are most aware of a soft area. By the time Sunday rolls around we'll have worked out the problem before it comes to the crunch in a game."

Madden works closely with his quarterbacks during the week. He wants them to take their orders from just one person—him—feeling the worst atmosphere for a quarterback is to be getting his advice from several people, all of whom may have different ideas on the same subject.

"When the week is finished," Madden points out, "I've been in touch with everyone on the team and that includes the special teams. To me that is one very important area, something that over the years we, as coaches, have given a lot of lip service to and then wandered off and sat down with the quarterback or with the defensive backfield.

"I make a conscious effort every week to get with them. The first thing we do is to watch their film, as a team. I run the projector and handle the critique and the discussion. On Friday, I present the special team game plan after my special teams coach puts it together. Again I'll run the projector and we'll review the previous week's game once more.

"We believe every detail is important. It's the only way you can approach your job. If you're honest and say that *everything* is important and you really believe it, then you've got to show equal interest. A coach who shows preference, interest-wise, in one phase of the game over the other is making a mistake, in my opinion."

There is more to Madden's preparation. He looks at an upcoming game with an eye to total picture. For example, when the Raiders opened the 1975 season with a Monday night game in Miami, Madden had the median temperatures for that date—night and day—thoroughly checked. If he had found the temperature to be oppressively hot, he was prepared to settle into Florida for a week's time and work under the prevailing conditions. It turned out that such drastic steps weren't necessary.

That was an opening game the Raiders won—one of only two first-game victories in Madden's tenure at Oakland. And that disturbs him a bit.

"How do you figure patterns?" he asks, shrugging. "We've had some long winning streaks. Our players have had a feeling we can win when necessary, and that might be one answer. Maybe in the openers there is a feeling it doesn't count, that they can make it up.

"I've studied this thing about as thoroughly as I can. We keep complete information so I know exactly how we've planned and prepared for fall practice, the dates and the times, the physical problems, the amount of work, just about everything you can think of. I've tried to change a few things here and there but I haven't solved the puzzle.

"One thing I will never do is to tell a team opening the season that the first game is a 'must' win. If we lose we have thirteen more problems ahead. Why start negatively? If we lose, we don't like it but we just go out to win as many as we can. We know it's a long season."

The Raiders probably are more famous for their passing game than their punishing ground offense. This fame was achieved primarily after Lamonica came to the team from Buffalo in 1967. In four seasons, he threw 111 touchdown passes; the club had gotten just 103 in the preceding seven seasons. The production numbers waned a bit after that, but when Stabler became quarterback, the Raiders' passing game became a feared weapon again.

"Many thought the zone defense had an effect on our passing game after 1970 but that wasn't true," Madden says. "Going from the ten-team AFL to a thirteen-team AFC alignment in a twenty-six-team setup in which everyone plays everybody else over a period of a few years, had a lot to do with it.

"We don't know all the teams any more. So much of a game is spent feeling out the opponent—like a boxer spending five rounds seeing what the other guy can or can't do. We always feel we can control our own destiny against any zone defense. Our receivers can either go deep and come back—which a receiver still can do against the zone—or get in front of those defensive backs for sixteen or eighteen yards."

Like everything else that is done, the patterns the Raiders run are well thought out, with a decisive edge given to wear and tear on the individual receivers. Thus you don't see a passing game geared to slant patterns where the lighter wide receivers can take a beating from heavier linebackers or get battered from good tackling angles opened to defensive backs.

"That's how you get receivers killed," Madden says. "We like to keep ours around. You'll generally find our wide receivers play every game because they don't get hit as often by big linebackers. That's how we can control our destiny and keep consistency in our passing game."

Madden, as Davis did before him, has Stabler and other quarterbacks take a different approach on how patterns are run, particularly on when the ball is released. The classic example is the quarterback who can release the ball even before his receiver has made a cut to the sidelines; ball and receiver should confront each other simultaneously.

"If you throw on the break or before the break, you get interceptions," says Madden. "We throw after the break, two steps after the receiver has made his cut. That receiver usually has an option between twelve and eighteen yards on the cut and we want to make sure he has somebody beat before our quarterbacks release that ball."

In Madden's mind, a good offensive line and a quarterback who can hold the ball add up to a good passing game. If the line can protect the Raiders' passer until the receiver has made his break, then the chance of a reception is greater.

"A quick release by the quarterback will get the ball there," he says. "We look at a quick release as when the ball is thrown, not getting rid of it quicker because of the pass rush. If our line protects the passer, that isn't necessary."

Madden often cites the play of Johnny Unitas in a 1970 playoff victory against the Raiders as a classic example of what a quarterback must do. Playing for the Baltimore Colts, Unitas completed only 11 of 29 passes that day—and only 5 of 18 in the first half.

"But the ones he completed were right in there under good coverage and the ones he didn't were thrown in a place where our defensive backs couldn't reach the ball," says Madden. "You see five-of-eighteen but those statistics are misleading. If receivers are covered a passer can do three things. He can throw the ball away, throw it in there and risk an interception, or he can get thrown for a loss, which often means losing field position.

"You don't want the interceptions and you don't want the loss. So Unitas did the best thing he could do. He threw it away; probably half his incompletions in that first half were that type. Those are the things that statistics don't show or that aren't understood by the fan."

Even less understood is the overall subject of defense. The Raiders have changed their approach under Madden, dictated by the rules (outlawing the bump-and-run) and personnel. Madden follows the same principles for establishing his defense as he does for the offense—personnel dictates what the Raiders can do. Then comes a fundamental approach, followed by the subtleties that make good defenses better.

"You've got to start by being able to do things the hard way," he says. "That means being able to cover man-for-man, to take on blocks and defeat them. Then you move on to the more sophisticated movements—the stunts, zones, multiplicity of pass coverage, situation substitution, and so on. But all of those are no good unless you can whip someone one-on-one."

Madden believes he upgraded the Raiders' defense with the sudden and complete transformation of the defensive line a few years ago. In 1970, Tony Cline, though a rookie, started at end; a year later, Horace Jones, also a rookie, started at the other end; and in 1972, Otis Sistrunk and Art Thoms replaced Tom Keating and Carleton Oats as tackles.

"We just stuck them in there and said we were going to go with this group and that if we had to live with it, we would," Madden says. "We didn't want to panic or have them think that we were going to panic. It was just such a philosophy that kept the unit together."

Though the bulk of Madden's coaching experience prior to becoming head coach at Oakland was on defense, he is not considered a "defensive man" as Tom Landry, Shula, and Noll are. Unlike Allen, he does not put all the stress on the defensive platoon nor does he spend the bulk of his time with it. This balance has helped him in maintaining his team's success.

It hasn't always been easy, either, because the tendency has been to downgrade the Raiders since they have appeared in only one Super Bowl. There are whispers about their great playing talent and there are constant expressions—justified or unjustified—about the team's lack of killer instinct to harness all its power for a push through the playoffs.

"If you or your players begin to believe they can't win the so-called 'big ones' then you can't be successful," Madden says. "People who play just cannot be subject to that kind of persuasion because, if they believe it, what will they do if people say they can't win on artificial turf or on Monday night or on a Sunday after playing on Monday night?

"We went for a period of time where people said the Raiders couldn't win on artificial turf. If we believe that—and we have five games on artificial turf—what do we do?

"We heard it a lot after we lost to Pittsburgh in 1974, but if we had lost to Miami, we would have heard it a week earlier. Did we change that much in a week? After all, the Miami game in the playoffs was a big game, too . . . big enough so that if we lost it, we were out. But we won and heard nothing. Teams just don't win ten or twelve games a year if those things affect them."

No one can deny the success of the Raiders and if Madden's rationale on shrugging off the loser's talk is correct, then his team rides an even track. Maintaining that success, he says, is a lot harder than it would have been to build it. He acknowledges the built-in pressures of his job from the moment he became head coach because he was handed success and he was expected to maintain it.

"The players know they must respond," says Madden. "They know that they either improve with us or we get someone else. We don't threaten them with this but they know it. Our off-season programs and training camps are successful because the players want to remain successful—more successful than anyone else."

The key ingredient, according to Madden, is to be sure that everyone—himself, his coaches, and his players—do not become self-satisfied. Madden himself loves to win—and, like Lombardi, believes it is the "only thing." As an overtly emotional man, he is euphoric when his team is successful. It's not unusual to see him racing down the sidelines with his runners or if one of his defensive backs intercept a pass.

"There is a distinction," he cautions. "I act that way because that's how I feel at the moment. But I don't carry it too far because my biggest guard is against becoming too satisfied when we win, and with maintaining my confidence if we lose. It's the coach's role to keep himself, and those around him, on an even keel and there are many times when you've got to put the joy of winning behind you and look ahead to what really is uncertainty.

"The only yardstick for success our society has is being a champion. No one remembers anything else. In pro football, only one coaching staff can be satisfied with itself, the one that walks off the field as Super Bowl champion. That means one winner, twenty-seven losers—twenty-seven guys [teams] who have all winter to think about it.

"I lived all winter with the playoff losses to Pittsburgh in 1974 and 1975, and to Miami in 1973. You can't skip over those to the game you won just before that one. You're only as good as your last game and there's nothing more important than your next game.

"You've got to view the season in that regard. You play the preseason schedule to get your team ready for the fourteen-game season. Then you play the fourteen-game season to reach the playoffs and the playoffs to get into the Super Bowl. But the team that wins the Super Bowl is not necessarily the best over a season but the best for one day.

"Over a fourteen-game season in 1974 the Raiders were best team in the AFC because we had a fourteen-two record. Or the same with the Vikings, who had the same record in the NFC. But on one day it didn't work out that way."

Madden favors a playoff system that would eliminate the one-game playoff. He notes that pro football is the only professional team sport that ties up its championship to one game and his feelings are not because of any lack of success in achieving that goal.

"I'd feel the same way if we had won the Super Bowl," he says. "If the fans thought about it, they'd demand we do it that way. Every year they build up their hopes for an exciting Super Bowl and virtually every year they are disappointed.

"It's no coincidence. Conservative football is boring football. But when you put everything on the line in one game, teams must be conservative.

"Look at the Raiders: All season we gamble when we feel the percentages are with us. We open things up and if we lose, so what? There was always next week and most of the time we figured to win. Now we get into a playoff situation and all of a sudden there's no tomorrow. If you gamble, the percentages may not have time to even up. And if you lose, they dig a hole and bury you in it. They say you can't win the big one, that you choked, and all the rest.

"Well, every team tightens up when the game comes down to winner-take-all. You don't play aggressive football. Instead of playing to win, you're playing not to make the mistake that could end up costing you the game. Execution becomes everything. The fans aren't just imagining those games are dull. They really are dull. And one reason is that you throw out a lot of plays for a championship game in the hopes of running only the ones you figure to execute the best.

"Hell, I know we used more plays in our first preseason game than the Super Bowl teams will have in their playbooks for that one day. That's what happens when you take one game and put everything on it. But if you made conference championship games and the Super Bowl both best-of-three, you'd start to see teams opening up offensively. You wouldn't mind gambling a little because no one mistake would cost you a championship.

"The pressure is hard to imagine when you get into those playoffs. It's unlike any other team sport because you can't afford a bad day and still win. You've got to be better than the other team on that field for that one day. And I'll tell you, it's a helluva feeling."

Still, Madden has not let his world cave beneath him because he has yet to guide the Raiders into the Super Bowl. For one reason: There is no one thing that has mitigated against the Raiders in the playoffs. In 1969, they beat Kansas City twice during the regular season, then lost the final AFL title game. In 1972, they had the Steelers beaten until Franco Harris's amazing catch pulled out a last-second victory. The next year, they beat the Steelers, then lost to Miami; in 1974, the process was reversed; and in 1975 they defeated Cincinnati, but again lost to Pittsburgh in the AFC championship game.

"It's happened and what the hell," he says, shrugging his massive shoulders. "It's the last game and you must live with it. There's no tomorrow, no saying 'We'll get them next week.' You've got to suck it up, take what the critics say, and go to work on next year.

"I can honestly say that it is not a frustrating thing. It's something that makes you anxious to get started again. People think that we get so close, lose, and get frustrated. The people who get frustrated are the ones who don't get close. There are winners and there are losers but the losers aren't the ones who go twelve-two, beat Miami, then lose to Pittsburgh.

"When I was a kid, the four-minute mile was the big thing. No one had broken it but there were guys who were running four-oh-one, four-oh-two, and four-oh-three and they knew they were going to break it. They couldn't wait to get back and run again. They weren't frustrated. The guy who was frustrated was the one trying to run the four-minute mile and was running four-fifty-two. Why should he want to get back?

"I've come to believe that once something is done, there are two things you have to do. One, you must evaluate what happened and, two, you must work towards it not happening again. That's what we do after every game, particularly after a losing game. And it makes no difference if it is the first game of the season or the conference championship."

Chuck Noll

"As you gain experience you mature as an individual, and along with that comes the ability to solve problems."

Television viewers who saw the Pittsburgh Steelers' dressing room following their victory over the Oakland Raiders in the 1975 American Football Conference championship game may have been a bit surprised. The game had been played in bitter cold, with snow flurries whipped by icy winds that accentuated the ferocious hitting by both teams—hitting hard enough to cause 13 turnovers and send a few players limping from the game.

You'd think that after such a struggle—one that went to the game's last play before being decided—the jubilation of the winners would be nearly hysterical, considering they had just won the right to defend their NFL title in the Super Bowl. But there were no phony champagne baths, no raucous noise making, no hugging each other in great glee.

To understand, one had only to see Charles Henry Noll as he came through the door of that dressing room. It looked as if he had just finished Wednesday practice, pausing only to shake the hand of one player who crossed his path.

It is the same look he has on the sidelines directing his team during a game. He does not scream or shout; he does not run up and down the sidelines as the play ebbs and flows. He always seems to be dressed the same—black jacket or sweatshirt with the white collar of his polo shirt protruding around his neck. His mouth always seems drawn in a tight line, showing at once determination, anxiety, and satisfaction.

If there is a descriptive word, perhaps it's bland. Like Tom Landry and Bud Grant, it's hard to know whether his team is winning or losing by watching him. In fact, the only time there has been anything approximating public jubilation followed the Steelers' victory in Super Bowl IX when Franco Harris and Joe Greene lifted him atop their massive shoulders and hauled him a few yards past the Pittsburgh bench. Then he displayed the warm, toothy grin.

In many ways, that is all most people ever will know about him. He is an emotional man in the singular sense of all men but the trigger mechanism that sets off those emotions is activated only at particular times and within the confines of whatever personal relationship is of that moment. No one will ever sit at his feet and hear great dissertations of football philosophy or gaze upon a blackboard filled with mind-bending formations. For one reason, he simply does not give away his football ideas lest someone find equal success with them—against him or another, that is not his style.

Yet this is the same man who used to be called "the Pope" by his teammates at the University of Dayton and with the Cleveland Browns because when he said a block should be executed a certain way or a play run in a definite manner, he was speaking without fear of contradiction . . . *ex cathedra* as they say in Vatican City.

Noll rarely made a mistake as a player and, generally was most correct in his pronouncements, as he is now. For one reason, he does not come off the top of his head with a statement of fact unless he truly knows it to be a fact. And he has taken great care throughout his life to accumulate facts, on anything from zone blocking to scuba diving. He has great curiosity. Some people around the Steelers' front office claim he is a better photographer than the professionals they hire. He learned to fly a plane after winning Super Bowl IX in order to take advantage of a family condominium in Florida and cut down his travel time. His cultural base is broad enough to allow him to be a regular patron of the Pittsburgh Symphony.

He is, in fact, a classical music buff. He loves the old masters—Beethoven, Bach, Mozart. His tastes peak at string quartets, like the Russian Bordin's quartet, the Budapest quartet, the modern Julliard quartet. He can speak of these with the same familiarity he does in detailing the Oakland Raiders' defense. In a restaurant or at home, he knows the precise (as opposed to merely correct) wine for any dish and knows enough about cooking to properly characterize his wife as a gourmet cook, an honor he disavows for himself though some have characterized him as one.

He is a voracious reader, finding books on "how to" and classical music ideal ways to relax during the evenings in a pressure-packed football season. He also reads everything written about him and his team, good or bad. Before the 1975 season, he picked up a copy of a book written by former player Lance Rentzel, read the introduction where Rentzel said the pressures of football were almost overwhelming burdens for any man, and pronounced the thesis "pure bullshit." Then he went on to tell why, speaking *ex cathedra,* of course.

Noll is not a know-it-all in the obnoxious sense of the guy who pretends to know everything then makes sure everyone knows it whether they want to or not. He is soft-spoken and articulate. He does not dabble over polysyllabic words but his language flows freely and without any hint of being forced. His speech gives a solid hint to the natural intelligence that has fired his intellect yet he is most basic when discussing the elements of his profession.

This basic approach is what really comes through, both with the man and with his football team. You could say the Steelers play football like vanilla ice cream—plain, old-fashioned, no frills. They are, in the self-descriptive words of Don Shula "about as subtle as a punch in the mouth." It is Noll's style too, though he is not nearly as pugnacious as Don Shula.

In fact, this style seems to be a tradition in Pittsburgh, perhaps the very embodiment of the town itself. There is little subtlety working in a steel mill or a plant that produces mammoth electric generators or railroad cars or any of the sundry items which flow from the heavy industrial complex that makes up the Golden Triangle. The quickest way to get into a fight in Pittsburgh, a man once wrote, is to step into a saloon and order Drambuie on the rocks. It's a shot or a beer or both.

Perhaps that is why Noll has found such favor in Pittsburgh. His team, after three long-suffering seasons, has been a winner but it hasn't stunned any opponents with fancy footwork or razzle-dazzle. The style of play is, as Noll characterizes it, "to win the battle of the hitting." Men who work in a steel mill seem to understand that pretty well.

Those who follow the Steelers and who have watched Noll since he became head coach in 1969, say the most impressive thing about him is the way he wins. He is a low-key individual who anaylzes everything he does unemotionally before doing it. He rarely acts on impulse. His approach to the game is logical. "Whatever it takes," seems to be his first and only commandment. And the Steelers are a vivid reflection of that philosophy.

Yet it would be wrong to characterize him as cold or aloof or unfeeling. His players are the first to put that idea to rest if Noll has not done it first.

"Football in itself is emotional," he says. "It's not a normal thing to run down the field and run into somebody. You have to convince yourself that is the thing to do. Nobody can be involved in a game and be emotionless because emotions are involved. People on television or in the movies portray emotion. But just because you don't portray emotion doesn't mean it's not there. I can be sitting at my desk and have emotion welled up inside me but you're not going to be able to tell."

He is, in fact, a deeply emotional person but, like his life away from the Steelers, he makes every effort to keep it highly personal and out of public view. Dan Rooney, the team's president and a man who knows Noll as well as anyone in Pittsburgh (or at least as well as Noll will allow anyone to know him), says that the coach is a very controlled person. He gives much thought to everything he does.

"Chuck doesn't talk much publicly about his football concepts," Rooney says, "because he doesn't want to give away any of his secrets. Nor does he want to take a great deal from the game itself. He never lets down his guard to allow anyone to really find out about him. Nor does he seek notoriety despite his great success.

"Basically I'd characterize him as a very good person."

If that's all a man's boss can find to say about him, then he must be doing something right. And it is no different elsewhere in football when people for whom he's worked are asked about his life off the field. They say Noll is a private person, a strong family man.

He spends most of his free time with his wife, Marianne, and teen-age son, Chris, admittedly "doing everything we can together." His scuba diving was an offshoot of trying to find an activity that he could relate to on a personal basis with a teen-age boy. Learning to fly fit right into his lifestyle, too. Now Knox can spend more time in family activity and less in actual travel and all the many hassles that travel presents.

Though he holds absolute control over his team, which may have more "superstars" than any other NFL team, he is fair-handed. It's that way at home, too, where his son prefers soccer to football and has never felt a moment's pressure from his father to change. Noll tries not to bring his business away from the playing field, at least to an extent where his living room is but an extension of his office or the film room. In his off-hours, he often can be found puttering around the garden of his home in the Pittsburgh suburb of Upper St. Clair or, if he is in Florida, he may be exploring the underwater caves along the Keys.

"My hobbies are whatever is around," he says.

That is all a part of his zest to discover. He recalls the first day he ever went snorkeling with his son.

"I got excited the first time I looked down there," he remembers. "So much life to be discovered. Discovery is the thing that's always excited me. A new wine, a new restaurant, an island in the Caribbean—it's all part of the same thing.

"I can do the same with football films. People wonder why I look at them so long. Every time I go over them I can see a new thing. You can look at the same one twenty times and then all of a sudden something will jump out at you. Again, it's the enjoyment of discovery."

It was like the time he discovered good wine and good food. It was at a place in Shaker Heights, a Cleveland suburb, called The Wagon Wheel. ("I courted my wife in the back of that bar," he says.) There was a French restaurant on the ground floor and the bar was upstairs.

"We used to see the people coming up the stairs from the restaurant below," he recalls. "Ladies in furs, perfectly tailored gentlemen. The guy who owned the bar, Doc Mangine, knew the two brothers who owned the restaurant. When they had tenderloin or tournedos or something left over, he'd get them to grind it up into hamburger for us. They'd mix a sauce in with it and it was delicious. We never could have afforded it, not at the five-thousand dollars a year Paul Brown was paying us.

"One night I was there with Mike McCormack and Don Colo, a couple of my teammates, and Doc treated us to a dinner downstairs. We ate from seven until eleven-thirty, everything they had on the menu, with a different wine with each course. The only thing I knew from then on was that I liked good wine and good food. It became a matter than of discovering the best and how to put them together."

In those days it was tough to afford the more expensive bouquets but he did keep a case of Sparkling Catawba ("at ninety-nine cents a bottle") in the trunk of his car. "In the winter it meant that I always had a chilled wine handy," he adds.

Being a connoisseur of fine food and wine is Noll's only real indulgence to some of life's more ribald pleasures. His life has a set of ordered priorities as can be ascertained by the importance he places on his family relationship. Neither is he so caught up in his own life, inside and outside football, that there is not room for others. He serves as a surrogate father to his widowed sister's children though few know it. One Steeler remembers the time he was in the midst of a divorce and seeing his life begin to fall apart. "Chuck stuck with me and did everything he could," the man says. "He's a helluva guy."

It is this all-out approach to everything that has enabled him to mold the Steelers from a chronic loser to two-time NFL champions. It was the key element that held the team to him in 1969 when it won its first game, then lost the next 13. He amazed not only the players who endured that season but the Rooneys, the men for whom he works. To this day, Art Rooney, Sr., marvels at that feat.

"I knew he was a good man before we hired him because every report we had on him told us so," Rooney says. "But you never know how a man will handle his first head coaching job. After that first season, when he lost thirteen straight games and never lost either his poise nor the ballclub, I told my boys they had hired themselves a great coach."

When he was being interviewed for the job, Noll told Dan Rooney, the club's president, that the Steelers had some good players but they were not a good team and it would take time to turn them around. He added it would take patience and a dedication to his way of building a winner to see it through.

"I liked that," says Dan. "A lot of the people we talked to about the job said they would come in and turn things around in one year. He talked about building an organization that reflected excellence from the front office to the locker room. This is something all of us take great pride in now."

This was something that had its beginnings back at Benedictine High School in Cleveland where Noll began to live his "whatever it takes" philosophy. He began his high school career as a running back but when the team needed a guard, he made the switch and wound up on the all-state team and with a scholarship to the University of Dayton. In college, he played tackle and when a weakness developed in the secondary, he moved back there. He was the team's captain in his senior year.

It was at Dayton where he acquired the nickname "the Pope."

"I guess one of the biggest problems I had as a player was that I had been coaching for a long time," Noll says, laughing. "The nickname was one of those things that just evolved. I was helping out one of my teammates one day and he got teed off at me. Since Dayton was a Catholic university, the Pope's infallibility always was being discussed. So he applied it to me on the spur of the moment and it stuck for quite a while."

Nickname or not, Noll was only the twenty-first draft choice of the Browns in 1953, a spot in the draft Paul Brown usually reserved for local players.

"A local sportswriter called me and said, 'You've been drafted. What's your reaction?' I thought he meant into the army because the Korean war was in progress then," Noll remembers. "I was not that aware of professional football and I wound up trying it because it was a five-thousand dollar salary for a six-month job while teaching and coaching in high school paid twenty-seven hundred."

Chuck was 21 when he began playing for Cleveland. With his youth and low draft status he did not figure to stay with the Browns for long. But Noll had the three key ingredients that Paul Brown sought in every player who showed a range of basic football skills: he was a "good person," he was extremely intelligent, and he had good speed.

"He was a highly intelligent person," Blanton Collier, an assistant coach with the Browns at that time, recalls. "Fritz Heisler, who coached the offensive line, always talked about how much confidence Chuck had in himself. He also asked a lot of questions and seemed always to want to know 'why' and 'how.'"

He was good enough to become one of the Browns' famed messenger guards for four years, during which time the club won a pair of NFL championships. "Chuck could have called the plays without any help from me," says Brown. "That's the kind of football student he was."

When the need arose for a starting linebacker, Noll again made the move. Collier always thought Noll was too small at 210 or 215 pounds to be an offensive guard; Collier suggested to Brown that Chuck should fill the hole at linebacker.

"He had great speed, agility, smartness, balance, was a good tackler, and had a good football mind," Collier says in ticking off the characteristics that caused the decision. "It took a little doing on Chuck's part to make the switch but he mastered the job."

He played linebacker for three seasons, then at age 27, after seven seasons in the NFL, retired as a player even though at the peak of his skills. It was not a particularly difficult decision he says, certainly not as tough as it would be for players of today in similar circumstances. The chief reason is the annual salary now, which is five and six times the amount players were paid in the fifties.

"You get players now who want to hang on and stretch out a part-time job because they can't make as much in a full-time job outside of football," Noll observes. "I could have played longer but the head coaching job at Dayton came open and I talked it over with my wife. I had done a lot of things in the off-season and decided that football really was where I wanted to stay.

"Originally I felt pro football was a part-time career, a stepping stone after graduating from college to what you would do in your life. I had sold insurance a couple of years, represented a trucking firm and went to law school, going there with the idea of getting a background, not a profession. I once had received some good advice about making something of your free time, even if you had to pay someone to keep you busy. The insurance business was very beneficial and in a sense I was paying someone by going to law school."

The idea of totally using his time accounts in large part for his great interest in doing something away from the job. You don't find Noll sitting around taking it easy.

Since he wanted to be a coach, going after the head coaching job at Dayton became the logical first step though he had no coaching experience. He was not hired. But with the AFL starting its first season, he wrote a couple of letters. Gillman hired him as an assistant for the then-Los Angeles Chargers, but only after checking with Paul Brown. Brown not only gave Noll a solid recommendation but also released him from any contractual obligations at Cleveland to pursue his coaching career.

Gillman says he knew about Chuck and his intense approach to football when Noll was a player. After hiring him he found him not only a man with strong convictions but one who was very bright. "A natural," Gillman still says because of Noll's intelligence, his background, and his desire to work hard. Nor was he ever at a loss for ideas in his role as linebacker coach and boss of the Chargers' pass defense.

"He had a great way with the players," says Gillman. "He had played and knew what to expect but more than that, he achieved the respect of the players because they knew about his reputation and he came true to form. If a guy didn't do the job expected, Chuck could climb on his back but always in a soft-spoken, low-key way where the guy would not be embarrassed but would get the message. He always was a low-key guy and that's how he coached."

Noll joined Don Shula's staff in 1966 and stayed until he went to Pittsburgh. Looking at his background—a player for Paul Brown and an assistant under Gillman and Shula and you have to say his football breeding was superb. Generally an assistant takes something from every man for whom he works and adopts what best suits his own personality and ability. Shula, who played for Brown and worked for Collier and George Wilson, is a prime example and he can cite the areas in each instance that were of greatest benefit to him.

Noll does not. He says it is hard for him to pinpoint any particular benefit. He claims he has tried to break down his own coaching approach and look at its origins and what comes out is that he has patterned himself after no one but he has learned from all—coaches, players, even equipment men.

"You start copying someone and you wind up doing a second-rate job because that's what a copy is—a second-rate imitation," Noll says. "That's why I never have limited my knowledge intake or my experience to a set of events.

"Perhaps the one general benefit of working for Sid was being exposed to more football in six seasons than I would have received in a dozen," Noll says. "He was one of the prime researchers in the game and had a great deal of time to bring all of the concepts and ideas to the fore. From Shula, there was great organization and the importance to attitudes. My contact with Paul Brown was as a player, not a coach, so I learned in a different way.

"But the main point is not what you learn from one person. You learn from everybody around you, not only the head coach, or his assistants, or his players. You take the learning experience as a group effort and if you learn from everyone as a unit, then you really don't know where things come from. All of a sudden they're in your mind and you believe them.

"It's almost impossible to pinpoint definite things coming from specific individuals. I've tried. It's easier to say, 'This is someone's strengths.' How it affected me, I don't know. Maybe that is the sign of having worked for good teachers because teaching is a tough process. You set up a situation where people must come in, be exposed to things, and learn for themselves. It's tough for the pupil to say specifically where that learning began."

Noll saw the difference in moving from player to coach. He said assistant coaches by nature seem to make a determined effort to note how the head man handles things and try to keep a mental catalogue—or list—of strengths and methods of their superior.

"As a player," he adds, "I was more concerned about doing my job. I was aware of a few things but when I became a coach, I became aware of how much I wasn't aware of as a player. It's one thing to teach yourself and something else to instruct another person and to get him to learn. The biggest thing for any coach is creating a learning situation.

"In school, Noll points out, "a person learns the philosophy of education but it is something else to see that the teaching and learning are accomplished. Coaching is teaching and an efficient teacher can get the job done. Efficiency is the prime objective from a teaching standpoint. A teacher, or coach, cannot wander because he works with attention spans that are short for what he must accomplish.

"The first and most important thing I learned as an assistant coach was that you must be organized in your presentation and that only comes when you know what you're teaching."

The net result became an awareness that the only way to play football was the basic way. That's why he says his team concentrates so much on fundamentals. "A fellow like Joe Greene doesn't run around blockers," says Noll. "He runs right through them. That is basic."

This was the approach he brought to Pittsburgh. It was one that he had practiced as a player under Brown at Cleveland and that Shula advanced in his coaching at Baltimore. So while Noll says he cannot point to any specific roots for his own football beliefs it would be fair to say that what was ingrained in him as a player and an assistant coach— at least that he accepted as correct—formed some of the foundation for all he has done with the Steelers. His own will formed the greatest part.

Again, veteran Noll watchers in Pittsburgh hark back to the time when he was being interviewed for the job. He impressed his soon-to-be employers with a cool detachment as he talked about coaching their team. Only the day before his first meeting with Dan Rooney, the Colts had been stunned by Joe Namath and the New York Jets in Super Bowl III and the residue of bitterness on that Monday was knee-deep in some NFL circles. But Chuck showed none in his morning meeting and got on with the business at hand almost as if he had not been a party to the previous day's shattering events.

"He had to be disappointed in what happened," Rooney says, "but never once in our talks did any disappointment or bitterness ever surface. He was totally logical in all of his points about the Steelers and knew a great deal about our people. You couldn't help but be impressed with his overall decorum as well as with his knowledge of organization and his concepts on putting the whole pro game together. He had his own ideas on every facet of being head coach, how players should be handled, how things should be run."

At the same time, Noll himself had been sold on the Steelers. He admits he was surprised that they had a first-class organization. Their talent department had improved with Art Rooney, Jr., devoting all his time supervising scouting and player procurement as well as participating in the BLESTO scouting system.

"It didn't take much to see that it was only a question of coming in and giving those players good coaching and surrounding them with even better players," Noll says. "The club always had been willing to spend money, contrary to what I had heard, and was willing to do anything. And ever since coming to the team I never have been turned down in any request I've made.

"We had to live with some bad practice facilities and an old office downtown but when I came Three Rivers Stadium was under construction and Dan showed me the plans he had for moving in. Coming into such a new environment was truly dramatic. I had set a goal for what situation I wanted as a head coach. If I wasn't able to go in and change something, then I didn't want it. I wasn't after just any old job. It's no fun for your family because you're asking them to do a heckuva lot. The pressure gets pretty great when you're not winning and it can become pretty miserable."

"People told me I was crawling into a graveyard of coaches when I came here. That was nonsense too. As a matter of fact it was part of the challenge, part of the reason I wanted this particular job. In the end you realize there just aren't too many winning situations available to a new coach so you're not always able to go with your druthers. What everyone likes is to go into one where you can get a turnaround very quickly. The reason the Steelers' job was open was because there were problems. I don't think you can go into anything and say, 'We must do this right now,' You must go into something and build totally with people who want to be winners.

"Becoming a winner is a day-to-day thing, teaching, learning, growing. A team must grow together and does not grow immediately. When you first meet the players, you must present your program, teach it, see how it works on the field, then make your judgments on all you have seen through that. Those judgments must concern coaches, players, personnel people—everyone down the line who is involved in helping make the team a winner. We want each department to think it is the best, has the best people, serves the most important function."

He brought his other basic coaching tenets into the job, all subdivisions of "whatever it takes." At the top of the list was settling on an overall process of development and the necessity "to have the guts to stick with it. We show people how to get things done. Take blocking, for example. We teach techniques on how to block. You know how and who, and the function then is reduced to a habit. So on Sunday a player doesn't have to worry about a guy's press clippings or his reputation or his size. He's able to concentrate on what he's doing."

It has paid off to the extent where one Steeler has said that Noll "is so smart he'll make a believer out of you. He teaches and teaches and teaches so much when you go to bed you feel, 'Oh-oh, I don't want to go to sleep. I want to get better.'"

Noll always has told his players they were going to be the best. Even during some horrendous times in his first couple of seasons, he worked them hard enough so they came to believe it though it might not have been reflected in the league standings. They say now they truly believed because they could see it coming to pass, at least the ones who still are there. The non-believers, hence the non-doers, are long gone. They fell victim to his "rotten-apples" theory. This is Noll's manner of applying the same set of standards to every member of the team, including the coaching staff.

"My job is never secure," he says. "Regardless of what I've accomplished, if I don't produce I can lose my job. Nobody can sit tight after winning the big one and rest on his laurels. You can't be complacent in this business."

That is the genesis of his "whatever it takes" motto. And that comes from his stern belief that he never knows what will happen in any one game. In fact, he says, no two games ever are alike because the problems in each game are totally different.

"A championship team is one that can solve these problems, whatever they are," he says. "But you must live the words, not just say them."

Long before a team reaches that point, it must cross other barriers. And even before those barriers arise, the team itself must be built so it can cope with the problems. As a player in Cleveland, Noll had seen the types of players who can achieve this; he saw it again in Baltimore and with the Chargers. He applied this experience in building his own team.

Noll liked some of what he saw on the Steelers' team. But one of his biggest problems was purging those who were to stay of a rampant feeling of negativism that had been built through losing seasons stretching back to 1963.

"There were some problems that losing engenders," he admits. "One was people interested only in hanging onto their jobs. Their goals weren't to be number one. They talked about it but didn't know how or what they were talking about. For a goal to be meaningful, it must be within striking distance. We didn't see it coming about with people who had set such limits as just being able to exist with us. So we had to go about putting together a team that could win. It's no fun if you're working with guys who can do nothing but simply *be* on an NFL team. Things get very bad under those conditions.

"Our goal at the start was not respectability. Our goal was to win a championship. The only thing that is worthwhile in this league is winning a title, not a nine and five record or being over five hundred. There's frustration involved there. We wanted to garner the kind of people and play the kind of football that would allow us to do that. It's not always measured that first year. We could have limited what we did offensively and defensively and won a few more games [they won only one] by being more simple. We lost a few that were close. But doing all of that wouldn't have helped us in the overall picture because we knew what it takes to win. We were trying to do that; trying to make judgments on the people who were willing to pay the price for this."

Don't think that Noll had given up any thoughts of winning each week. He directed those efforts the way he knew a championship team wins: by being sound in every phase of its game. That meant a total dedication to teaching sound, fundamental football without yielding to the temptation to forego the basics and slide into an extra victory or two. Noll does not subscribe to a theory among some coaches that a team that has been a chronic loser must win a few games so it knows what victory is like; and that this awareness will help increase the total each season. Nor does he believe that a team must particularly win its last game because that is the one that stays with it through the off-season. Every game is approached the same way, from the most recent Super Bowl back to the opening game of the 1969 season, Noll's first year with the Steelers.

That game was a victory, a 16-13 decision over the Detroit Lions. Then the Steelers lost their next 13 but Noll, all around him agree, never lost faith. He stuck with his plan of schooling the team as he felt it should be schooled. He insisted it go out and "win the battle of the hitting." Quite often the Steelers did but they lost the game because of the mistakes they made. At the same time, he worked to continue the gradual improvement, to correct the mistakes and to maintain the physical approach to each game.

"There was frustration among the players because they were trying to achieve what we wanted and many times came close," Noll admits. "The big danger was avoiding any finger-pointing. We told them that if anyone was going to point a finger, point it at the mirror. We said the attitude has to be, 'If we are not winning, it is my fault.' That's the way it should be. We have to have everyone doing that, even now. With that attitude, everything falls into place."

That is not to be construed as an exercise in positive thinking, something that Noll disavows in the context in which the Steelers rose from the ashes. It was, he claims, a matter of working on the things necessary to make the team better.

"You can talk about things positively but if you're not working on things to improve then you won't be going in that direction," he says emphatically. "No amount of positive talk does a damned bit of good unless there are sound, basic fundamentals to back it up."

All of that takes for granted there are the players to carry out those fundamentals. The Steelers have been unbelievably successful in acquiring quality football players since Noll became head coach, a tribute to his determination to adhere to the program he felt would bring a championship. It is one laid directly on the draft. The Steelers are a home-grown team and the growth has been through a carefully selective process that has eliminated major mistakes.

This can be a slow process because the burden for developing these players rests solely on the team. Quality can speed up the process but there still must be a large infusion of patience during the growing years, particularly for a team like Pittsburgh which had little to fall back on while these players improved.

"It did not take much patience on my part," Noll says. "It took some on the part of the owners and the fans because when you build through the draft it takes a little while. You're going to make mistakes and there is a tendency to remember those mistakes."

Noll says he felt pressure-free during this time because he wouldn't allow pressure. All pressure, he claims, is self-induced (part of the reason for his scathing denunciation of the premise in Rentzel's book) and he was fully aware of every element in the course he charted for the reclamation of the Steelers. Still, he had the full approval and cooperation of his team's management so there never was any temptation to try to speed up the process.

It helped that the Steelers drafted people who showed great promise for the future. The direction then, as now, was not to draft to fill a position but to go after the best available athlete, even if it is a player who is skilled at an already fully stocked position.

"It doesn't matter whether we need someone at a position or not," Noll says. "You make a mistake in the draft when you panic and say, 'We haven't someone at this spot.' Then you draft someone who is not as good as someone else and the other guy makes all-league some place else. When you get to a point where there is no particular standout, then you go by position. But we'll always find a spot for guys with size, speed, and physical ability. If we can upgrade the team at any spot, we're going to help ourselves."

There are no great secrets to the Steelers' drafting success. Noll admits luck has played its role because drafting a player from college is nothing more than "guessing what he will do in a different element. We try to leave no stone unturned to get information to make a reasonable decision. Mostly, though, you're taking someone else's word."

The Steelers feel it's unrealistic to grade more than 150 players, or enough for the first five or six rounds. The club collects as much information as possible from their play during the collegiate season, then places great importance on their work in the various postseason all-star games. These games help in taking away some of the guesswork about moving a player from a familiar situation to one where he must blend with others.

If Noll never was to participate in another draft he would probably be best remembered for picking Joe Greene in 1969, the first one that he directed. Greene was no darkhorse. He was recognized then as the best collegiate defensive lineman in the country. But the Steelers were known to be favoring Terry Hanratty, a Pittsburgh native who had finished three spectacular seasons as Notre Dame's quarterback.

The Steelers even had brought Hanratty into Pittsburgh for a medical examination of his injured knee and had made no effort to hide the fact that he would be their top pick. But Noll was hired the day before the draft and had surmised that perhaps the club could get Hanratty in a later round. Of course, that's what happened. Noll wanted Greene, and got him; then he made Hanratty the first pick of the second round.

One Pittsburgh newspaper headlined: "Joe Who?"

Noll was not bothered by Greene's lack of recognition. "We reasoned that we needed the immediate help that Greene would bring a lot more than we needed a quarterback," he said.

It worked out that way. The following year, getting the draft's first pick, he selected quarterback Terry Bradshaw. In later years the Steelers' first-round draft choices included such players as Franco Harris, J. T. Thomas, and Lynn Swann. In fact, only four players on the 1975 Steelers' Super Bowl championship roster were not drafted or signed as free agent rookies. There were eight of the latter as well as 22 players who were selected in the first five rounds.

The Steelers do not disavow trading for players, though John Fuqua and punter Bobby Walden are the only players acquired in that manner who played for the Super Bowl X champions. Often, Noll prefers another team's draft picks and six Steelers on his 1975 AFC champions came in that manner.

"When I first came to the Steelers there were people who wanted the few good players we did have," Noll recalls. "They wanted to give us their second-line guys who weren't real quality and couldn't carry the load. I said, 'You're asking for a starter and giving me second-line players.' And they would say, 'Well, our second-line players could start for your club.' But I don't believe in building a team in that manner.

"What we try to do is to gather all the quality people. You won't have forty-three but we try to have them in different stages. We may have some young ones and there is a chance whether or not they'll come along. Those are the ones you get in the draft. We have established, quality people and then guys who are good backups. If you're going to trade, you want to trade in the same category. You don't want to give up a quality guy for one who can only be a backup. So you must evaluate your people.

"But you may want to give up a backup guy for someone who is not quality right now but who has the potential to be. Or you trade quality for quality, particularly if you're loaded at one position, to get people for a position where you don't have a quality guy. Even there you've got to be careful. Most teams are reluctant to trade quality players. If they have one up for trade, it's because he may be unhappy in his situation. You must measure that—whether you can satisfy him or help him with his problem."

No one unloads their problem children on Pittsburgh any longer. Noll is like Paul Brown in his insistence that a player be a "good person." To him, that is a player who will do his job by utilizing his ability, a willingness to work and a maturity that will allow him to accept all that is asked. He makes a point of shunting players who are not willing to face up to and solve problems. In other words, the immature ones.

"As you gain experience you must mature as an individual," he says, "and along with that comes the ability to solve problems. I'm a problem solver. There are problems in every organization and part of my job is solving them. That's what makes it all worthwhile. The problem may be solving a particular defense, mastering a coverage, or dealing with a player who is bothered by something off the field that is hampering his work with the team. A person either faces up to what it takes to do all this or he runs away. Anyone who keeps running is in for a life of misery. And the people who are not good people are those who try to run away from their problems."

Noll makes frequent reference to the word "problem" when he discusses his coaching style and his relations with his players. It is not that he has an inordinate amount— probably less than any team in the league, according to those in the NFL. But it would seem that any ripple on his pond is viewed as a problem and there is no differentiation as to size or scope. It is his view that a coach is a problem-solver in his role as supervisor, organizer, and teacher. In this role Noll is not a martinet who demands total conformity. He fully disdains running a football team like a Marine Corps boot camp but believes in dealing with mature men on a mature basis. All that he demands is that they understand that they are responsible for their actions.

"I'm guided only by what's good for the team," he says. "I don't want a team whose players are more afraid of the coach than they are of their opponents."

He has established that balance, though his players say there is a fear of botching a play on the field, particularly if it should involve a mental error. One player remembered a muffed punt by Mike Collier during the early part of the 1975 season. Collier tried to come off the field at the far end of the Steelers' bench, hoping that Noll would be too engrossed in the game to find him. But he was wrong. Noll watched him all the way and started in his direction even before he crossed the sideline. He had chewed out Bradshaw on the sidelines and marched onto the field to get after his offensive line.

Still, Noll attempts to maintain the low-key, straight-ahead posture in dealing with his players that is his public demeanor. Sometimes it works, sometimes it doesn't and he makes no apologies for either stance. He does not consider himself out of balance in this area and most likely would find it one of the keys to his team's superb style of play.

"Everyone gets excited," he admits. "Whenever a problem arises, I first try to identify it. Often that's very elusive but once you find out what it is, then you can solve it. That's something I learned in law school, 'What really is the issue?' But I can't do it by myself. I get with the person who has this problem and work it out with him.

"For example, if you're losing, you try to find out what really is causing it. You want to make the effort to find out but at the same time you don't want to panic. Sometimes panic does set in, your motor starts racing, you start hyperventilating. But most times you really want to sit down calmly, find out what the problem is and take a course that will solve it. Then you convince everyone that is the right course."

That is the verbal solution. Those who have seen him translate it into positive action say the approach is direct and with little effort to slide past the facts at issue. For one thing, he does not get close to his players "other than to help them solve their problems." His other coaches are in the same capacity. They're problem solvers too, and if they can't handle the job, then Noll takes over.

"He gets plenty of respect from every player, from Joe Greene and Terry Bradshaw down to the last guy on the roster," one former player says. "He's helped by the type of organization he set up for the team. Everything is programmed, the same every day so the players know what is expected of them, get into a groove and stay there. There is little opportunity for guys becoming disenchanted because they're being jerked around."

Noll rarely criticizes his players publicly—and then only in the heat of a game—but he can play a torrid number in the privacy of his office. He never worries about their affection for him but he knows he has it. Part of the reason is his willingness to get right down on the ground and do all the exercises, to get wet and dirty as they get, to wear nothing heavier than they wear when it's cold, to observe the same rules away from home as they do.

Noll is not a stoic. Mostly he is serious on the practice field but he'll joke around on occasion, say his players.

He also has a system of fines but the till has been empty since 1971. That is a tribute to the respect he commands and which he has engendered in each player for the other.

"You can fine people for silly things but you also can show compassion," says Dick Conn, a former defensive back with the 1974 NFL champions. "He's been in the game and he knows. Sometimes you can't make it to practice on time because your wife's sick or there is another serious reason. As long as you call him and let him know, you're okay.

"One day I had an accident on the way to practice. My roomie was with me but he hitched a ride and went in to tell him what happened. We always met together at the start of each day and he would make some announcements. So this day he said, 'It looks as if Dick Conn has decided an accident report is worth getting fined today,' But he just laughed and he never fined me. He understood that such things can be unavoidable."

Nor does Noll harass the players about their dress. Indeed, the room clerk at the Steelers' hotel in New Orleans for Super Bowl IX told one Pittsburgh sportswriter, "Your team has to be the lousiest-looking, worst-dressed of any of the teams that stop here." There is no embargo on beards and the clothes range from barely adequate to John Fuqua's many-splendored threads, which include shoes that have goldfish swimming in their elevated heels.

"Chuck doesn't give a hoot how they look or what they wear," one Steelers' observer notes. "All he cares about is how they play. You look at him and he seems to be the epitome of conformity, certainly not a man who at first glance would seem to be in charge of a team that is totally individualized in their off-the-field styles."

That is the "maturity" Noll has referred to, maturity in himself. He has managed to transform that same maturity to his players by demanding only what he feels is important. At training camp, for example, he doesn't mind if they drink a few beers "because beer is one way to replace body fluids." At Super Bowl IX, the Minnesota Vikings were segregated from their wives but Noll imposed no such restrictions.

Noll also was not upset when one of his players said the Vikings were inferior to at least three other teams in the American Conference just a couple of days before they were to play Minnesota in that Super Bowl. "We have freedom of speech on the Steelers," he says. "All I ever tell my players is that they might have to suffer the consequences for what they say. That is their responsibility and they must act as mature men in facing it."

Naturally, Noll comes across in different ways to different people. He knows there may be some who wish he was a little warmer, perhaps would like him to get closer to the team personally because that would fit their own personalities and make a relationship more comfortable. Linebacker Andy Russell is not one who shares this view and if he hears it, he has a rebuttal.

"I can remember when we were closer together on and off the field but we didn't win," says Russell, who joined the team in 1963. "Noll is warmer than others might think. More importantly, he's exceptionally fair, applies discipline only where it really counts but has a knack of making you play your very best by conveying the point that it isn't what you've done for him last year or a week ago that counts. What counts is what you can do for him today or in the next game. It's the same for me as it is for the newest rookie and I certainly don't quarrel with that reasoning nor think it's wrong."

This must be reflected to others, too. Gillman points out that Noll has concentrated on the team concept and though he has an abundance of great individual players, every man seems more concerned with the team effort and puts it ahead of their own self-glory. It accounts, he adds, for the Steelers' steady approach to every game.

Babe Parilli, who was an assistant under Noll for several seasons and who played with him in Cleveland, thinks that Chuck did indeed acquire some of his finesse in dealing with players from his previous stops with the Browns, Chargers, and Colts. Perhaps so. Noll admired Gillman and the way Gillman pushed players who needed it. And Noll points to Paul Brown's record when someone tries to tell him that his former coach "couldn't handle men."

"Look at his record," he'll say. "When I hear people talking about a football coach who is a great guy, loved by all, I wonder how long he'll be employed. Coaches who want to be loved usually are losers."

It was something Art Rooney, Sr., saw in Noll's first season when he had to endure 13 losses. He marvels at the steady-handed approach he has maintained since.

"If that's him and that's the way he's done things, I don't know that it's bad," says Rooney, who has seen his share of screamers and veritable slave-drivers working as Pittsburgh head coaches. "I don't say that being low key means a guy will be successful but in Chuck's case, that's his nature and he should be that way. I've seen tough coaches who were tough guys, like Dr. [Jock] Sutherland who had players saying their day off was the day of the game.

"He was very successful that way but then I've seen guys who were tough and just couldn't make it. And I've seen it the other way—guys who were easy-going and who were successful and easy-going guys who failed. The difference always seems to be how the players take to a coach, how much respect they have for him. I believe the biggest part of coaching is getting the best out of the players and a coach must get it out with respect."

Rooney, who knows athletes as well as anyone in football, having been around them for a half century, has seen the respect and confidence the Steelers show toward Noll. He saw it begin in 1969. "At no time did Chuck lose his poise or get exasperated," says Rooney. "He always was the same guy. He never changed one bit from the opening game victory through the thirteenth straight loss. He never lost the respect of the players and he never lost his hold on them. It was still there the day we won our first Super Bowl."

That might have been the toughest part of Noll's job, tougher even than working against any complacency that often occurs on a team that has just won the NFL title. Noll had no such problems during the 1975 season because he had built a sound emotional base long ago.

"There comes a time in any person's life when he must say, 'This is tough for me to do,' but he still must do it," says Noll in explanation of his approaches to building positive attitudes. You face up to it and say, 'I'm going to do it,' and you do. That's a great maturing thing."

It must have been difficult for the 1969 team to go out Sunday after Sunday as its losing streak continued, particularly after having suffered through some horrendous seasons before Noll came. There had to be times when many of those players were exasperated, but the ones who kept responding became the bulwark of the teams that would win the titles. Ten members of the 1969 team were on the 1974 Super Bowl champions and eight of those were starters, including the two kickers. Three more, including two starters in Super Bowl IX, from the 1970 team that won just five games.

"We're looking for men to play professional football because our goals are winning and to be the best," says Noll. "To do that you must be able to face your obstacles and be able to solve them. When we got the kind of men on our football team who could do that, we were all right. If we get a group of children, we're not going to win."

Noll doesn't worry about the latter happening. For one thing, he won't allow it; for another, neither will his players. The Steelers grew up together and the leadership on the team is spread throughout so that no one man becomes indispensable in this regard. Noll feels that every man must be his own leader. Thus it is not up to Joe Greene or Terry Bradshaw or any one particular player to become a rallying force.

"I think anyone who is a good football player is accepted," Noll concedes. "His actions have a great deal to do with what is happening. These people must be quality people, to want to be the best and to want the team to be the best. We have a lot of players who fall into that category, not just Joe Greene or Terry Bradshaw or anyone else, particularly. Any time you have people who are producing, the respect in the locker room comes from performance, not from any talk or politics. Everyone accepts a good player.

"He may even have some lousy habits and people don't even want to get close to him. But if he is a good football player then they look on him differently. The respect ultimately comes from a player doing his job and doing it well."

Obviously, this has been the case with the Steelers. So many players perform well that there is room for a variety of approaches in the area of leadership. Thus far, all are compatible with the team's overall objectives. It wasn't something that came only with success but was marshaled through those losing Sundays and in the weeks between games when Noll really built his team. The belief in each other actually came as the players worked to eliminate the errors that were costing them victories, Noll says. Preparation for each game got better and everyone began to have confidence in each other.

"What we try to do at all times is to teach fundamental football," Noll points out. "No amount of talking is going to do that. It really gets down to, 'Can you handle your job?' That is the problem for each man out on that field. As coaches and teachers we must teach them the techniques that will allow them to cope with those problems. If they don't have the techniques grooved they're going to have trouble. The answer is being a good technique football player and being a team with good football techniques."

Success does not necessarily breed motivation but it certainly makes playing football a lot more fun. That is the course Noll has charted. Football should be fun, he says, echoing other successful coaches. It's only fun winning and you only win by being properly prepared and doing things correctly.

"If you don't," he adds, "it's miserable, and that should be motivation enough. But then, some people like misery. Every situation they're in, every relationship they engender, creates misery. Those people can't be a part of our organization because we don't want misery. We want people who will work to an end."

Noll does not tell his players, "Do it my way or you're gone," or, "If you fail you're gone." He does not rule by fear and he certainly does not openly motivate by fear. He doesn't think such means are assets to good performances though he admits they may be built in to the structure of professional football—that the player who does fail too many times will not help the team and consequently will be released from the squad.

"I never felt it as a player. I never felt any fear for my job and if I had I don't know what I would have done. Fear of failure can restrict a player; it can kill him as an individual. If he continually worries about failing, he'll get so damn tight that he will fail. Panic can kill anyone. Fear of failure is the worst thing that can happen to an individual. There's nothing anyone can do about it if it creeps into a person's mental attitude.

"I tell my players that; I try to warn them against worrying about failure. We want to be properly prepared for anything in a game but we don't want to worry about losing the game. If we lose it, we'll find out why but one of the reasons shouldn't be that we were so tight we were afraid at the outset. That's terrible."

That was Paul Brown's approach when Noll was a player but he does not draw on those experiences with the Browns as the prime source of relating to his own players. Today's pros don't care whether their coach played or not, he claims, but are interested only in learning about the game for themselves. Noll takes that self-interest as a starting point in laying out the necessary ingredients. Then, he draws on his experience of what it takes to win and how a team must go about using those means.

One example is the manner in which he runs his daily practices. He does not want his players on the field during the week "just to pound somebody into the ground. We want to be efficient with the idea that this will prepare us to do what we must do on Sunday. I must assume they will accept this.

"Now if I find someone who will not accept it and won't do what is necessary to win, then it becomes a picking process. You must get rid of the ones who won't win for you. I'm not in a cat-and-mouse game with anyone. But I will assume they are following our program until they prove differently. And we give them plenty of the benefit of the doubt. We'll stay with people and stay with people assuming they still are not sure what they must do. We figure that over a period of time they will fully come around. If they don't, they go."

Many former NFL players who became head coaches after achieving excellence in playing the game, have been shocked that their own players do not have what they consider similar outlooks as they had as players. Noll is not one of them. He puts the onus for winning on the coach himself, not on the player. Some say that is akin to signing your own death warrant but holding it in your pocket until the right time.

"A coach's only goal must be to help his players be the best they can," says Noll. "If you don't do it, they will know; if you do, then you can be a very big part of what is happening.

"The selection process is the difference. If you have more people on your team who are not willing to pay the price to win, you won't win. That's a coach's decision. He knows who they are and he must take the means to see that they change or that they don't play for him. You can't expect to line up a team and say, 'Okay, here are the plays. Let's go play.' A coach must demand certain things, things that he knows to be the means for winning. He must see that the players accept them. If they don't, he must get men who will.

"The NFL is a league where winning is the important thing; to be the best is the important thing. That is what pays off. That's what I mean by getting people together who will do that and why the selection process is the biggest part of coaching."

That selection process probably is toughest on the rookie player. It is not uncommon for a rookie at all but become a recluse during his first training camp because he lives in fear that the next knock on the door will be the Turk telling him to come, bring his playbook, and say good-bye to everyone. That also is part of pro football's built-in structure, a nine-week galvanizing process that goes a long way toward toughening a player's mental resolve so he can better cope with the most pressure-packed situations.

Noll is not insensitive to some of the problems young players encounter as they come into professional football, but he does not offer himself as a security blanket or as a psychiatrist's coach. It is the coach's job, he says, to make the player's football environment as good as possible and to support his players to the fullest extent possible. After that, the player must do the rest for himself.

The crucial time often is during a player's early seasons. Noll says that a head coach puts his job on the line by staying with a player through his development and, even though it may not seem that way to the outsider, there can be a great many problems in developing a player. It is one reason why he supports the Rozelle Rule that says a team losing a player because he has played out his option should be compensated by the team with which he signs.

Noll's first great test in developing a young player was Bradshaw, the first choice in the NFL's collegiate draft of 1970. Bradshaw was a quarterback and the focal point of the team; he drew the most notice and criticism. Terry came from Louisiana Tech and while he was coached by Mickey Slaughter, a former pro quarterback at Denver, he still had to learn some painful lessons for himself. Two dozen interceptions in his rookie season did not make him an instant favorite in Pittsburgh and neither did some misunderstood emotional outbursts that were fired by his own frustrations.

"When you bring someone like a quarterback along it's inevitable that he will make mistakes and people always will remember them," Noll says. "Joe Greene never had the problem because people don't see the mistakes of a defensive lineman. Certainly Joe made some when he was a young player but who, outside the team, ever knew what they were? Learning the quarterback trade is a difficult thing because you're out there in full view and if you throw an interception, everyone sees it. They might not know why it happened, or if it even was the quarterback's fault. But they'll blame him and they'll remember."

Noll does not dwell on those first couple of seasons with Bradshaw and actually is quite evasive in making specific comments that might hinge on hindsight criticism. He emphasizes that Bradshaw copes with his problems very well after a half dozen seasons in the NFL. Noll still deplores the public comments and insinuations hurled at Terry during the week prior to Super Bowl IX about him being a "dumb" quarterback.

"Terry came into a tough situation in Pittsburgh," Noll says, "tougher than, say, a Bart Starr, who came to Green Bay as a seventeenth-draft pick. When a seventeenth-round draft pick does something, everybody looks and says, 'Hey, that's great,' There is a little less pressure on a guy like that. It's not that way with a top pick, particularly one who is a quarterback. But anyone who is a top pick must be ready to endure that pressure.

"Everyone has his ups and downs coming in. It's never a straight, level flight. One of the things I love about football is that you have the full run of emotions and pressures. In fact, every chance I get to talk to any young man, I encourage him to get into athletics, football in particular. It shows you yourself. You must function under pressure.

"There is nothing wrong with that despite the fact that many people attack the game and say that part of it is bad. That is not bad. Some place along your life you are going to have to function in a pressure situation and if you can learn to do it in a game where the results are not life and death, you can come to a situation where it *is* life and death and be better able to cope. There are many parents who shelter their kids and don't want them to make a decision. They make the decisions for them and what happens? They wind up with a twenty-eight-year-old child.

Noll's critics claim his philosophy of dealing with people epitomizes much of what is wrong with football as a game. But Noll has no problems in either communicating or being credible with his own players. They are the ones who must bear the brunt of his thinking and his overall rating with them is at a high level.

He works at being credible in the sense that he never will say or do something that will cause disbelief among his players. He fully believes the prime coaching maxim: "If you say something that's not true and the players find out, then it's all over." At the same time, he adds something of his own: "You can't say, 'I'm the coach and don't know much about the game.' Your credibility will go down just as fast."

He passed his first and most crucial test of credibility during the 1969 season and he has maintained the same level ever since. Dan Rooney says the evidence is in his total control of the team.

"Chuck's done it by being honest and not saying anything that is not true," Rooney points out. "He gives each player equal treatment but can be critical of anyone when necessary. He tries to treat everyone right and they seem to understand this. But he does not try to be their friend so there is no emotional hurt when he does get on them."

To be sure that everyone always has a means of understanding that he is indeed the coach and indeed does know more about football than anyone on the team, his channels of communication always are open. Again, the player must make use of it. Some are reluctant to approach a head coach and prefer to discuss matters with an assistant. That's fine with Noll. "As long as we get it," he says.

"The assistants will let me know about it. If someone has a better way of doing something, we're open to hearing it because we want to operate the best possible way. We encourage our players to come in and talk."

Noll draws on his brief time as an insurance salesman in dealing with communication. His key is to encourage a response.

"If I'm making a spiel," he says, "and I'm saying, 'This is the way it is,' and you as a prospective customer have an objection, I want to hear it. I really can't convince you about something unless I know the objection you have. It's the same thing in teaching, which is nothing more than selling. If a player sits back and says, 'That's not right,' but keeps it to himself, goes out on Sunday, and doesn't follow what was laid down during the week—well, that just kills you.

"I'd rather someone say, 'Coach, that's not right. It should be this way.' We don't have all the answers. At the same time, if it's not right and you know it's not right, then go through and point out the pitfalls from your experience. Soon you'll have believers."

Noll has gathered a lot of support in his relatively brief time as a head coach by knowing what is correct and then proving it to be so. As Gillman noted, experience and maturity as a coach has shown Noll that there is something to be said for listening to other views. Nor is he adverse to changing his mind once a decision has been made that he sees not to be valid.

The best example came during the 1974 season when he awarded Joe Gilliam the starting quarterback's job over Bradshaw after the two had run almost neck-and-neck during the preseaon. This became a source of discomfort in Pittsburgh, including some ugly racial insinuations after Bradshaw regained the job.

Noll tried to keep the matter on a purely football level but one day at a meeting, he remarked to one of the team's officials, "Don't they [fans and media] know that I want this matter settled as much as they do? There is nothing racial about it. I liked the idea of Gilliam passing, but we just can't operate as efficiently as I think we must that way."

In the sixth game, with the Steelers' record at 3-1-1, Noll returned Bradshaw to starting quarterback. "Noll realized," the official says, "that ball control was the way to win and Terry understood this phase of the game better than Gilliam. He could have gone with Bradshaw right at the beginning but Gilliam had done so well in the pre-season. His decision to make Joe the starter only backed his own philosophy that almost anyone could lead the Steelers but he didn't become so stubborn about it that he wouldn't change because he felt a change would help the team more."

Noll takes the same even-handed approach in the matter of discipline. He will jump on a player if the situation demands but he says he doesn't like much of that. In those times, Noll never talks down to the player or demeans him, but tries to approach the man in an intelligent manner.

"Many times when I yell at someone I'm sorry about it later," he says. "If I have to talk to someone sternly—I don't consider it chewing out—I'll do it on a person-to-person basis. I don't scream at anybody or try to embarrass anybody. But we want to be sure we get things done the way they should be. I'll come down hard on them if I think it's necessary. The best way you can come down hard on them is by shipping them out."

It is easy, his players say, to tell when he is displeased. He has what they call "a certain look," and the muscles around his eyes and mouth tighten. When things really are going badly, he'll get that same look, then suddenly explode with a couple of expletives. An instant later he's regained his composure and is back to functioning normally.

"I'm not going to jump on someone and say, 'You broke this rule. You're fined! You do this, you do that!'" Noll says, "That just adds to the problem. I want him to understand that he does have a problem, that he must solve it, and that we're there to help him.

"We have rules that we're going to stick to. Players must obey the rules and stay with them. But we also try to forewarn everyone that the rules are to help everyone live together in harmony. When everyone knows what everyone else is doing, then no one is guessing and you have that harmony. If we have people who are trying to beat the rules, we don't want them around."

A few years ago in training camp, Greene went out to get a pizza and missed curfew by five minutes. "That pizza will cost you fifty dollars, Joe," Noll told him. And it did.

Team rules are something that Noll stressed the first day he met his team in 1969 and which he has stressed every year since. He tells his players the rules are not for punishment and not to take their money in fines, but only to establish a system under which everyone works to the same standards . . . to the same disciplines.

"Discipline means no guessing," says Noll. "We follow a patterned system. That means you know where your help is coming from. You don't gamble or try to out-think your opposition. It's a little more demanding because it eliminates guesswork and requires our players to know more defensive plays. You must know your assignment. When you change to fool the opposing quarterback you also have to be sure that you're not fooled along with him. The basic premise is: you do precisely what is asked of you so that you have two things to remember—where you have to be and where your help is.

"There was a philosophy in the game at one time that said defense was a game of reaction. If that is true, you won't win. Defenses would sit there and read the offenses and their blocking patterns as they came. If you do that, you give the offense the edge and you must be a super kind of athlete to defeat it. What we try to do now is attack the offense at the snap of the ball. We're coming and everything is taken care of. We're reading as we're moving, not sitting and waiting. We take the game to the offense so we can be aggressive."

Noll feels that defense is the ultimate in team function because it must be played as a team. He says it takes a special kind of man to be a defensive player, one who must get great personal satisfaction from doing his job well. It's a profession where a good performance is not always noticed; but make a mistake and everybody seems to notice.

"This is an unnatural way to live," he admits, "but I think it's unnatural to play football. It's not the customary thing to run around and smack into other people. Not everybody wants to do it."

Though he had played defense at Cleveland and was a defensive assistant at both San Diego and Baltimore, he did not set that phase of the game as the top priority when he became head coach in Pittsburgh. Actually, the Steelers arrived defensively a little quicker than he figured because their player drafts were so excellent at the defensive skill positions. Nine of their starters in 1975 were on the team by 1971, including the remarkable members of the front four—L. C. Greenwood, Ernie Holmes, Dwight White, and Greene.

"You can't program what you will get from each draft because you don't know what's available," says Noll. "You can't look at your team and say, 'We need this, this, and this.' They may not be there. The decisions are based on the facts and those are ever-changing. That is one truism in this sport—you never arrive and you never can be satisfied. The real reward is striving. Our basic premise has been to get the best people we can, in all departments."

That includes the coaching staff, in his first seven seasons, he had a dozen coaches working for him. They were not old pros or others who have bounced from job to job as the programs around them collapsed. Noll never had met Bud Carson, who is his defensive coordinator, until he appeared for an interview. They went into a room, closed the door, and it opened eight hours later. Carson got the job.

He is demanding with his coaches in meetings and on the field. Players say that Noll begins each practice as nothing more than the overseer but he never stops coaching. If something goes wrong, he'll stop practice and make sure it's straightened out. He gets right into a drill if he thinks the proper techniques aren't being emphasized and he'll point out what they are. Some of his former coaches think he gets involved too much. One said Noll never has gotten over his being an assistant coach and simply finds it difficult to stand back and watch others coach. If nothing else, he keeps his other coaches on their toes and the result is an absolute compliance to what he wants done.

Noll shies away from discussing his relations with his coaches, saying only, "I let them do what they have to do." He is not close socially with any of them, his reason being that the entire staff spends so much time together at training camp and through the season. This reluctance for social contact enables him also to keep a clear view on any hard decisions he must make just as it does in his relations with his players.

Noll acts as overall offensive coach, but puts special emphasis during the week on special teams. Like many head coaches, he shows those films himself. Everyone watches and players say no one ever goes in worrying about being embarrassed. If a player does his job, he tells him. If he doesn't, he simply says, "That's terrible."

"Having him run those films has a strange effect on everyone," says one of the special teams players. "I think that may be one reason why Pittsburgh has such good special teams play. They know the head man is interested and he gets everyone else interested. When you join the team, he tells you he has twenty-two starters on offense and defense and everyone else is a starter on the special teams.

"He means it, too. There is no second team. If you're a real good safety, but not good enough to start regularly and can't play special teams, then you're gone. The Steelers may not have any better personnel than other clubs' special teams but they have a desire to get the job done because if they don't . . . well, they just do."

Noll himself seems to enjoy the reaction of the entire team as it watches some of the spectacular hitting that takes place in special team play.

"He can enjoy those moments," the player says, "but he still is able to stay enough above you as coach to player without looking down on you. When he makes the comments, everyone listens and the words have impact."

Pittsburgh's offense has come to be almost as well-regarded as its defense because it also is able to wear down an opponent. With Bradshaw, Franco Harris, and a highly competent offensive line, the Steelers play with the same rough-hewn determination; they're not always smooth and they're not always clever but their power and force is always apparent.

If there is a hallmark of Noll's teams, it is remarkable. This is the product of Noll's concentrated efforts since he began gathering the nucleus of his championship team. There was a time, particularly during Bradshaw's first two seasons, when the Steelers relied mostly on passing. When Harris came in 1972, Noll was able to begin shifting that overload to a point where, in 1975, the team ran the ball 581 times and threw 337 passes.

The Steelers' running game is not pure power alone. No team in the NFL runs more trap plays than the Steelers, triggered by some misdirection maneuvers that set up good blocking angles for its offensive line. And no team in the NFL has a more versatile interior line.

"I don't know of anybody around the league who alternates players as much as we do," says line coach Dan Radakovich. "Our guys are pretty close in talent, so it's hard to pick one over another. If there is a wide difference then the guy who is better will play most of the time. It's not that way with us, so I play them all.

In 1975, five players alternated at three line positions—the two guard spots and center. Jim Clack played left guard in the first and third quarters, then shifted to right guard in the fourth quarter. Gerry Mullins played right guard the first three quarters. Sam Davis played left guard in the second and fourth quarters. Ray Mansfield played center in the first and third quarters, Mike Webster in the other two. The two tackles, Jon Kolb and Gordon Gravelle, usually played the entire game.

Bradshaw handles all the play calling, a firm belief of Noll's that the quarterback should be in charge on the field. This belief is not born of any resentment from watching Paul Brown call the plays for Otto Graham and ferrying them into the game during his first three seasons in Cleveland. He finds no fault with Brown's system, nor with his play calling.

"I just happen to believe a quarterback should run his own game and be given help only when he needs it," Noll says. "That doesn't mean we haven't called plays in our games. We have. My theory is that a quarterback and the other players on my team study all week long for an opponent. If he isn't prepared by that time, very little will help him. Besides, practically all the teams stunt their defenses so much a quarterback must revert to last-second audibles and adjust to the situation.

"A quarterback depends on his teammates to be successful. A lot of people try to equate his role with that of a pitcher in baseball but they're vastly different. A good pitcher can completely dominate a game. A good quarterback still has to depend on the line in front of him, his backs, and the men he throws to."

Though his quarterback runs the game on the field and his defense is controlled by two veteran linebackers, Andy Russell and Jack Ham, Noll still maintains a strong hold from the sideline. His "game face" is a smile, or at least the hint of a pleasant expression, reflecting either his confidence when the team is winning or masking his inner turmoil when things aren't going well.

He isn't totally emotionless, though. Terry Hanratty remembers him during the final 73 seconds of the Steelers' 1972 playoff game against Oakland. Ken Stabler had just scrambled for a 30-yard touchdown to put the Raiders ahead for the first time.

"Chuck very seldom gets emotional," says Hanratty. "But when I looked at him after Stabler's touchdown, I saw he thought we'd win. He called those final pass patterns very calmly. He knew something would break. It was weird." In that game Harris made his incredible catch of Bradshaw's deflected pass and ran for the winning touchdown with a half-minute to play.

Noll is calm in the dressing room before and during a game. Parilli seems to think he copied his decorum from Paul Brown because he is totally unemotional and all business. If the team is not playing well, he'll tell it so at halftime; if things are going okay, he just asks the players to eliminate some of the mistakes they may be making. The harder he grits his teeth—Noll seems to grit them when he's smiling or talking— the more serious the mistakes are, his players claim.

He is not a locker room orator of great note. He hardly said a word to the team before it went onto the field in its first Super Bowl appearance. In fact, Noll says he thoroughly enjoyed the locker room experience that day because his players were loose and confident. To him, it was the end product of what he had tried to achieve throughout the season—"to enjoy playing the game no matter which one it is."

That attitude was reflected in the 1974 playoffs, when the Steelers defeated Buffalo, Oakland, and Minnesota in an astonishing display of consistency.

"We were concerned that we might have been too conscious of our disappointments the preceding years," he says. "So we had to make sure we did not get out of sync. Our team went into the playoffs with the idea that it would not be denied and it played exceptionally well in every game."

Most surprising was the manner in which it handled the pressures during its week of preparations in New Orleans for Super Bowl IX. This often has proved the undoing of teams never before subjected to the four days of media sessions, the constant reminder that they would be playing for $15,000 per man, an NFL title, a championship ring, and sundry other reasons; to say nothing of the fact that they were about to play the most important game of football in their lives.

Noll had been through the Baltimore Colts' disaster in Super Bowl III. The Colts were overwhelming favorites to beat the Jets; they heard it every day during their interview sessions, and saw their hotel become a madhouse of families, friends, and well-wishers. Football was all but forgotten during that week, and the result was reflected in the game against the New York Jets. The Colts were over-confident.

"I'll never forget it," Noll says. "The first day we were down there it started with people saying, 'Gee, you guys are so great. What makes you so great?' If you hear this enough pretty soon you're thinking, 'This team we're playing is nothing.' You've talked yourself into over-confidence. No football game is that way. You lose your edge.

"In January of '75 we didn't want to go to New Orleans and lose our edge. Knowing we weren't going to lose the edge, we knew what we had to do. In a sense, there was not a lopsided attitude. It was one of those things—if Minnesota wins, so what? Pittsburgh never had been in a Super Bowl before. All we had to do was prove it the day of the game."

Noll himself set the tone. He was quiet, confident, and totally cooperative as though he had been in three or four of the games as a head coach. He seemed to thoroughly enjoy the necessary distractions and so did his players. He still laughs remembering Ray Mansfield chasing after a writer when an interview session was terminated, pleading, "Hey wait a minute, I'm not finished."

"I learned something down there," says Noll. "I remembered something that newspapermen must have learned their first day in journalism school: write or speak of something you *know* well and you'll *do* it well. The first question every day was, 'What about the pressure?' Well, the only ones down there under pressure were the media. They had pressure of deadlines, the pressure of new material. They knew more about pressure than anyone.

"Hell, this was just a football game and we had played twenty-two by that time. It's not a new thing but everyone wants to create it and make it something more than it really is. They're under the pressure to do that so that's why they want to talk about pressure."

Noll probably had laid the ground work prior to the AFC championship victory over Oakland two weeks earlier, when he kept his team aware of the pounding the Raiders had given the Steelers in the previous playoffs. That 1974 AFC title game was their Super Bowl, "a kind of inspiration," one says, "because we beat them all over the field. We knew the AFC was stronger than the NFC and there was no doubt we would win the Super Bowl."

Noll was not aware of the confidence, or at least he will not admit seeing it if he did. For one thing, he says, he long ago gave up trying to figure a team's readiness and state of mind from the way it practices. He's seen his team go through some fantastic practice weeks and lose. His most vivid memory in this respect was the Steelers' loss to Oakland in the first round of the 1973 AFC playoffs.

"They ran us off the field," Noll says simply. "Why we lost is a good question. We may have left our game on the practice field because we worked awfully hard and had good practice sessions all week in Palm Springs. But we certainly didn't play very well. You have those days and that's when you've got to go back to fundamentals. In a sense, that may have helped us in 1974, that and our regular season loss to Oakland the same year. It pretty much set the tone for our playoff game out there. It also worked to our advantage to have everyone conceding Oakland as the AFC's representative in the Super Bowl and the Raiders' game against Miami as the only worthy game."

Noll thinks the Steelers were ready as contenders before 1972, despite 5-9 and 6-8 records the previous two seasons.

"I knew it was coming," he says. "I knew that our players believed it and I know that our opponents believed it. The only ones who didn't believe it were the press and the fans. So the 1972 season was a big surprise to them because sometimes your image lags behind when there is a long history of losing."

If the players believed it, says Terry Hanratty, it was because of Noll's very patient approach in bringing them to contending status. Even in the throes of the 13-game losing streak in 1969, through the frustration of those two other losing seasons, Noll acted as if he knew good times were ahead.

Noll does not deny it.

"I guess it's a philosophy," he admits. "I don't concern myself with eventualities. So I never worried if I'd get fired. I just did it the only way I knew how. There's nothing else."

Dan Rooney feels that Noll has been the Steelers' catalyst because of the way he approaches the job—particularly in his role as a teacher—as well as in his intelligence and solid character.

"He teaches players and gives them a chance to develop," says Rooney. "Though the Steelers have a great drafting record, it is Noll's ability to give a guy a chance to develop that really complements it. He does not run them off the first time they make a mistake. He doesn't berate them but tries to bring them on. He keeps them in training camp a lot longer than many coaches will. He encourages them and insists that his assistants do the same thing.

"I've seen coaches run off talent that turned out to be good but Chuck never seems to do this. Anyone who winds up playing for other teams simply did not have a place on the Steelers."

Whatever the reasons for the success of the team and himself, the glory to him still is in the striving.

"I know the feelings of coming out after playing a game," he says, "and being depressed as hell. You get yourself worked up in the week's preparations, play the game with all its excitement, and then it's all over and a lot of people are saying, 'Let's savor the victory.' Well, everything's all over, and it's either a victory or a loss. I still feel that letdown now. Everything has to come from the working or the striving."

His ability to transmit that feeling and insist on its execution was a prime reason why the Steelers did not falter in winning a second straight Super Bowl. Noll knew, and reminded his players going into the season, that every team would attack them harder than any other opponent because they were the champions. It was never a negative psychological block and, if anything, he seemed to relish the challenge—again, the striving.

"Everyone asked me how I would attack the problem of staying on top and when I told them that was fun, they looked at me kinda funny," he says. "But it sure beats hell out of being at the bottom. Having everyone shooting at us was a plus, not a minus. That's the way it should be. We had to prove we still were the best. You've got to be able to take it as you do winning and losing.

"One of the things I've talked constantly to the team about since I came to Pittsburgh was the danger of thinking they had it made. There is no such thing and if a person thinks that way, then he is a fat cat. We preach—I preach—that you can't dwell on the past. Today and the future are all that count. You spend too much time lingering on what you've done and you get nothing done. There's only one way to coast and that's downhill."

Perhaps that's one reason why he says he savors a victory no longer than the walk from the bench to the locker room, his Super Bowl triumphs being exceptions because "there was nothing coming afterward so you could hang onto those a bit longer."

"One thing I learned very early," he says, "is that you never relax, never rejoice very long. What happens on the day you win is great. But the next day, there is another problem to confront. That's where you direct all your attention."

The day after the Steelers' Super Bowl IX victory over Minnesota Noll was asked how it felt to have won the NFL title. He replied quietly and without much emotion, "It's a great feeling. Pleasant."

"That's all, just pleasant?" someone asked.

"Right," he replied. "Pleasant. It's the same thing as when somebody asks you after you've had a birthday, 'Do you feel any different?' "

Later that year, people asked Noll if his life had changed.

"I told them how my wife, Marianne, puts it," he replied. "She says she's just finished doing the laundry and is in the middle of ironing and still has the cleaning to do. Well, that's the way it is with the coaches. We spent our time going through scouting reports, watching films, and preparing for the 1975 season."

It was the same after he became only the third coach ever to win successive Super Bowls, following Pittsburgh's 21-17 victory over Dallas in Super Bowl X. He made no attempt to minimize the feat yet at the same time he shrugged off attempts to immortalize him. When someone asked how it felt to be placed alongside the late Vince Lombardi and his old boss, Shula, as the only two-time Super Bowl winners, he gave a throaty chuckle, then said, "I'll leave that to you historians." But Noll obviously is proud of the feat.

"Winning is like a tight-rope act," he says. "If you look down you get dizzy and you can fall. If you look straight ahead, always toward an objective you must reach, you keep going. I'm not against winning. In fact, a lot of people in this country apologize for it and that's been a problem with us as a nation for too many years. I don't believe in that, either in football or in life. Some people work like hell to be the best and it's wrong to put them down."

He did not merchandise himself as a banquet speaker nor milk the deluge of requests for personal appearances. "The only value I can see to being well-known is financial and I'm not at all interested in merchandising myself," he says. "That's not my way of doing things. I'm a teacher and the most important thing is teaching my students."

As a teacher, he makes sure his students learn from defeat as well as from victory. An example is the way the Steelers seemed to visibly sag in the 1972 AFC title game when the Dolphins' Larry Sieple ran for a crucial first down on a fake punt. Noll points to such mistakes and tells his team, "There it is. That's the thing that is killing us!" They first had to know the problem before they were ready for the solution.

"In a sense, we were looking for something like that to happen," he says. "The thing that a winning team does is that no matter what happens adversely, it can counter it. Something like that play shouldn't matter because the game is played for sixty minutes and you have to keep playing it. Things have a way of evening out and you still can get the things done you must to win."

Noll allows a defeat to stay with him about as long as he endures a victory. He is not a bitter loser. His first reaction is one all good coaches respond to: find out what happened and see that it doesn't happen again, if possible.

"We're striving to get our goals accomplished and when they're not, sometimes things go all to hell," he says. "But if you let it affect you, you're in trouble. Just as if you take a victory and think you're a world-beater, you're going to fall right on your face the next week. I pretty much take it all in stride. When you win, that's the way it's supposed to be because you've worked and done what you should do. When you've lost, then you've done something wrong.

"It's the only course you can take. I've been in professional football a long time and it's been proven again and again. Sometimes you forget these things and you get a rude awakening. I've forgotten them myself sometimes. And my awakening always seems to come the next week."

That's when he goes "problem solving" but the way he and his team have progressed, there have not been too many "next weeks" in recent seasons. Nor are there likely to be with the tight rein he holds on a team. He may never admit it, but you just know his football breeding had something to do with it. As Art Rooney, an old horseman from way back, puts it, "Noll is out of Paul Brown by Don Shula and Sid Gillman."

He has won pro football's Kentucky Derby—the Super Bowl—twice with that blood line.

Bum Phillips

"You must win but you also must have
fun—or what's the use? Football is but
a small part of all of our lives."

The Houston Oilers didn't create many ripples in professional football when they named the successor to Sid Gillman as the club's coach and general manager after the 1974 season.

The new man's name was O. A. (Bum) Phillips. If there weren't ripples around the National Football League there sure were frowns. O. A. (Bum) Who?

Eight months later everyone had a much better idea of exactly who Bum Phillips is and their original surprise was nothing compared to their astonishment when the Oilers—the sad-sack team of the National Football League during the first four seasons of the seventies with a 9-45-2 record—became playoff contenders.

Until Houston finished the season with a 10-4 record, the impression Phillips seemed to have made around the NFL was reflected in wisecracks from cynics who caught their first glimpse of the man and couldn't quite believe what they saw: a crew cut that was a carryover from his Marine Corps boot camp shortly after Pearl Harbor and western clothes—baby-blue cowboy boots to a 10-gallon hat.

They had their chuckles. Then they saw his team play football and became aware of something a lot of Texans had known for a quarter century; Oail Andrew (Bum) Phillips, in only his second major head coaching job at age 51 was nothing to laugh at as a football coach.

Bum Phillips—they've called him Bum since his little sister found it impossible to pronounce "brother" and his friends found it handier to remember than Oail—also happens to be a delightful man. His speech is rich with the flavor of his native Texas, and it becomes even richer when he plugs a tobacco chaw into his cheek. He has a ready wit and a mind that can cut through conversation to pick up what is important and offer the same in reply. Sitting behind a desk in his paneled office, he looks bigger than he does standing along the sidelines. His chest is broad and his upper arms are powerful, showing the results of some days spent wrestling oil rigs as a young man.

He is without pretense. You want to talk about coaches and their importance to a team, and he says with a wink, "Coaches are very important. Hell, you can get the players off the back of a Wheaties box."

Of course, he doesn't mean it because players—his players—are just as special to him as his son Wade, now an assistant with the Oilers. He treats both the same: with respect and affection.

These attitudes do not set Phillips apart from the coaching crowd but the means he uses to reach his players do. Such as a mid-week beer bust and dominoes tournament at which he is reigning champion ("or else we'd be playing something different"). Or how about a training camp without a single full-scale scrimmage session. Or a training camp that has no rules about when players must be in their rooms with lights out?

Try in-season practices, the longest of which was 94 minutes, and generally run no more than 75. Or practices cut to three days late in the season when the team begins to sag?

Some might say he is coddling his players, giving in to their inclinations to shun the drudgery of practicing. But the results tell a different story.

The fact is Bum Phillips relates to his players. Not long ago he saw a notice tacked on the players' bulletin board inviting all to come to the home of quarterback Dan Pastorini for a "moving party"—lugging the Pastorini's furniture and personal belongings to new quarters in exchange for an ice box filled with beer.

Who was among the first to show up? Bum Phillips.

"Okay," he said, "let's get the damn stuff moved. The quicker we do it, the sooner we get to that beer." And he hoisted a large carton atop his shoulder. Afterward, he sat in the new living room, sprawled in a chair with a beer in hand, and listened to country and western music with everyone else.

Phillips shocked a few people on the first day of training camp when he brought the two writers who cover the team for the city's two major dailies into the team meeting. He introduced them and told his players, "These men will be covering us throughout camp and through the season. It will be beneficial to you and to the Oilers if you will cooperate with them in every way." Then he invited the writers to stay during the meeting. Throughout that season, he never complained when they were critical and he always found time for them—as well as for media from around the country.

His 3-4 defense, which helped the Oilers reverse their slide in 1974, proved equally tough in victories over Miami, Washington, and Oakland. It was ranked first against the rush in the American Football Conference. Most importantly, people began filling the Astrodome again.

There was a time, following his graduation from Stephen F. Austin College in 1949 when he was nearly 26 years old, that coaching was only a part-time avocation. He was married, the father of two children, and he had bills to be paid.

"I was going to coach for a couple of years, get it out of my system, then go back to the oil field, or buy a farm or a ranch somewhere, and settle down for the rest of my life," he says. "But I coached in high school until I was thirty-four. At that time colleges were hiring guys like Darrell Royal and Jim Owens, who were twenty-eight, twenty-nine, thirty, as head coaches. At thirty-four I never felt my chance of getting a head coaching job in college was that good."

Phillips joined Bear Bryant's staff at Texas A&M for the 1957 season, then returned to the high school coaching for another six seasons. When he finally left that phase of his career for good in 1964, he had been through it all, in cities and towns such as Nederland, Port Neches, Jacksonville, and Amarillo. In between, he spent the 1962 season as head coach at Texas Western (now the University of Texas-El Paso), where he had a 4-5 record. Phillips quit because there not only wasn't much money for recruiting, there wasn't anyone to spend it on.

Phillips was an assistant coach for two seasons at the University of Houston before he joined Sid Gillman as a defensive line coach in San Diego in 1967. Gillman believed in hiring an assistant from college football whenever possible to take advantage of the college coach's skills in teaching and conducting drills that mold important fundamentals. Bryant and other coaches had recommended Phillips among the best in the college game.

"I don't think any head coach should overlook a man who has these skills," Gillman says. "Drills and techniques are methods of doing things. You drill for execution and a team really doesn't execute unless it is drill-oriented. That is college football's major contribution to the pros and it is something the pros did not put too much stress on until several years ago. Coaches looked around and found the teams that stressed teaching—like Paul Brown's teams and Vince Lombardi's teams—were the ones who were so dominant. Now you won't find a successful team without coaches who can teach the various drills."

Phillips brought along the 3-4 defense that he had learned in 1950 from observing Bud Wilkinson at Oklahoma and that he had perfected at various stages during his high school tenure. The Chargers used it at Phillips' insistence in 1969 and he also was successful with it when he returned to his home and for one-year assistant coaching stints at SMU and Oklahoma State before rejoining Gillman in Houston.

He certainly didn't come into the NFL's head coaching hierarchy as any wunderkind. He's never written any books on techniques, and he's not a celebrity at coaches' meetings. But if he's asked about something he'll say why without any false modesty and in understandable terms.

"He doesn't hesitate to volunteer information," says one friend. "He never tried to improve his image yet he was so candid about some things that I don't think he ever could besmirch the fine reputation he has built. Imagery is not part of that reputation. He points to his own background, where he has jumped from head coaching jobs at high schools, colleges, back to high schools without fear of damaging his reputation because he believes a person has to be his own man."

Phillips has often said that he "would rather coach a good situation at Nederland High School at twelve thousand than a poor situation in the pros at fifty thousand." It's one of the reasons he chose to work for Gillman, knowing that Gillman was among the most demanding of all coaches in demanding time, effort, and attention to detail.

"I'd known Sid for twenty years so I knew the kind of guy he was to start with," says Phillips. "To me, being a high school, college, or pro coach isn't that important. But when it comes down to working, there are just some people I wouldn't care to work for. I'd rather go back to high school or back to the oil fields—anything. The guys I work for are the ones I want to work for, not because I need the job."

The feeling obviously was mutual. Gillman didn't hesitate to recommend him as a successor following the 1974 season. What did he see in a man who had just one season as a head coach outside of high school?

"In my mind," Gillman says, "he was head coaching material. That was foremost. He was knowledgeable in certain aspects of the game and I knew he would acquire those he did not have. He also had shown me he could handle any adjustment because he was wise and clever. On a personal level, I felt we had licked the problem of a lack of continuity that had been the biggest drawback to success with the Oilers. I had established a good system and hired Bum to maintain it so the players could continue to learn."

But Phillips did not feel morally obligated to maintain the same program Gillman had established. Nor did he feel any trepidation in stepping into a situation that had proven to be quicksand for past coaches: He's the ninth head coach since the team was established in 1960.

"Pressure is part of this game," he says. "Pro sports is entertainment. People demand to see a winner and they deserve to do so. If you don't have one, somebody's gotta suffer. If you want to dance to the tune, you've got to pay the old fiddler."

He made it easier on himself, first cutting down the volume of offense that Gillman had laid on his team. The Oilers' playbook under Sid was as thick as that city's Yellow Pages. We had almost everything everybody had in that book," he says. "I mean almost every play *every* team had. We just simplified things a bit."

That practical approach pretty well sums up his overview of coaching: he advocates simplification not complication.

Though football is his profession, his life has a much broader scope. This probably goes against the stereotype of Texas football coaches as being nothing but purveyors of a system that grinds up young men and spits them out in some totally different image and likeness. Phillips was that way a few years ago—until one of his high school players, who had been chosen to his all-state team as a sophomore, came to him before his senior season and told the coach he was quitting because football wasn't fun anymore.

"How could it have been?" Phillips says today. "I had been driving that team two-and-a-half to three hours every day. I had thought winning would make it worthwhile. This started me thinking. What I came up with is the firm idea that you must win but you also must have fun—or what's the use? My approach now is to let the kids play and enjoy it and let the coaches do the work.

"Don't get me wrong. Winning football games is important but I don't think it's the only thing. There's a whole lot of things in the world more important than winning football games. Just take a walk through Texas Children's Hospital sometime and that will convince you that there are more important things.

"No matter what happens on the football field, we still can look forward to playing golf, going out to honky tonks at night, a lot of things. But a kid with leukemia or some crippling disease—he's got nothing to look forward to."

So life is not only football to Phillips as it is to some of his peers. Gillman for example, was known as totally dedicated to the sport every waking moment of the day, which always began early. Though he demanded the same dedication of his assistants, Phillips always managed to keep a balance in his life and now he tries to pass it on to his players.

"Football is not all I live for," he says. "I've told my players many times that football is but a small part of all of our lives. We can learn a lot of lessons from it that we can't learn in school or anywhere else. Now if you play it right, that's all you're going to get out of it. Everyone will forget you when you leave the game and all you will have left are the things it has taught you—to sacrifice, to work hard.

"There are a whole lot of people who don't know how to work. But they play football and they like it well enough to get some good work habits because they work at getting better. When they get out in the world, they find they're not lazy any more. They've developed some good work habits such as getting after a job when it must be done. Without them knowing it, football has trained them to do some good things, like not giving up when things are going bad—there's just a jillion things that football does for you.

"That is all you are going to carry out of it, not the money which you will throw away or spend. So what good is money? All those other things will help you all your life. You may quit playing football when you're twenty-eight but you don't quit living."

That is a lesson he tries to teach his players. Teaching really is Bum Phillips's life and in any discussions with him about football—professional, college, or high school—the natural bridge between all three is teaching. A major failing of many professional players who want to become assistants in the pros is their lack of teaching ability. They know what to do but getting it across to the players is the problem.

Phillips does not have that problem. He began coaching in high school with two other assistants, which meant they had to know and disseminate a great deal of football knowledge. By his seventh year as a high school coach, he had eight assistants, as many as most NFL teams now use.

"We had enough to do a job," he says when someone expresses amazement at such a large staff for that level of football. "In high school it's even more important than in pro football. You must have enough people so you can isolate, teach what you want taught. If you only have three coaches and sixty players, obviously you can't break down into enough groups. It must be that way with the Oilers, too.

"A lot of people say, 'That's too doggone many people.' But they forget we're picking up free agents and those free agents aren't great football players or they wouldn't be free agents. Somebody must teach those guys. In days past, when there were twelve teams, you could get by with four assistants because you had better talent coming out of college. Now with the expanded league, you have less talent coming onto your team that can play right away so you must do a heckuva job teaching. It certainly has paid off with the Oilers."

Phillips easily draws the comparisons of coaching in high school with his work in the NFL. One of the benefits of the former is the fundamental teaching experience; another is the patience required to be sure the slowest member of the group is as well schooled as the smartest.

"When you start out in high school," he notes, "you must take whoever is out there and play with them. You start by saying, 'Okay, put this hand here, that foot there.' Then you adopt your offense and defense—everything—to those people. In pro ball, players already have techniques they can use and if it's successful for them, it's fine with me."

Phillips remembers the day Curley Culp came to the Oilers from the Kansas City Chiefs. Houston was to play Cincinnati the following Sunday and Culp asked him, "How do you want me to play?"

"Just control the center and go to the football," Phillips replied.

"How do you want me to play them?" he asked Phillips again.

"Hell, you've been playing six or seven years. You should have an idea."

"Beautiful!" Culp said, and a huge grin spread across his face.

"With guys like him," Phillips adds, "you don't need that much teaching. But you must get the players disciplined to play the team defense. Being pros they want to make all the tackles and all the sacks. It's a team defense and you must sell them, as well as discipline them, on the necessity of doing that. We can't win any other way unless all of us are on the same page."

For those who are not Curley Culp, the need for teaching never lessens in pro football. Phillips has noted a great tendency among pros to say, "I'll do it the way I like to do it and can get it done better that way." All of which is okay if the player knows what he is doing. If he doesn't, then it's up to the coach to figure out why and how he can get it straightened out.

"That's where teaching comes in and teaching is nothing more than selling," says Phillips. "But a coach must study the problem first, analyze it real well and be sure he knows how to correct it. Once that's done, then he's got to sell the guy on the idea that his way will make him a better player.

"A coach needs patience to do that and you've just got to learn that in high school coaching. You teach there by explaining something over and over. Many times they don't catch on quickly to something because they don't have the ability. You can't say, 'Okay, the devil with you, we're going to trade you, or we're going to cut you.' They're all you've got so you just learn to be more patient. That, not method, is the most important talent in coaching football.

"Everyone's method is good and there is no certain way to do one thing. There are a multitude of offensive sets but you can't run all of them. You must narrow them down to what you can do best and what fits your people the best. The quickest way to learn that is coaching in high school."

Phillips agrees that his experience in high school and as a college assistant makes teaching almost automatic in professional football. Like other successful pro coaches, Phillips approaches each season with total concentration on the basics, "just as if we didn't know anything." He does not insist on a heavy technical approach with a player who is competent through experience. A Culp for instance, doesn't get the "put-this-hand-there, that-foot-here" treatment. None of his players start that way, in fact.

"The first thing is to get them to listen to you," says Phillips. "The easiest way is to let them do it. If they can't get it done and are having some trouble with some phases of technique, they *want* you to tell them how to correct it. They want to do good so now they're listening to you. If you start out telling them everything, then they just blank you out. You must use psychology with a guy to get him to listen to you in the first place."

He does not try to impress players with great secrets. And he doesn't show his players how and why. Even in high school he didn't do that. He coached the *coaches*. He does the same thing in the pros.

"You have a practice going on where the position coaches have five or six drills in progress at the same time so someone must be able to see what's happening," he says. "Someone must get an idea how the continuity of the practice will continue the next day so the people who need the most work will get it. You work to strengthen your weakest link, not worry about the strongest one.

"Gillman's way was different. He worked with one unit, so he didn't know what was going on in the other drills. Sid always had his mind made up at the start just what would be. I'll stand in the tower or walk around and perhaps see something from fifty yards off that will help a coach's drill. A lot of times a guy running a drill can get so close to it that he really can't see what is going on.

"The idea is that if everyone has an equal amount of playing talent and all practice the same amount of time, then you must get more done with your people in the same amount of time than the other guy. That's why there must be someone to coordinate it and put it together."

Bryant's influence is very strong here as it is through much of his approach to the job. For example, Phillips does not believe in stepping into a group drill as Gillman did because of something he learned at the time he worked for the Bear ("and I say 'for him' rather than 'with him' because that's your relationship on his staff").

"Even before I joined him at Texas A&M, I found out why he never got in the drills," says Phillips. "He told me that if he got in there, the players would listen to him and if that is the case, then he certainly didn't need the other coach. Bryant said it would be like telling his players, 'That man doesn't know what he's talking about. I'm in here to tell you.' Whatever you do, he told me, the players must have confidence in the guy who is telling them something.

"I'm not interested in everyone saying that I know something. If the assistant coach is telling them what I want told, I don't care whether they think I thought of it as long as they do it."

There are some who might think such an attitude is just a way to mask an inadequate knowledge of the game's fine points but don't ever mistake that with Phillips. He ran hundreds of unit drills as a defensive line coach in four collegiate jobs. He also was defensive coordinator, which meant he not only had men working under him but he had to know all possible about every facet of the defense—line, linebackers, and secondary.

He worked under Bryant, Bill Yeoman at the University of Houston, Hayden Fry at SMU, Jim Stanley at Oklahoma State, and Gillman—coaches who feel an assistant should be left alone to accomplish his job once a course has been charted.

"That's how you must treat assistant coaches," Phillips adds, "because they're like players. You can't stay on a guy all the time. Every time he does something, you can't be correcting him or before long he'll be thinking, 'Gosh, I can't do anything right.' It's important for an assistant coach to think he's good just as it's important for a player to think the same way."

Of all the coaches he worked with, Bryant is the only one he consciously imitates, particularly in the manner of getting people to do things. Bum says Bryant is a master in the proper use of psychology to achieve this, perhaps explaining some of Bryant's mystique.

"I found out how he motivated people," says Phillips, "and it was different than anyone else's methods. He always took all the blame. Anything that would happen, he would say, 'My fault.' Regardless of what happened, he never was one who would blame another person. The coaches and players who kept hearing that after awhile began to think, 'Well, it wasn't *all* your fault. I could have done something better.' That was his method of getting more out of people. He was a master at it."

Phillips agrees with that approach, too, if for no other reason than he knows the degree of appreciation an assistant can feel for the boss who takes the blame for his mistakes. He also knows the amount of effort the assistant will generate to be sure the mistake won't happen again because he has not been the fall guy.

"In the long run," he says, "if you want a guy to get better it will happen a lot quicker if you don't blame him for everything. For one thing, he's not going to stand being charged with everything. For another, the head coach can't expect him to correct his mistakes unless he is willing to admit he made some. And for a third, and maybe the most important, if the head coach takes the blame in most cases it will work the opposite way and the assistant will try to do something about it. I can say that from personal experience."

Phillips found another important technique in Bryant's methods: positive communication. "He'd also talk to his teams, which is something I think is important. You've got to sell what you're doing and he could talk to them better than anyone I've ever seen. He could get a squad's attention and keep it, though he never would talk unless he had something to say. And it seemed like he always had something to say and it always was important. It wasn't long but it always was to the point.

"He'd always start by complimenting the coaches or the team on what they did. You'd think, 'He's *got* to be right because he's saying something good about me.' But he has your attention. Then he'd name a couple of things—never too many—that we would have to work on the next day. By starting out with good things, he really had their attention and got them conscious of correcting things.

"Now he could have gone in with the idea of just correcting—and a lot of people in coaching make mistakes by doing this because they think the good things don't need mentioning. This is wrong because there is mental attitude. Though what the coach says may be correct about a player or a team's faults, if he says it day after day, they're just going to get used to hearing bad things. But Bryant would just brag on a couple of good things before he'd start on something else."

The bottom line from all of this, Phillips adds, is that it's not what a coach knows or what he can do but what he can get someone else to do or learn.

Phillips has adopted some of Bryant's techniques because he has found them workable and they are reflected in the relationships he has molded within his own team. To do this he also added, perhaps unconsciously, some of the salesmanship Bill Yeoman used as his personal motivating technilue.

"Bill is a total optimist, a salesman who dwells on the positive while Bryant is lowkey," Phillips says. "Bill's the kind of guy who puts up a play on the board and says, 'There is no way they can stop this play.' And on the blackboard there is no way you *can* stop it—unless you have the chalk last. Bill's a good talker, a good recruiter, and that's necessary in college football. Bryant would be a good recruiter, too, but he doesn't bother much because his assistants do it all."

You also can see one of Hayden Fry's strong points—his great belief in players—in Phillips's method of working with his players.

"Hayden believed in people like Jesus Christ believed in people," Phillips declares. "No matter what a person did, he could overlook it or excuse it, at least off-the-field stuff and that is where the real loyalties are built. I think that's the only way you can get a guy to do something better than another guy might get him to do it."

Phillips takes great care—and particular pride—in his off-the-field relations with his own players. Those relations are a good object lesson because no one has tried to take advantage of either him or the rules he has laid down for the team. When he told the players there would be no specific time for lights out, and that bed checks would not be on a regular basis, they offered to police themselves. There were no known violators.

His philosophy is not to bother them, not to try to play God. For one thing, he says, he is not smart enough to decide who can do what off the field so he never has really paid a great deal of attention to the nature or extent of his players off-the-field activities. Nor has he ever had any complaints about any of them.

He also takes great pride in his players' willingness to give their time to various charities. Once or twice a month, 25 or 30 players go through Children's Methodist

Hospital and Rehabilitation Center for the Crippled in Houston. And they do it on their own, every player participating at various times of the year.

"It's in something like that where I feel that if I haven't taught a guy something about helping people, it doesn't matter how much football I've taught him," Phillips says. "I failed him. I owe him something other than football because he can get football anywhere. I talk to them about such things. I teach them to get along with their fellow man—the other players. If you don't teach that in coaching, then you're not coaching. I don't care how many plays you diagram, that's not coaching.

"Coaching is making a better man out of a guy you have on your team. It's a matter of being able to look back and think you've been able to help him somewhere. Teaching a guy to kick the football just lasts four or five years. Developing good attitudes in people, the ability to take the losses and the ability to come back as well as the proper emotional approach—well, those are the things he must live with for the next forty or so years after he leaves football. Those are the things that are important.

"We have some players on the team who aren't church people. I don't mean they are atheists but they don't go to church on Sunday and aren't religious in the same sense other guys have been brought up to be. I try to encourage them but I don't set any standards as to what a guy should or should not do. I just believe that you can't be wrong by going to church.

"If I go to a player and say, 'I think you should do this,' and if he doesn't do it, then there is something wrong somewhere because he has no respect for what I would say. I try not to get a 'no.' If I get talking about something like that I want to make sure I get a 'yes' before I force an answer. I think that's part of my obligation—not my job, my obligation—to help guide a man. Who in hell can help guide them better than me? I make more mistakes than all of them put together. And if I haven't done it, I know ten thousand people who have. I can sure tell them what not to do."

Building a mutual belief between player and coach has its positive spinoff on the football field, too, he believes. He places a high priority on dealing with the real essence of a man and he uses that same tactic to help the player do something that he might be reluctant to attempt or accomplish at someone else's bidding.

This is where a player can develop a personal edge on an opponent by becoming better. Developing "the edge" was something he heard Gillman talk of constantly, whether that edge be his way—from personal physical conditioning—or by a team working longer than its opposition—Gillman's way. Phillips's method is to get a player feeling he must play better because he wants to.

"He's got to play for his pride, you've got to pay him well, the fans must be behind him and then you give him that something extra, a feeling of playing for someone whether it's his teammates, the coaching staff or whatever," says Phillips. "He must want to be doing something for someone other than himself. And it happens twice in football. The first is when you're behind thirty-five to nothing and he doesn't want to allow someone else to be embarrassed because he knows that he's beaten. The other is when he's in that clutch situation—when it's fourth and goal on the two-foot line and you must make the doggone touchdown. He's got to reach for something extra. When it comes down to one shot, he's got to make it happen.

"In order for it to happen, there must be loyalty and it goes both ways. A player must feel that a coach is loyal to him and a coach must expect the same loyalty in return. He's got to think you believe in him if you expect him to believe in you."

In addition to achieving the edge, Phillips also found a tenacity in Gillman that refused to accept defeat, plus a mature way of coping with the myriad personalities on a football team that often are made even more complex by changing traditions and styles. Sid often had a stormy relationship with many of his players but Bum gives him high marks for defusing situations that could have become volatile. Phillips has applied both qualities in more measured ways, but he still acknowledges his former boss as the one who helped show him the way.

"If there is one thing you can say about Gillman it is that there was just no give-up in him," says Phillips. "Almost anyone has sense enough to quit when they're beaten. But you could beat him right to the ground and he still wouldn't quit. The rest of us can look at the clock, see there are thirty seconds to go and we're behind thirty-one to nothing and we give up. Hell, Sid wouldn't give up.

"He also was good at handling people. He wasn't bothered by unimportant things, like length of hair or style of clothes. Lance Alworth was the same good kid playing for him with long hair as he was playing for Arkansas with short hair. So was Dickie Post. I found out a guy's own personal business was his own life. I'd help in some way if I could with his manners or in his dress. But before you ever can do that you must get the players in the palm of your hand. If you ever get them there, you can suggest something to them and they do it. But you can't make rules for them to live like you want them to live. You can't make someone be like you are no more than you can be like them.

"I've got to confess, when I went to San Diego to work for him in 1967, I had some definite ideas on how people ought to be. To Sid, those things were immaterial and he could overlook them. I learned to overlook them for the same reason."

Phillips remembers one day at a Chargers' practice when one of Gillman's players bad-mouthed him with some heavy profanity. Sid got mad, the player got mad, and it looked as if a violent confrontation was about to take place.

"Wait, wait, hold it," Gillman said suddenly. "Just a second. Don't you say anything more and I won't say anything more. I'm going over to another group and you go work with a group on the other side of the field. Tomorrow we'll talk about it."

Gillman had defused a serious situation. He could have suspended the player but it would not have helped either the player or the football team.

"In other words," he adds, "you must be a big enough man to overlook things. You could say, 'Boy, I'll show you.' You might show him but you'll kill him, too. You'll ruin his career, your team, and everyone else just so you can say, 'I won't let anyone else talk to me like that.' Sid was a big man that way. He was a disciplinarian but there also are times when you must call a halt. The alternative is to force the issue and just make it worse. A school superintendent I once worked for told me, 'Don't ever force a guy to tell you, 'no!' If it's real important to you and you can see you might get a 'no,' don't force the issue. Walk away. Sid, in that instance forced the issue but he was man enough not to penalize himself and the player."

Phillips tells his coaches the same thing. He warns them about the times they will come in from a game or from the practice field disappointed, hurt, unhappy with their players' performance. Those often are the times wrong words are spoken and when the response can get out of hand. Phillips practices what he preaches, too. In 1975 Phillips was forced to defuse a touchy situation between wide receiver Billy Parks and an assistant coach. The two had gotten into a shouting match coming off the practice field. Bum stepped into the situation, heard a quick capsule summary, then sternly told Parks, "Go on home. Get out of here right now, go home."

Billy insisted on being heard and Phillips listened. Instead of going through a dispassionate recital, Parks began shouting at the assistant coach again. This time Phillips sent him off. The problem, it turned out, began during an offensive drill when Parks asked to look at the ready list of plays the Oilers were working on. The assistant thought Parks wanted to check when the pass plays were scheduled so he could run them and duck the running plays. One remark led to another and this triggered the shouting match.

"The next day Billy came in and apologized right away," Phillips recalls. "I already had asked the coach for his side of the story and got Billy's side. I said to him, 'You wanted to run all the pass patterns.' 'No that's not true,' he told me. 'Ask the coach to look back. I wanted to make sure that I *didn't* run all the passes. I'm a second teamer behind Ken Burrough and I wanted to make doggone sure that he got to run some passes. I didn't want a workout where I ran nine of the twelve pass plays and he would have to play the whole game having worked on just three pass plays.'

"Now that was just the opposite of what the coach thought and if you knew Billy, you knew that is the kind of guy he is. Everyone who really doesn't know him would think just the opposite, that he really wanted to run all the passes. It was like the time at Dallas when he was supposed to have refused to go into a game because he thought his presence on the field would deprive a black player of an opportunity to play. In this case, he didn't want to do anything that would deprive Ken Burrough of a job. He's wild and he's a bit weird at times but he has a feeling for the other guy.

"That's why I say things work themselves out if you don't let them come to a head. It's why I didn't force the issue and continue the argument the instant it happened because it ultimately might have come down to a decision. In an instance like that, the coach has to be right and I would have told Billy, 'You're either going to have to play for us or I'm going to suspend you.' He was so mad I just knew that would have been the end result.

"I also wanted him to understand that we don't want any raised voices around our team, not in anger anyway. If he or anyone else has a question, they know they can come to me or to anyone on the staff to get a straight answer. The only time I want anyone mad around me is on Sunday afternoon and then we all can be mad together at the guys in the other jerseys."

Many around the NFL shook their heads when the Oilers scooped up many of the so-called problem children like Parks, Tody and Bubba Smith, Al Cowlings, Steve Kiner, Mike Montgomery, Morris Stroud, and Culp from other teams. Gillman brought many onto the team when he was head coach and some still are left for Phillips. Those who stayed, like the Smith brothers, Culp, Kiner, and Parks, all have played well and are not problems in the locker room or on the field. Nor did Phillips ever look on any of them as so-called "problem children" when they came or during their stay.

"I know that Tody and Bubba Smith were raised by Willie Ray Smith and I know he was tough on them," Bum says. "But he never insisted they say, 'yes sir and no sir,' He just insisted that they do what he told them."

According to Phillips, all it takes to deal with Tody Smith, who had stormy times with the Dallas Cowboys though a top draft pick, is to believe in him. Do that, treat him fairly, don't get upset when he flashes his hot temper, add some patience, and he'll play football to his capacity. If a person took personally everything Tody has said in anger, then it would be hard to get along with him. Bum says he understands this and knows that he does not mean the things he says. He found out once he got to know him.

"We're dealing with grown men, not ten- or twelve-year old kids," says Phillips. "They've already formed their habits of whether or not they will say, 'yes sir and no sir,' and some of them do. There are certain people I say it to because I've been trained that way. I don't think about it, I just do it. Some of those players are trained that way and they do, regardless of who they are talking to or if the person is older than them."

Phillips also knew Parks at San Diego where he had a reputation of being somewhat of an odd-ball. He wasn't, Phillips maintains. He was like many young players at that time, with different ideals than older persons. Bum has nothing against ideals or players who believe in them but he asks they recognize the times when they just are not workable. Sooner or later, he adds, everyone "has to join the establishment."

It is in the area of player relations where Phillips perhaps takes the most radical approach—or at least an approach some of his peers feel is most radical. He gets as close to his players as he can and never even considers where there might be a line of demarcation between player and coach. For one reason, he says he never had any reason to think about it. He wants the players to be willing to come to him in trouble just as he would be willing to go to them.

"If I have to tell a guy, 'Do it!' because I'm the head coach, then there is a little bit of doubt whether or not I am," he adds.

He can assume this stance because he says he never has had any trouble dealing with people during his years as a coach, on any level. Naturally, there were some people who didn't like him just as there were some he didn't like. But he never had any trouble getting along with his players. His rule: Treat them right.

"That's about as good as I can do and that must be good enough," Phillips says. "If that's not good enough, that's still all I can do."

Many coaches feel the toughest part of their job is to first get to know the 43 or so different personalities who work for them, then find a way of blending this diverse structure into as cohesive a unit as possible. No one ever has reached perfection and every coach lives or dies by his own methods.

Phillips's philosophy follows through in his relationships with the men who work in the locker room, from the players to club president Bud Adams, a man who supposedly is not easy to work for. Phillips hasn't had any problems and he waves off those who tell him of past situations. For example, he says, Adams never has interfered with any matters bordering on player personnel.

"He's a businessman, he's not supposed to know players," Phillips has said when this charge is raised.

Phillips gets along just as well with his players. Gillman must get partial credit for at least conceiving some of the ideas, such as the Thursday afternoon beer busts and dominoes tournament. Sid liked to get his players together and found this a good way for them to congregate and stay around and socialize a bit. The interaction meant defense players would get to know offensive players and offensive players would mingle and get to know those who did not play regularly. The end result: a stronger team togetherness fostered by a genuine liking for one another.

The idea of a beer bust should not be misconstrued into something resembling a good, old-fashioned fraternity party with kegs lined up against the wall and guys falling over each other. There is not enough beer to bother anyone, no more than a couple or three cans apiece and always there are soft drinks for those who do not prefer beer. The whole bash lasts about an hour or 75 minutes, though there is no time limit. These sessions usually dissolve of themselves because the players have to go home to their families.

"We have a lot of fun, a lot of laughs, and there is a lot of real, happy banter," Phillips says, laughing. "Our bunch is the cut-uppingest group you've ever seen. They are so funny and really get a kick out of each other. They ride each other and they ride us. We all get along good.

"Yet when we say, 'Let's go do something,' there's no problem. They get after it. When I first began coaching I used to think that I was up here and the player had to be down there, otherwise they would take advantage of you. That is, until I coached my own boy. There wasn't any doubt in his mind that I loved him but I never had any problem with him because he knew I loved him. He did what I told him to because I was his coach.

"From that day on in 1962, I quit worrying about whether a guy liked me. If he knew I liked him, I didn't care. And," he adds, "some people confuse respect with liking someone. Many coaches say, 'I'd rather have someone respect me than like me.' But I want to be liked. If they like me, they're going to respect me."

Through all of this, Phillips establishes a solid base of friendship in the locker room and success on the field. It was something Vince Lombardi established through totally different means than those used by Phillips but with the end result that he once described as "love for each other." That's a solid base for producing winning teams.

Again the edge for Phillips is that his players genuinely like this aura and enjoy playing for his team. He agrees that there can be a built-in fear within the soul of each player. Rule violations or haphazard play will force him to leave this happy environment. And all the Oilers have found there is what amounts to a "waiting list" of other NFL players who want to come to Houston because of what the Houston players themselves have said about their treatment—and their record.

Phillips had several World Football League refugees come to his team for tryouts when that league folded but he says he did not even work them out during the season because he did not want to disturb the roster he had assembled in training camp. In fact, only two players—wide receiver Elmo Wright and substitute punter David Beverly—were waived from the Oilers' roster from the 43 who started the 1975 season. Two more went off because of injuries and a fifth, linebacker Ralph Cindrich, was signed as a free agent after the season began, then later was released.

Phillips guards his squad very tightly once it has been formed. He says he "wouldn't sign the best football player in the world if it meant cutting our forty-third player. That's the way the team felt, that's how I felt, and I didn't care if it hairlipped everybody. That is how it will be each year, barring injury.

"We had those guys from the World Football League come by after it folded simply because our players sold them on our program. Our guys aren't afraid of competition, most pros aren't afraid of someone coming in and beating them out. They all think they're better than they are anyhow—all of us, coaches and players alike. That is how it was in the war. You always thought the other guy was going to get killed, not you. And you gotta believe that way, whether you're landing on some Pacific Island [he landed on five during World War II] or going into football training camp."

Phillips is not blinded by loyalty or friendship when it comes to making the selection process, regardless of his intention to stay with his final roster. He will cut a player only if he feels the man who replaces him is more important to the team. He cut running back Vic Washington before the 1975 season began, despite the fact that the team had given up a high draft pick for him the year before. Elmo Wright was waived after the season began. He told both players, "I hope I'm wrong for your sake," and both later played with other NFL teams. He wasn't necessarily wrong in cutting them because he kept the people he felt he could win with and the team's record proved he was correct.

Adams gave Phillips Gillman's dual role of general manager-head coach but Bum gave Tom Williams the day-to-day general manager's duties. Nor did Phillips, unlike his predecessor, sign—or even attempt to negotiate—any player contracts. He says he doesn't even want to know what a player is making and he doesn't care.

"I don't even want the player to tell me," he adds. "I want to be able to believe the same way in everyone who plays for me. I don't care if he's making twenty thousand dollars or one hundred thousand dollars. I expect the same thing from him. In coaching you've got to have mutual trust and understanding and you won't get it if you argue money, or if you begin to consider one player over another because of what he is paid."

He has achieved that end, all of his players agree. Dan Pastorini, who was inconsistent as a quarterback before Phillips began to simplify his offensive load, is totally sold on Bum's methods. That means a great deal because he is one of the team's leaders, on and off the field, and his reactions carry a great deal of weight when translated into positive action.

"He is the best coach I ever played for—high school, college, or in the NFL," says Pastorini. Before Phillips became his head coach, he had said that only about his coach at Santa Clara, Pat Malley. "Bum is the type of guy who will not lie to a player; he's straightforward, honest, and he does not demand a lot. He also is the kind of coach who will make you realize what is important and help you to think for yourself. He motivates you by making you realize your own potential. Bum's biggest thing is saying that if you were hanging off a cliff on a rope, you'd want to be sure you had a friend up there holding the other end. We've made that our slogan—'Hold onto the rope and don't let our people down.'"

Pastorini says he appreciates Phillips's own individuality in dealing with players. He will talk to a player when he feels like it, regardless of what is going on. He is not afraid to express his feelings; there are no pretenses. Nor does he forget the people who helped him get him where he is today. He is not modest about what he has done but neither is he conceited nor ungrateful.

Pastorini recalled an incident near the end of the 1975 season when Phillips called him into his office.

"I guess this was a year where we both kind of felt each other out," Bum told him. "You're a helluva guy and a helluva quarterback. I plan on being here a long time and you're going to be my quarterback as long as I am head coach."

"He surprised me," Pastorini admits, "but at the same time he also made me feel secure. He's a helluva guy to do something like that."

Don Hardeman, the Oilers' top rookie running back in 1975 and one of its two first-round draft picks, says that Phillips "shoots it straight from the hip. He's the kind of guy who is not afraid to tell you he doesn't know the answer to a question if he doesn't."

"He communicates with his players," says Elvin Bethea, a player who lived through some of the team's most tumultuous seasons. "He's always thinking of our comfort and welfare and he makes us want to play for him."

Fred Willis, another of the team's running backs who also played for Paul Brown at Cincinnati, said that Phillips was the first coach he ever had—in high school, college, or the pros—who was completely tuned into the thinking of the players. He treated them as mature individuals, Willis added, and dispelled the idea that there must be an almost antagonistic environment to build a successful team.

Skip Butler, the Oilers' placekicker and player representative, set up a grievance committee with himself as go-between for the players and coaching staff. He had only one complaint during the 1975 season, he says, and that was a player complaining that he had nothing to gripe about.

Phillips, for his part, would just as soon do away with any committees and doesn't believe in investing one or two players with a special mantle of leadership. For one thing, he says he has no special messages he wants carried back and forth. Anything he has to say, is said to everyone or to the man for whom it is intended, and in person. If the players have something to say, they don't hesitate to tell him in the same manner.

"I don't want it any other way," he says. "I'd rather a guy come to me if he doesn't like something and say, 'Coach, I wish we didn't do this.' If I don't want to change it, I'll tell him why."

Outside of the team captains, there are no specially designated team leaders on the Oilers. Phillips remembers handing out the ballots for selecting team captains prior to the 1975 season—a departure since they had been appointed in the past.

"Curley Culp was the first to get a ballot and I told him to vote for any two guys on defense to be captain," Bum recalls.

"Why?" Culp asked. "Are you going to count them?"

"Sure I'm going to count them," Phillips told him.

"Well," Culp replied, still unconvinced, "you're going to pick who you want."

"Curley," Phillips said with a hint of exasperation in his voice, "just put two names on the damn sheet and I'll count them. Whoever gets the most votes gets to be captains."

"He looked at me kinda funny and said, 'That's different.'" Phillips recalls. "Well, he was elected one of our two defensive captains. Zeke Moore was the other while Mack Alston and Pastorini were selected on offense because that's how the votes came in. If I was going to appoint them, I would have gone ahead and done it. I never would have asked someone to elect them and then decided on my own who would be captain.

"The point is, we don't need really to elect captains to find out who the leaders are. Curley was a good leader the previous season though he was not a captain at that time. We have a lot of guys who are leaders though they don't go around saying, 'Hey, I'm a leader.' Or they don't go around trying to act like one. They just lead because they do it."

There are many who express surprise at such warm and genuine relations between players and coaches, particularly after the firestorms that have swept the professional sports scene in the form of player strikes, walkouts, and pickets. Phillips does not see any radical changes in the players on his team now and the ones he first got to know back in 1966 at San Diego.

"In fact, their competitive instincts are the same now as they were the first year I began coaching in high school," he says. "They go about it differently because they are better players now than back in those years. The big change from my first year in professional football at San Diego is that players now are more conscious of their future once their careers are ended.

"The difference isn't the money," he insists. "The money—and this may sound funny but it's true because you must be in the dressing room with a guy to know—didn't mean a thing to those players after we lost to Cincinnati by two points early in the 1975 season. I'll promise you, there wasn't a single player in that locker room who wouldn't rather have won that game and given up all the money it might have meant to them.

"At least that's how they felt right then. Maybe the next day they felt differently but reward is a personal thing. Money is important just like it is to all of us but that day I felt the same way they did. I would have given all I owned to have won that ball game."

With outlooks of players and coaches so positive and directed toward a single objective, discipline isn't much of a problem.

By the end of the 1975 season Phillips had collected a total of $220 in fines, which amounted to about a half dozen broken rules by 43 players over 22 weeks.

"What good does it do to fine a guy two thousand dollars for staying out?" says Phillips. "The object is to get him where he won't be out at all. Maybe the threat of a two-thousand dollar fine would prevent it from starting but after you've been around for a year or two then you shouldn't have to fine them. If you must holler or threaten after that much time, then you're in trouble.

"Now if a guy is screwing up, I'll come down on him. But I'll tell him like I would in any other way. I don't believe in threatening people because I don't like to get threatened. I'd much rather have someone tell me what they want me to do and if I don't, then fire me. I just don't believe in hollering or arguing or getting cancer of the throat bitching about something."

Late in the 1975 season, Bethea and Culp were late for a morning meeting, the first time it had happened all season. Phillips didn't say anything to them because he felt they didn't miss anything "I couldn't have told them in ten seconds." After the meeting Bethea came up to him.

"Coach," he said, "I have to tell you something."

"What is it, Elvin?" Phillips replied.

"Coach, I can't lie to you. You have been awful good to me and I was just late. I didn't have any reason," the giant defensive lineman said.

That was the end of it.

After a preseason game in New Orleans, Pastorini and Willis received permission to stay over with the proviso they be back in training camp when everyone else was due to check in. They agreed but the next day they missed the flight home.

"We didn't miss any meetings," Pastorini remembers, "but we felt like a couple of heels because he gave us permission to do something and we let him down. He fined us about fifty dollars apiece but what hurt was our letting him down."

That, Pastorini adds, is how he gets to people—his making a player feel that if a rule is broken the team suffers. He tells his players they should be able to take care of themselves after the age of 21 and he wants to reflect his belief in them by not being a slave driver or by fining indiscriminately.

"He puts you right on the spot from the day camp opens," says Pastorini. "You know that if you do something against the rules you have put yourself ahead of the team and no one likes to be thought of as selfish. Particularly, not after he has established such a great rapport with you and everyone else is working to stay within the rules."

Phillips is most understanding of the ordinary foibles that are found in any football player. He agrees that if someone comes in late to a meeting or misses one altogether, some punitive action must be taken. But if a guy makes a mistake because he couldn't help it he will not penalize the player. Those things fall within the realm of human nature and he tries not to let them upset him.

"But," he adds with a rare ominous tone in his voice, "if I thought a guy was dumping on me, there's no telling what I'd do. I'd be bad, though; I mean really bad. I wouldn't start half way. I'd suspend him, at least. If a guy is going to try to do something bad that will hurt the team, I'm just not going to allow him to do it. That's the difference—a guy deliberately trying to hurt the team versus one who makes an unintentional mistake."

His ideas on discipline spin right off his approach to motivation, which really isn't much of an approach at all because he never has seen it as something that must occupy a certain amount of time in his day's work. All Phillips asks of his players is that they get better every day. He sells them, as he puts it, "on the facts of life . . . that we have the same number of players as everyone else and have an hour and thirty minutes each day to prepare on the field as does everyone else.

"Motivating during the week means they can motivate themselves on the weekend. And it will happen if you don't take it out of them during that practice week by playing or practicing them to death."

He does not spend a great deal of time trying to come up with different ways to motivate his players. He can get certain ones fired up during practice very easily. He does this particularly if a practice session is dragging. He'll simply say to a couple of players, "Practice is dragging. We need some help." They spread the word and soon the drills are going at a good tempo.

"I'd rather have preparation than motivation," he says. "The only way they won't be motivated to play the game is if you have taken it out of them on the field. Everyone likes to play and no one likes to practice. Elvin Bethea told me after the 1975 season, 'I'll play for ten more years. My legs felt better than in any previous season.' Well, he used to have to work two-and-a-half or three hours in training camp twice a day, plus all the practice and playing during the season so there was no way his legs could hold up under that."

Phillips vividly remembers Gillman's last training camp in 1974. The Oilers reported four weeks before their first preseason game and stayed with two-a-day workouts for 43 days—until the preseason schedule was near the halfway mark. Not only that, the club—because of the player's strike—also underwent three four-a-day workouts in that span. The coaches were on the field at 8 A.M. and, except for time off for lunch, did not come off until 6:30 in the evening as the 135-man roster went through its paces.

In contrast, Phillips worked his team just two weeks prior to its first preseason game in 1975, with a week of "double-days," plus two days the following week. After that, the team followed the same workout schedule as it did during the season.

"With two weeks of practice, then six weeks of games, you have eight weeks to get ready for the regular season," he maintains. "If that isn't enough time, either your coaching staff can't coach or your players can't play."

On-the-field workouts, while important, do not have overriding priority in his training camps. The main thing he tries to accomplish is to get the players to know each other, a deficiency he ranked number one with past Oilers' teams. Outsiders think players all know each other because they play together, meet together, practice together, and sleep in the same dorm during this period. But often a player will have four or five friends he runs with, and with all of the programmed routines of camp, it is difficult to really get to know other players on their own team.

"A player could play for me—for money, for pride, whatever—but he also will play for the team because he doesn't want to let his buddy down," says Phillips. "We want that buddy system spread throughout all forty-three players, that a guy with eight years' experience will play so he won't let down a rookie he just met that summer, and vice versa."

To help achieve this objective, Phillips established a curfew when the players had to be in their dorms but not in bed with lights out. Late in the evening everyone would be in, and then they would order pizzas and hamburgers. Sitting around together forced them to know each other better. None were ready to go to sleep so they were thrown into a social situation where some sort of interchange took place. The net result was that Phillips got the offensive players having a feeling for the defense and the defense establishing feelings for the offense.

"We got our football work done, you do that anyhow," Bum says. "But it's just as important to be rubbing shoulders with guys who you are counting on. If you know a man better, you like him. And football players play harder if they like their team-mates. They try harder not to disappoint each other. I always felt that you could put a football player to bed but you couldn't make him sleep unless he wanted to. My job is to convince them this way is worthwhile. If he goes out at night it's my fault because I wasn't very persuasive."

But few, if any, did. When the players saw they weren't going to have a bed check they put in their own and said they would turn in any violators. None appeared, mostly because he had told them beforehand they were in an entirely different situation and could go two ways with it. They could be men enough to do their own self-disciplining or they could undergo a lot of criticism because this method didn't work. Phillips ran some checks—as he told them he would—but never on a regular basis and he never found any violators.

His approach to football work is just as different, with the shorter time in camp and the modest amount of time on the field. No workout was longer than one hour and thirty-one minutes.

Some people criticized Phillips for not running a full-scale scrimmage but he never has believed in putting his own offensive unit against the defense. "We don't have Houston on our schedule so there is no point in playing Houston," he says simply. "When you do have one of those intrasquad scrimmages, someone is going away with the feeling that they didn't do too good. You don't want them to lose confidence. We try to get our tests of a player's abilities in one-on-one drills. I don't think you need test a guy's courage. You can find out after just a little bit whether he has enough courage to play. Why force him to prove it every day?

"You also can get much more taught that way. And you don't suffer the injuries. If a guy knows he's going to be on the field only a certain amount of time and knows what you are telling him is important, you get more out of him. We started with the idea that we are not going on the football field unless we have something to do.

"Short practices also are important. You might help one or two staying out longer, but those two probably won't start for you anyhow. So you'll hurt a lot more than you'll help. It's best to get the ones who will play for you totally prepared and off the field. You should gear everything to the guys who will play instead of the ones who are not going to play, even if you keep them out there two and a half hours.

"There are a whole lot of people who did it the other way. If you don't win you're wrong. New Orleans, for example, scrimmaged every day and look what happened to them. Our first scrimmage was against them in the Superdome and we beat them. But if we do lose, it won't be because of the system. It will be because of our method of teaching. If you feel you can get more taught scrimmaging every day, then obviously that's the way to do it. But your job is to teach something.

"I would never say there would not be a time when I felt a team needed scrimmage work. If they did, I wouldn't hesitate to do it but it would be done only on that basis—not because everyone else does it that way."

Phillips takes the same ordered approach in programming playing time in preseason games. He feels a coach who brings a player to training camp is obligated to give him a chance—a chance to do something, even if the player does not last until the first preseason game. He wants any player who is cut to be able to say, "I had my chance." And if a player stays long enough to practice for a game, then Bum says a coach just has to play him.

There were instances when he knew he would cut a player, regardless of whether he played in a game or not. But he made sure the man played so he would know, too, and so would his teammates. He thinks the latter is a valid factor because then everyone knows who the best players are. Not players at the same position necessarily but, for example, the backs would know who the best linemen are, who should be cut, and who should not.

"I think it's important for team morale," Phillips emphasizes, "because everyone should feel that our final squad is the best group we can assemble. The players will know because they saw for themselves in the films after each preseason game. That way, there is no reason for everyone not to know what the other guy is doing."

Cutting those who did not make it became the hardest part of Phillips's job as a head coach in pro football. Before his first season ended, he desperately wished there was a way he could avoid it but he knew it just wasn't so. He had watched Gillman delegate that responsibility because he was so occupied with every phase of the team's play he just didn't have enough time. Those with the team said that Sid was interested only in the players who would stay, and he didn't care about the guy who couldn't.

"I think the player deserves the right to be told by the head coach," says Phillips. "There probably are a lot more who don't do it than who do and if I could find a way to get out of it and still keep my conscience clear, I probably wouldn't do it. It's particularly hard if a kid stays with you four or five weeks, goes through everything and does all you ask of him. By God, the least you can do is to tell him.

"And they are going to want to know why. The Turk can't tell them why. Whether or not they agree with it, you owe it to tell them why one guy was kept over them. The head coach is the only one who can tell them that. Some may not agree with your reasoning and say, 'I think you're wrong, coach.' I say, 'I hope you're right.' As I told both Elmo Wright and Vic Washington when I had to cut them, 'Nothing would please me more than for you to prove me wrong because it would do two things. One, that gets you back into football where you ought to be. And secondly, I wouldn't mind being proven wrong if you came out good.'

"When you have to cut a player, it's not necessarily that he can't play, it's just that he may not be able to play for you. You're telling him, 'I've got someone I think is better for the team; who can do more to help the team win. It's not that you can't run fast enough or are not a good enough running back. We have someone here who I think can do more things.'"

Phillips says there is a vast difference doing something like this in the pros as opposed to college. A college coach can tell a boy who has tried out for a team he will not get a scholarship but the boy still can find work to pay his way. In the pros, when a player is cut, "you are cutting him, his family, his kids, his bills. You are putting him out of work and he usually doesn't have something he can go to. That makes it harder, particularly if it is a guy who has been in the league for a few years."

Phillips gets visibly distraught just talking about such things. Perhaps the toughest cut he had to make in his first season with Houston was defensive back Mike Simpson, who had played for him in high school and at the University of Houston. Simpson played on the same high school team with his son, Wade, and was a close family and personal friend.

"It was like cutting my own boy," Phillips says, "but he took it a lot better than I did. He consoled *me*."

Before such decisions are made, there is the grading process and Phillips does that a bit differently, too. He calls it "grading by eye-sight," because there are so many things a coach can judge during five days of practice sessions each week. He remembers the Oilers almost cut defensive back C. L. Whittington before the 1974 season because he wasn't as fast as some of the other players. But Whittington turned out to be a superb special teams player that season and was even better in every role asked of him in 1975.

"If you time him and live by what that stopwatch says," Phillips notes, "you've always got that in the back of your mind. Yet when he is in the game, he always seems to outrun all of those guys who beat him in the forty-yard dashes in practice."

He uses the same "team approach" in allowing a starter from the previous season to defend his job. Anyone who comes onto the club at that position must prove himself better in practice and in the game. Carl Mauch had been regarded as an outstanding center at San Diego but when he came to the Oilers he had to line up behind incumbent Fred Hoaglin. Mauch eventually won the job "but he won it the way he wanted to, not by just having it handed to him.

"You could look at a rookie like Don Hardeman," Phillips says, "and see he was going to be a great running back. You can take that greatness for granted and start him the first day in camp. But that's no way to run a stable team. What would the people who played that position last year think? I have to be concerned about that because they will be making contributions for us, even if they don't start. It goes right back to keeping faith with them and they'll keep faith with you."

Phillips applies the same philosophy in working with his assistant coaches. They do the bulk of the planning for an upcoming game, each looking at their specific area so that Phillips has an accumulation of some 80 hours of work in each area of play. He then sits in on the pasteurizing process that is necessary so that each coach knows what the other is doing.

The whole process begins in February with an analysis of opponents for the upcoming season. Then during the summer, a game plan is built for each one, and when it comes time to play that team the plan is brought out and updated from its recent performances.

"It's a great time-saver during the season," he agrees. "Time is one of the two things you fight in football—time and the scoreboard. We don't make too many changes from the plan we originally draw up because your opponent will do the same things year-in, year-out that have been successful for him. If he's not successful, many times you must make a complete change; or there may be partial changes because of some new thinking on his staff. The good teams don't change a lot."

In the past few years, the other teams found themselves with more preparation problems facing the Oilers than did Houston facing them. One reason was Phillips's total immersion in his 3-4 defense, one not yet accepted by every NFL team. If a team faces it just once or twice a season for an entire game, then the preparation efforts become difficult because players somehow must acclimate themselves to playing against people who aren't where they normally should be.

In the 3-4, there are three down linemen backed by four linebackers and four defensive backs. The key, Phillips says, are the two linebackers in the middle and he prefers to call it a 3-2 defense. The two middle linebackers give more and quicker pursuit than one, as in the 4-3 defense. On pass coverage, the three-man rush enables eight defenders to cover instead of seven in the 4-3.

"Everyone who plays four linemen ends up in an overshift or undershift," says Phillips, "and that makes the same alignment we're playing to start with. No one hardly plays a straight four-three. Almost everyone has the odd-man front. Besides, it's not how many hands you have on the ground when the ball is snapped, it's how many you can get to where the ball is by the time the ball gets there.

"You can do more with the three-four than any other defense. It's the best run defense there is. They say you can't rush the passer but we finished third in 1974 in sacks and fourth in 1975. You get a lot more pursuit out of it and can do a lot more stunting with it. You have more variations in coverages.

"Besides, it's a lot easier in pro ball to find three linemen and four linebackers than it is to find four linemen and three linebackers. One of those linemen generally isn't as good as that missing linebacker. So it comes to adapting to the people you have and that's where the fundamental background of coaching should begin. That's where you can learn to innovate things to fit your people. It's not what *you* can do; it's what you can get those players to do. You can't ask them to do something they're not capable of doing."

He has played more 4-3 defense in his time than 3-4 but he has seen the latter used with success at Oklahoma and at Texas A&M. He used it in high school and tried it at San Diego when he found he had more good linebackers than defensive linemen. Gillman wasn't sold on it and eventually the Chargers went back to the 4-3 without good results.

"I told Sid before I came to Houston that I wouldn't take the defensive coordinator's job unless he allowed me to put in the three-four," Phillips says. "He told me I could use whatever I wanted. All I believe in is getting the best eleven players on the field. I don't really care what we have to play. I coached the four-three four times as long as I coached the three-four but you still must play with your best eleven players regardless of what you use.

"To me, the logic of what the defense can do makes it worthwhile. It makes more sense, for example, to defend against the pass with eight people than with seven. In a four-man pass rush, you lose one of those people. As for defending against the run, it's just about as easy as with the four-man front because you rush one of your linebackers. It baffles the quarterback because you can get so much more variation with eight people behind the down linemen. Quarterbacks also are used to seeing a middle linebacker and reading their keys off him. With two middle linebackers, their keys are harder to pick up and the pass protection messes up."

He points to the problem of pass protection. With a tackle playing over the nose of the center, the center has problems immediately. Once he snaps the ball, he must raise his shoulders and get into his pass blocking stance. By that time, Phillips claims, the nose-man is past him. Thus three people—the center and two guards—are tied up looking to protect the middle against one man's pass rush. Add a blitzing linebacker through that area, and the problems multiply.

When Culp first was asked to adopt to it, he didn't like it and along with Bubba and Tody Smith and Bethea preferred the four-man line. Generally, it's man-for-man in the four-man front but Culp didn't like the double- and triple-teaming that takes place in the Oilers' defense. Once the Oilers began winning, however, there were no problems.

"If we were winning with a two-man front, I'd like that too," Culp says.

It pleases Phillips to see other teams going to the 3-4, if only in situation defenses such as second or third down and obvious passing situations coming up. The NFC champion Cowboys did it in 1975 with great success, utilizing top draft pick Randy White as a blitzing linebacker or end because of his great quickness. Cowboys' coach Tom Landry, who perfected the 4-3 defense, sees the 3-4 as a very workable alignment.

Despite his concentration on defense in the past, Phillips spent more time with the Oilers' offense in his first season as head coach than he normally would have because he wanted to find out more about his personnel. Actually, he always thought himself a better offensive coach and went to Texas A&M in that capacity. His college background at Stephen F. Austin also was on offense, as it was in high school.

"Funny thing," he says, chuckling, "but I spent all my time on offense before I got to A&M. But when I left there I was supposed to be a helluva defensive coach."

His offensive approach is built on a basic: to take what the defense will give him. He also likes to repeat plays that work well. Gillman wanted to score on every play and often Phillips would go into a meeting, put up a pass play and say, "Coach, that's a helluva play." Gillman would look at it and say, "Hell, anyone can drum up a pass play for a first down."

"The way I look at it," Phillips says, "is that enough first downs get you right down into that end zone. Sid had such great belief in man-for-man football and if you used that defense, he'd kill you. That's because he wanted to score on every play. But if you put up a zone against him, then you'd kill him. It seems every time we'd get the ball on the fifteen-yard line, we'd put the ball in the air for four plays. That's one reason why we had such a bad running attack."

One of the Oilers' priorities in their first preseason schedule under Phillips was to improve the running game. In each game, the offense would get a certain number of runs and they would concentrate on those until the coaching staff got an idea of exactly why that phase of the game was not functioning. There was no heed paid to the score. The same thing happened with the passing game so that when the season opened, there was more offensive balance than ever before.

"You can find a lot of things to work in the preseason," says Phillips, "but in the regular season when that other team is ready, you can't go around grab-bagging. You've got to develop something. We finally had a pretty good rushing attack to go with our overall offense. The good football teams are the ones who can run the football; who can advance it and use the clock because that's just that much more time the other club has to play defense."

Phillips is not bland in his offensive approach. During the 1975 season, Houston had a play it called "Bumerooski," one that he conceived during his first seasons at Nederland High School and used at Texas A&M. He originally had called it "fake punt right" or "fake punt left" but Bryant dressed it up a bit and called it "Bumerooski." In a game against Pittsburgh that season, with Pastorini out of action with an injury, the Steelers had the Oilers third-and-22 on Houston's 19-yard line.

Pastorini also was the team's punter so when Phillips sent him back into the game, without the regular punting unit and ordered him to take the snap from a modified punt formation, the Steelers' defense didn't quite know how to react. Feeling he would pass rather than punt, they did not drop back and Dan booted the ball 68 yards to Pittsburgh's 13-yard line.

"We were thinking kick," Phillips recalls, "but if they had dropped one or two safeties downfield, then we would have audibilized to a pass. We have a whole series of routes to run from that formation and with Dan as a kicker we also can throw from it."

Even with the improvement by Houston's offense, Phillips feels that an offense must concentrate as much on beating the opposition as not beating itself. He found his team improved in this respect in his first season but there were times when he had to inject himself quite strongly to see that it happened.

In a 20-19 Houston victory over Miami, the Oilers had the ball with 1:40 to play. Pastorini came to the sideline on second down and said he felt a play-action pass would go.

"I know we can do that," Phillips told him. "But we ain't. We're going to run two downs, then punt and let them try and come back at us the length of the field. We've got the game won and the only way we can lose it is to give it to them."

"And that's what we did," he says. "I'm not interested in how many yards we make. I'm interested in winning the game. I have to get my quarterbacks thinking that way all the time."

This idea strikes a responsive chord—as all of Phillips's ideas seem to do with his unflappable logic—because the players work only on those things that will help them to win.

Phillips plans his time carefully. He says his team probably works less time than do most others in the NFL, and that includes the coaches. Phillips has disciplined himself to do all of his work within the 12 or so hours he allots to football every day. That cuts down on idle bull sessions, long and often fruitless discussions, and being tempted to try to overachieve. A radical departure is the entire staff being home on Monday night— often the busiest night of the week in other NFL coaching offices—by 7:30 so that all can watch the Monday night NFL game. That is not a mandatory assignment but because football is their profession and they are interested, they all watch.

The coaches never work later than 9 or 9:30 in the evening, again a radical departure from many NFL staffs, which often work past midnight. Since the staff already has built a game plan prior to the season, much of the detail work is eliminated. In fact, the work load on Thursday and Friday off the field generally is concerned with polishing up a plan for the following week's opponent.

"We put everything together on Tuesday, practice it on Wednesday, eliminate the part that won't go or that we won't get to and have everything polished by Friday's practice," Phillips says.

He tells his players that the quicker they get things done correctly, the quicker their practice day will be over. The result, Pastorini says, is the players shun any thoughts of simply going through the motions but put forth a totally concentrated effort.

"How can you argue with that man's ideas?" says Pastorini. "He puts it to us so we can understand it and appreciate it. When a guy says he wants to get off the practice field as badly as we do and go have his fun just as much as we want to go have ours, then you know where you stand. He doesn't slough off things, either. He knows, and we know, that when he finally sends us in everything is as it should be."

Bum admits he's about as crazy for practice as his players, "which means I don't like it either. I'd rather coach seven games a week than one. But you have to practice so it must be done the way all of us can get the most from it, and that even means enjoying it as best we can. At every level, that gets harder. You can take a high school sophomore out and practice him three times a day and he'll love it. You can't work that much with a college sophomore and it's even harder in the pros. Hell, if you started working them that hard they'd start asking questions; they wouldn't be any kind of men if they didn't."

The players' response at Houston is just as you'd expect under such humane conditions. So was the injury list, perhaps the lowest among all 26 teams when the 1975 season ended. He does not fully ascribe his team's excellent health to diminished practice time but points out that "if a team practices five days a week on the field and plays another day, then it has more of a chance of hurting itself than the opponents do.

"It's not that you can get badly hurt in practice," he adds, "but you can get a player bruised just a little bit and that causes him to get hurt worse in a game. My object is to get them to where they will be ready to play the ball game and be as healthy when it began as when it ended. That goes back to something I remembered Bryant saying, 'I'd rather have a guy ready to play the game, not have worked out a day, and have him in super condition so he can play on pride.' Conditioning is important but sometimes we coaches overstress it.

"There is a belief that if a team is not in super condition it will let down in the fourth quarter. We played Washington in the Astrodome after not having run thirty wind sprints all season long, but our defense never came out of the game. There was not a single substitution in that game on defense but they were stronger in the fourth quarter than they were in the first.

"Knowing George Allen, I'll bet a day doesn't go by when they don't run twelve striders after practicing two-and-a-half hours on the field. So conditioning is in the head and in the heart, not all in the legs. It's how you think you're going to do, whether you're in the game or not. If you're in the game, you won't let down or get tired nearly as much. But if you're dead mentally you're going to be dead physically."

Phillips's game plans are uncomplicated. His offense consists of plays he feels will work best against the defensive tendencies of an opponent in certain situations. His rule of thumb is that he doesn't change what he does best and, he reasons, neither will the opposition. So you prepare for a team knowing basically what to expect.

Phillips admits he does not like to play against teams that concentrate their offense at one major point of attack. He recalls breaking down a Denver Broncos' film several years ago when Lou Saban was coach.

"I saw him run to one place over and over against the Chiefs, seventeen straight plays to the left of their defense," Bum recalls. "He scored, got the ball back and then ran eleven straight plays to the same hole of the other side, and scored again. Denver did not call one sweep or one pass; their backs just kept breaking inside the hole, outside the hole or into it. Miami is the same way. The Dolphins just hammer and hammer at you. They won't vary a lot, just keep coming at certain people you have on defense until they get what they're after."

Pastorini believes Phillips subscribes to that theory because he preaches execution. He must, because his game plans are uncluttered. "He does not try to do a lot of things in a game," Pastorini maintains. "He said if we have only one play we would run it in practice until it was right, then go into the game and do it the same way. He is a great believer in execution, mostly because we do not have long game plans. He wants things short, simple, but always with a different look."

This basic approach carries into the locker room on the day of a game. Throughout the week he has told his team that it wastes a day if it does not learn something from practice. On Sunday, he tells the players to go out and apply that learning—it's that simple.

"It is, too," says Phillips. "If we have been practicing terrible then we'll play terrible. We always go out and play like we practice."

His pregame exhortations are usually dispassionate. There was one exception to that in 1975 and Phillips feels it cost his team a game.

"That was our Monday night game against Pittsburgh in 1975," he says. "We really didn't think the Steelers were as good as we were. I was convinced and always will be convinced that we were better. We felt we lost the first time that season in Pittsburgh simply because we didn't play well. So I told them during the practices for that second game, 'I don't want to beat 'em. I want to kill 'em.' And all week long we practiced like that.

"And we did kill 'em—and lost the damn game. It wasn't until I looked at the film that I saw that I had gotten everyone so damn fired up we forgot our basic techniques. We charged like we never charged before on defense, completely ignoring the guy in front of us and that's poor technique. You must control a guy and do something with him. We didn't do that, we were going to kill him. We played out of control and it was my fault.

"In all honesty, that night Pittsburgh would have beaten us but it would have been something like thirteen to seven, not the runaway [32-9] that it turned out to be. They were a better team that night but we made 'em look a helluva lot better."

Phillips is careful to control his emotions on the sidelines, too. One of the truly expressive scenes in his first season came following the end of the Oilers' last-play victory over Oakland. NFL films caught Phillips leaving the bench, visibly heaving a sigh of joy and relief, and lifting his cowboy hat to wipe his brow. It was as expressive as he had been throughout that exciting game.

"Show me an emotional coach on the sidelines," he says, "and I'll show you a team that will mirror everything he does. That means, the players will be emotional if he is, they'll holler at the officials when he does. I want my players as consistent in their emotions as they are in their play. I also want them showing the same consideration to the officials that I do.

"Oh, I want an emotional team but who can tell what emotion is? You watch one team come out on the field before the kickoff, jump all over each other and then see the other team come out and do the same thing. But the first team gets beaten forty to nothing. The alumni and the fans say, 'Boy, that second team really was ready to play today.' But they forget the other team looked the same way. Emotion is not something you can put your finger on. If you run down under the kickoff and you still don't feel a desire to play, then all the hollering in the world isn't going to make much difference."

Phillips believes losing can teach powerful lessons. A loss to the Cincinnati Bengals in the first meeting between the two teams in 1975 is a good example. The Oilers trailed 21-17 late in the game, had a first down on the 1-yard line and didn't score. They lost 21-19. Phillips told his players afterward that they might have won more than they lost in the game because they learned that no losing game ever boils down to one particular play. As he likes to say, "there were a million things that could have changed the outcome if we had done them differently. But if you can say a loss helps a team, then you can say that game helped make a mature team of the Oilers. It made them realize, 'Boy, you gotta do something extra in the clutch. You just can't do the same old thing.' At the end of the season, I looked back on that game and I truly felt that had we not lost to the Bengals the way we did, then I don't think we would have beaten either Miami or Oakland under the same set of circumstances."

His victory celebrations are directed toward his family. Two of his daughters are cheerleaders for the Oilers and his wife is as emotionally involved in his work. That is why he spends his glad times with his family; they mean more to him than any partying. His idea of a good time after a winning game is to send out for some fried chicken, crack open a couple of cans of beer, and talk over the game with his family, including two son-in-laws who are high school football coaches near Houston.

Though he may have tried to downplay his emotions, his players say they could see the rising tide of excitement as the Oilers stayed in contention through most of the 1975 season.

"We never gave up in one game during the season, which was different from the Oilers of the past," Pastorini says. "He was just amazed that we never quit. He said it made him prouder than anything else we had done. In fact he told me that if we had lost all our games, he would have been disappointed in losing but grateful for the kind of effort we gave him every week. We played our hearts out because we loved him."

No coach could ask for more.

John Ralston

"I'm a self-improvement nut. I think
people want to get better so I explore
every avenue. You grow or you go."

The scene has been a familiar one on television the last few years. There's John Ralston, in the middle of the playing field with his kicking team, leaning into the huddle, moving around, getting that final hand clasp before the game begins. It seems . . . well, it seems out of character for a head coach. Head coaches don't get *that* involved . . . do they?

In the first place, you have to understand that Ralston does not consider himself a coach so much as a manager. He readily admits he delegates the authority to his assistants for putting Xs and Os in their proper place, before and during a game. He becomes the orchestrator, the man who approves the plans, organizes the practices, supervises the work, and, on game days, becomes the chief cheerleader around the bench with ancillary duties of telling the team when to kick, keeping track of scoring combinations, approving key substitutions, making final decisions on penalties, and coordinating halftime strategy changes.

He is an admitted "self-improvement nut" and utilizes the motivational approaches espoused by the Dale Carnegie Institute (he's an accredited instructor), American Motivation Institute (AMI), and the Success Motivation Institute (SMI). In other words, he preaches the power of positive thinking. There is no more positive thinker in the National Football League than John Ralston. He told the Broncos they would go to the next Super Bowl when he became head coach in 1972, and he told them the same thing in 1973, 1974, and 1975. He will tell them every season until, as he says, "it inevitably happens."

Football is Ralston's life but it is not his obsession. He agrees that it has limited appeal for some youngsters. His own son, whom Ralston wishes were a player, broke into tears after his freshman year in high school and told his father, "I just don't like to play football." Ralston said that's when he began to realize that the game wasn't for everyone.

"To each his own," he says. "There are many other great lessons you can learn in other ways. Yet I've always been a great believer in the ability to work in an emotional atmosphere and in the physical contact of football. Some thrive on it, others can be spectators, and still others don't give a damn for two seconds about it."

He does not subscribe to what he terms the "authoritarian" method of coaching because he's never considered himself authoritarian. His methods always have been successful on every level so he's satisfied that his ways are best. Ralston is a master of the soft-sell, though don't ever say "soft-sell" to any of his players who have just made mental errors.

Ralston is truly unique among coaches. He tells you that as a football coach, he's never really considered himself working a day in his life, that he literally runs to work each morning. He is rather self-effacing in playing down his role in the success of his teams; he never criticizes a player in public and he takes full responsibility for anything that goes wrong, whether or not it was his doing; and he has a wide range of phrases and sayings that pop up in conversation, interviews, or books and articles he's written.

He uses terms such as "comfort zone," "positive expectancy," and descriptive phrases such as "vividly imagine". . ."ardently desire". . ."sincerely believe in". . . and "enthusiastically act upon." Yet with all of these, he also had a mini-rebellion on his hands in his first Broncos' training camp because he worked his players so hard. One player did rebel openly, team cocaptain Dave Costa, and Ralston traded him without hesitation.

He readily admits going home with his family after losing games in Denver, replaying the low points and, before the discussion is finished, engaging in a full-scale weeping session. If he loses on the road, he'll cry, if he feels he must, right in the locker room. Conversely, his exultations are just as high as his depressions are low. But both are momentary.

There are many things about Ralston that make him different from his fellow NFL coaches, but he also has the same basic qualities found in the most successful. The marked distinctions are his approach to the game and the fact that he came to the NFL directly from a head coaching position in college football. In the latter regard, he was among the vanguard of six college coaches who came into professional football in the early 1970s; Bill Peterson, Dan Devine, Tommy Prothro, Chuck Fairbanks, and Don Coryell were the others.

His success in making the transition reflects the flexibility with which he approaches his job. Unlike Devine, for example, he did not come to the pros determined to prove—or die trying to prove—that college coaches were better. Unlike Peterson, he brought a straight-ahead approach (in fact, he got the job at Denver when Peterson, The Broncos' first choice, had to renege because of a prior commitment in Houston) and, unlike Prothro, he adjusted his ways to his players rather than declaring they would have to adjust to him.

He still preaches his theories on motivation, still tells his players that football "is a game and should be fun" and hires talented assistants to put the technical aspects of the game into execution. It is a practice he has followed since his first high school coaching assignments in northern California in the early fifties and which was refined and perfected during winning seasons as head coach at Utah State and Stanford. His former college players say he has changed little in these fundamental outlooks.

This thread of continuity that runs through his professional life began, he says, when he was 11 years old and living in Norway, Michigan, a rural community in that state's upper peninsula. A man named Allan Ronberg lived "a nine-iron shot" from the Ralston house and was the high school coach. Young John, who was called "Jackie" then, used to watch the coach walk to school every day ("he never owned a car through his entire life," Ralston says) and became enthralled with watching him work with the school's teams.

Ralston's former friends and neighbors in Norway say he was a very talented and naturally gifted athlete. The boy skied, but just casually; he ice skated like everyone, but only for exercise and only occasionally. Young Ralston excelled in football and the other team sports, where interaction is important.

More than anything, he looked up to Ronberg and the esteem generated by him in the eyes of that small Michigan community. Everyone in town called him the "Old Grey Fox," and he was the school's coach for 33 years.

In contrast, Ralston has moved often, but his moves have been with a purpose, always upward and, so far, always successful. He was a self-described "nondescript" linebacker on California's Pacific Coast Conference championship teams in 1950 and 1951 "who was lucky to get into a game." But he was fortunate to have Lynn (Pappy) Waldorf as his head coach. His learning process began on those practice fields, continued for one spring football session, and, after five years as a high school coach, continued for another two years as an assistant coach at Cal under Pete Elliott.

Of the three men he worked for—Ronberg, Waldorf, and Elliott—Ralston found Waldorf's style most attractive. "Our personalities are more similar," he says. "Ronberg was a volatile type of guy; he'd explode and rant and rave. Lynn was an even-tempered man and my coaching roots had taken hold in that direction when I came back to Cal to work under Pete Elliott. I still tend to coach like Waldorf in the manner of approaching players and dealing with them on and off the field."

Ralston had an impressive record as a head coach in college football.

His Utah State teams were solid, leading the nation's major colleges in both rushing offense and in scoring in 1960 and rushing defense in 1961. In four seasons, his teams twice were cochampions of the Skyline Conference and bowl participants. He produced such players as Merlin Olsen, Lionel Aldridge, and Clark Miller, all rugged defensive linemen who later were exceptional professional players.

Ralston went to Stanford in 1963 and, after one losing season, ran off eight straight winning years, capped by back-to-back Pacific 8 championships and Rose Bowl victories his final two seasons.

In college, Ralston has the reputation for using sophisticated, pro-type offenses and defenses. He disdained the run-oriented offenses and often would throw on first down or run on third down. He helped develop quarterback Jim Plunkett at Stanford, a Heisman trophy winner and the top selection in 1971 NFL draft. When Plunkett left Stanford, he was college football's all-time passing leader.

A measure of Ralston's work was seen in the January 1, 1972 Rose Bowl. Stanford and Michigan battled to a 10-10 standoff until three minutes remained to play. Then the Wolverines were awarded a safety for a 12-10 lead. Stanford stopped Michigan after the ensuing free kick and came back as Rod Garcia kicked the winning field goal with only 12 seconds left to play.

Denver owner Gerald Phipps already had contacted Ralston about becoming his team's head coach and admitted, after watching the last-minute poise and execution displayed by Stanford, that he was certain he had the man he sought. If there were any doubts, Ralston eased them later at a breakfast meeting. Ralston's power of positive thinking concepts so enthralled the Broncos' owners that they gave only a cursory hearing to Don Coryell, their other candidate.

Ralston got the idea of becoming a professional coach after his first Rose Bowl victory in 1971, over Ohio State.

"I've always been one to build on things and set goals," he says. "After that game I said to myself, 'Well, now what are we going to do?' Then Tommy Prothro and Dan Devine went into the NFL. It seemed to be a natural career progression.

"I had reached a crossroads after sixteen years of coaching. I had been a head coach most of that time and I enjoyed the recruiting but it was either stay as a head coach or go into athletic administration. I wanted to stay in the arena, so never thought in terms of leaving coaching.

"I also had the feeling that you can coach longer in pro football as compared to college football. That means pure coaching, working with people, getting the job done on a day-by-day, hour-by-hour basis. The tough part of college coaching is relating to young people, not the recruiting, which is nothing more than getting on that road and staying there [his wife Patty estimates he was away from home nearly 85 percent of the time as a college coach].

"A guy can run out of gas after awhile so I began to consider pro football during my last three years at Stanford. There were some things to learn but they weren't really difficult. The most noticeable difference in pro football was the longer season, from the Fourth of July to Christmas and later. You must budget your energy and enthusiasm. Another is understanding the moods and attitudes of the professional athlete. He is so much more mature than the college person, an adult with outside interests and a family who can be distracted by things that never come up in college."

Ralston said the biggest area of education came in learning personnel. The football plays were not that much different, but the people who made them work were. He found out most about people on the practice field, seeing those who had tremendous internal motivation, and others who had great natural ability but not too much push from within. When he pushed them after a hard practice, he found which was which.

At first he didn't believe San Francisco coach Dick Nolan, who told him it would take two years before he really got to know his own players, but that's exactly how long it took. Devine had told him the same thing after a year at Green Bay but he also advised him not to hesitate to take college assistants to Denver as he and Prothro had done. This was one area where Ralston showed more restraint, hiring only three.

"There were many adjustments, of course," Ralston says. "At every level, the game is the same but the stresses are different. The adjustments you are required to make in your own situation in college year after year are fantastic. There is more scoring, for example, in college football because the pros emphasize defense more. But the pro game is more skillful and the fan is interested in how it is played now.

"Draw the bottom line and it still doesn't matter, because in the end, you coach to your personality. I came into professional football intending to do things the same way I always did, knowing that no one becomes Vince Lombardi overnight, and that a loss in the NFL is no different than a loss in college. It still hurts as much.

"The big thing when I came to the NFL—and it hasn't changed—is communication. Young people want to know why. A coach not tuned to answering the 'why' is in trouble at every level of competition. It's the same with emotion. That is very important at every level because this game still is an emotional type of game."

Randy Vataha, a wide receiver at Stanford before joining the New England Patriots, doesn't feel that Ralston stressed the aspects of football as a game (and as fun) so much as he did lessening the appearance of the sport as pure business.

"He was very reasonable about his approach to the game," says Vataha. "If there were classes in the spring you needed for your major, you were excused from spring practice. He did not have a mandatory physical program class like many schools do. He would advise you to follow a program if you had the time. He also realized you had outside lives and outside interests and knew they were important to you. But when football came around it was a serious approach every day and we had to dig into it that way."

Plunkett, Vataha's teammate at Stanford and with the Patriots, never felt football was a business at Stanford. "To me it was just a whole lot of fun, particularly compared to the pros," he says.

At Denver, Ralston's approach has met with a mixed reaction. Floyd Little, for example, was an unabashed believer in his ways and still spares no effort to tell anyone who asks. He also admits that there is a faction on the team that does not buy the approach yet contributes enough to make the team successful from a won-lost standpoint.

The degree of success in each instance is the difference in how Ralston's programs are accepted. Plunkett and Vataha combined with other players at Stanford to win a Pacific-8 title and the Rose Bowl; the Broncos under Ralston, have had just one season, 1973, in which they contended for a title to the last day of the season. In 1974 and 1975 injuries took a toll but Little claims these could have been overcome in stronger measure by a full acceptance of Ralston's dictums.

This is in line with Ralston's approach to his profession. He believes the attributes of a good coach start with the player's athletic ability combined with a positive winning attitude. Then comes a constant stress on fundamentals.

"You don't do it with a lot of rah-rah," he adds. "You do it by understanding your people. Then you must find a way to motivate them to get that five or ten percent extra from them."

It is his fashion to be very expansive, almost scholarly in approaching this subject. He has given it a great deal of thought and he has put together what he believes to be an unimpeachable credo. First, a coach must practice personal integrity in his associations with his team and in his personal life both on and off the field. At the same time, he must develop early in his career the ability to cope with adversity and not blame his staff or players.

"If one takes the bows or applause," he says, "he must learn to accept defeat with humility. However, the ability to bounce back from extreme adversity and to hit the practice field with renewed enthusiasm is a constant requisite. A coach must realize that the only way to reverse the tide and to get back on the positive side is to work even harder in his teaching, preparation, and attention to detail."

He must, in Ralston's mind, be other things, too—colorful and imaginative, a good disciplinarian, a good organizer and administrator, flexible in his coaching methods, techniques, and system and have the ability to operate under the public's scrutiny with dignity, good appearance, and as a true sportsman.

Is there such a man? Ralston thinks so and he strives every day to make himself fit his own qualifications.

Ralston's preparation begins with his own organized methods of setting up a program, then dealing off that which must be done to assistant coaches and explaining the aims and desired results. It is a method he learned the hard way, once having tried to do everything himself. He did this through his first few seasons at Stanford until he found himself getting bogged down to such an extent that his overall perspective and personality had become distorted.

It was then that he assumed for himself the same game day responsibilities he still manages with the Broncos. Plunkett remembers him as a great coordinator who preferred pumping up people, something that is his nature and which he truly believes in.

"He was more than a cheerleader or an armchair coach," Plunkett adds. "He was the guy who directed that staff and our practices to the most minute detail. He did much of the verbalizing and let his coaches handle the technical aspects."

In Denver, Ralston has tried to focus his role as head coach and general manager in purely football aspects. He'll take the responsibility for all that happens on a day-by-day basis within the organization but he has delegated others to handle non-football aspects.

"You can't allow yourself to be so bogged down with distracting details that you lose the power to adjust and take advantage of what you see in the films, on the field, and with the players," he says. "I've got an extremely capable staff and they do ninety-nine percent of the game plan. I understand this is a bit different than methods followed by other coaches but it is one that we find very workable and most comfortable."

He also refuses to worry about things over which he has no control, which are, in his estimation, a sheer waste of time. Instead, he utilizes part of that time away from the nitty-gritty details to engage in what he terms "the creative thought process, trying to come up with more effective and more efficient ways of doing things." He tries to allot at least one morning hour to this. If that doesn't work, he'll try to get the thinking time in late at night when all the day's business has been concluded.

When he first came to Denver, much of his time was spent this way. As a result Ralston made many discoveries about his football team. He found many players willing to accept the fact that the team was losing football games though they were doing well individually. The Broncos, for example, had led the NFL the previous season in sacking the quarterback yet really had nothing to show for it on a won-loss basis. On offense, the Broncos had scored just 18 touchdowns in 14 games; by comparison, the Super Bowl champion Cowboys had scored 50.

"Obviously we had to come up with ways to get more touchdowns because, for one reason, people enjoy watching the ball go into the end zone," Ralston says. "So we traded for quarterback Charley Johnson and raised the total from eighteen to thirty-eight. It could have been the loss of Dave Costa and Rich Jackson but it boiled down to our having to rebuild the front four and the linebacking.

"The main point is that you must put priorities on what must be done first and foremost. We knew we had to back up Floyd Little so we got Otis Armstrong in the draft; then we went after the best athlete and got Reily Odoms on another draft even though we didn't need a tight end. We just concentrated on trying to upgrade the total quality of our personnel. But before we could do any of this, a plan had to come forth. Something like that is my ultimate responsibility because the success or failure of the team rests upon how well it is conceived. And you don't think clearly with a million and one details boggling your mind."

Perhaps it explains why Ralston never has had a winning season the first year—at either Utah State, Stanford, or Denver. One reason is that he's never jumped into a winning program ("a coach generally is replaced in a losing situation and it takes a year sometimes to turn it around," he says). But he thrives on that experience and Bob Gambold, who has worked for him in all three places, says that once the first season passes, "look out!"

"I don't know any other way," Ralston admits. "Utah State was the first major college job I applied for because it was the one I thought I could get. I was one of seventy-five candidates. After three years there, I applied for the head spot at Nebraska and California and didn't get either. After my fourth year, I applied for just one, Stanford, and was one of more than two hundred candidates."

How Ralston accomplished the task of turning around a losing team is what sets him apart from other coaches. It's what makes his coaching style distinctive from theirs, too, because he places so much stress on the motivational techniques widely used in industry rather than going to the blackboard and setting up mind-boggling formations and alignments. Some of his sources are the Dale Carnegie Institute, the power of positive thinking people; SMI, an organization with headquarters in Waco, Texas, whose approach is to teach the dynamics of personal leadership through goal-setting; and AMI.

There are those who consider these techniques "canned" in that they have been scientifically developed, tested, proven, and are available in tapes, movies, and book forms. The user is expected to operate within certain guidelines and limits in their utilization.

Some claim this cuts down the spontaneity but Ralston disagrees, insisting that they provide direction and leave to the user all the innovation he wishes to utilize in their application.

"I'm a self-improvement nut," he says. "I like to think people want to get better so I explore every avenue. You either grow or you go. In industry today, they have people whose job is to figure out how to get two or five or maybe eight percent more out of a firm's employees. That's nothing more than another form of management and what is management? It's getting things done through people.

"When you talk about the functions of management you talk about planning, direction, organizing, and controlling, something we as coaches have been doing for years but never with any formal training. The problems of industry are no different than those of a football coach. It's just that when you talk about getting desired results from people, you open up an area that has not been heavily explored in its football applications.

"So I've taken every program that's been offered to learn everything I can about this phase of my profession. I've used these approaches not only to help myself but to help others. And why shouldn't football tie into them? Players always are practicing to get better. That's self-improvement too. Boiled down, it's nothing more than grass-roots human relationships whether you're applying it to everyday talk between people or to football."

Ralston says the whole point of learning how to have better human relationships is to increase your own understanding and confidence.

"Football isn't all a game of plans and finesse," he points out. "Down on the field it can be as physical as a street fight. A team has to feel like a team. It must believe that it has been better prepared for each game than the other team. It's up to the coach to provide this preparation and to supply the motivation that gets his players ready to produce a top performance."

One of Ralston's chief reservoirs of this motivational thinking is the Success Motivation Institute. Its credo is: "Anything you vividly imagine, ardently desire, sincerely believe in, and enthusiastically act upon must eventually come to pass."

"They don't say 'believe in' but "*ardently* believe in;" not 'imagine' but "*vividly* imagine." Think about the words a little. The ability of the mind to conceive of something and make it a reality is an amazing concept. If you believe in something strongly, start pressing the positive buttons, and work to achieve it, then why shouldn't it happen?"

Ralston calls this visualizing. He tells his players to "visualize" what the scoreboard looks like after they win as opposed to what it looks like after they lose; to "visualize" how they will react in the locker room after a winning game as opposed to what they will be like after a loss. Chuck Knox has adopted some of the same concepts in Los Angeles, though he applies it in a stricter football sense when he has his players visualize performing their assignments.

Ralston wants players to go on the practice field each day with the idea that when they leave it, they will be better. He extends the self-improvement theory to everything—to meetings with coaches, film sessions, blackboard drills, and meetings.

200

"It must be an outgoing process," says Ralston. "I subscribe to Cabot Roberts's theory that the real professional loves what he's doing and wants to get better every single second of every single day. To get involved in self-improvement is an easy thing. The Dale Carnegie approach goes to football's blocking and tackling, which outside of football would be the fundamentals of human behavior. Any coach who looks at film to find out why he won or lost will appreciate the fundamentals."

Ralston doesn't give regular classes in self-motivation to his players. The philosophy is part of the team's everyday life. But his favorite teaching story has to do with a rich man's twin sons, one positive and one negative. For their birthday, the pessimist got a pony, the optimist a pile of manure. An hour later the pessimist already was worrying about how much work it probably would take to care for the pony and how he'd probably die anyway. The optimist was poking through the manure. "I know there's got to be a pony around here someplace," he said.

He also will hold up a glass with water halfway up the side. He tells his players that anybody who thinks the glass is half empty is negative. Anybody who thinks it's half full is positive. At the same time, he does not disregard the realities of life, particularly life in the NFL. Reality there often can be measured by the bounce of the ball or the pull of a muscle.

"We have to live that way," he says. "All of this isn't foolishness. We strive to eliminate all the negatives yet we add the lessons we've learned from our disappointments. For example, we contended for a title in 1973, then got rocked by injuries the next two seasons and were pretty much out of it. That was a lesson in realism. And that adversity also taught us some fantastic lessons that we should use to our own advantage whenever we get into tight spots in the future."

He had to do it those two seasons as well as in his first year, when the team fell out of contention for a division title. His approach then is to talk about the idea of creating an edge.

"The attitude will stand in there though the incentive is gone," he maintains. "If you rely strictly on incentive and talk only in terms of winning a championship, you've lost everything. If you talk about an attitude where you must be the best in your position, that when you go on the practice field you become better, then it begins to pay off. That's when attitudinal motivation takes over and gets you to the highest possible level. What you have is taking all the negative things that happen and turning them into something positive."

Broncos' placekicker Jim Turner remembers an afternoon during the 1975 season when an electrical failure cut off all the lights in the team's dressing room after practice. It was impossible to dress and the players began moaning and complaining that they never would get home.

"John threaded his way through the place in the darkness saying, 'Don't worry, don't worry, the light will be back on in a few minutes.' Sure enough, the lights came back on almost immediately and he gave everyone the business for being so negative."

Ralston began to use "positive" methods during his second season at Stanford, but some people who played for him before that claim he always coached this way. He had been following a program of goal-setting, along with some of the other points these various programs stress, but never with any formal training. Once he stepped into a formalized program, he extended it through football to a point where he now tries to have his players get a visual picture of where they'll be when they no longer can play football.

But his greatest application still is in the day-by-day relationships with his players. Some began thinking of it as a back-slapping, hail-fellow-well-met approach, which is totally wrong. There is a great deal of sincerity—as much as Ralston can muster from his ample spirit—and the conveyance of this is most important. For example, he'll open every team meeting with, "A *pleasant* good morning (or afternoon or evening) to you all!" Or he's been known to start his meetings with, "Hey, today's the best day of your life and tomorrow may even be better."

He's got a litany of little slogans that he uses as germs of positive-thinking ideas, such as "act enthusiastically and you'll be enthusiastic," or "success comes in cans, not in cannots." Often, he'll ask his players to repeat them in their minds.

Joe Dawkins, a former Bronco who was traded to the New York Giants a couple of years ago, admits that Ralston's slogans sounded "corny" at first. But after awhile, he said, players found themselves telling the same thing to people outside of football, or often to each other within the locker room.

"There are two reasons for that," says Dawkins. "First, we heard them so often and, second, they proved out. In 1973, we won our first game, lost the next three. After the third loss he said we would not lose again and would win so many games we soon would be tired of winning. Everyone sort of shrugged but we were unbeaten in our next seven games in a row and then, everyone believed."

Other former players still draw on these motivational insights long after they have left him. Both Plunkett and Vataha still remember the slogans; more importantly they have found the ideas Ralston implanted from his motivational teachings of some value in their professional careers.

"I don't ever remember doing a lot of the visualizing at Stanford," says Vataha. "But in the past few years I've found myself doing it without even realizing why. So consciously it may not have an effect but it stays with your subconscious. I can look back over my NFL career now and remember times when some of those techniques would come to mind and be of some help."

A favorite of Ralston's is having each player set down his personal goals and what he hopes to accomplish in a game the night before it is played, something espoused by SMI. Many players may do this automatically but after awhile it becomes an integral part of a man's final mental preparation. Vataha still finds himself doing it.

Plunkett remembers visualizing the scoreboard after a victory and a defeat, then being asked which he'd rather have. A player, he says, makes the logical choice but then doesn't think about that scoreboard reflecting a winning score when he is playing. But he does think about it when he's not playing.

"That's how I still reflect on things," Plunkett says, "and I haven't played for John since 1970. The difference is that I'd rather feel happy about things and this has an effect on my preparation. It helps me. It makes me feel confident so that I know if I go out and do the job properly, I'll win. Even when I came to professional football I felt that way, though I also found out that it's not quite that easy because you don't always have quite as good a team as the one you left in college.

"But it does help your confidence and you must maintain those positive-thinking attitudes to be successful as a professional. I had some of that before I met John at Stanford but I kept a lot of the others he gave me and still think about them."

Both remember Ralston talking about Stanford winning the Pacific-8 title and Rose Bowl each year just as he tells his Denver teams it will win the Super Bowl. In Denver, this optimism has caused Ralston to operate under a great deal of pressure. It was the same at Stanford.

"The criticism from the alumni bothered him but only in that he couldn't understand why they weren't as positive in their outlooks as he was in his," Vataha says. "His enthusiasm in this regard flowed right down to the players and it had a very positive effect on how we approached each game. The fact that we just missed the first year I was there, won it the next year, and won again the year after Jim and I left has to prove something."

On Ralston's desk, there is a printed sign: "Go To and Win the Super Bowl," as if he needed a printed reminder of the goal of every NFL team. But he believes that a goal sometimes is not worthwhile if it is out of sight and that sign is a constant reminder of what each day on the job must ultimately produce. He has one on the sun visor of his car and often will paste one on the mirror of his bathroom so that when he shaves each morning, he will get a forceful reminder of the long-range goal of his day's work.

Ralston often has admitted his own visualization process has seen himself coaching in the Super Bowl, seen the scoreboard at the end of the game that shows the Broncos winning (though he won't reveal the score), and has placed him in his team's dressing room, with NFL commissioner Pete Rozelle, his bosses, the Phipps brothers, and the huge Vince Lombardi trophy. He also has his acceptance speech prepared.

"I'll thank everyone . . . the team, the Phippses and say it was because of a superb all-around effort by the players and my assistant coaches, and the great support of the owners and Denver fans that achieved the victory," Ralston says without hesitation.

"I've got to see it!" he adds with almost an emotional emphasis. "It was like that with the Rose Bowl, too. Talk about an obsession with something! I had this total, all-encompassing obsession for eight years to get to the Rose Bowl. And I won't attend a Super Bowl game until we play there. Until we get there, we really haven't done anything; we haven't won anything. I said we would win it in the first year, and every year since, so we're way behind schedule.

"Probably what we really found out ["we" means him] is that everyone else is good, too, and has the same goal. The ones who win and get there or get into a position of going to the Super Bowl, work every bit as hard as we do. I guess you could say they work even harder than we do—or at least are more successful in getting their work done.

"I know people wonder about these things but I have a theory. If you think you are going to lose, the chances are you will. My slogan is: 'See yourself successful.' Not a day went by in my eight years at Stanford that I didn't picture myself coaching on the sidelines at the Rose Bowl. It's been the same way at Denver. Everyday I can see myself on the sidelines of the Super Bowl."

At Denver, he's had motivational experts speak to his coaches (and even to his personal secretary) on the techniques of interviewing so as to facilitate their means of getting inside the heads of the players. In his office is a row of briefcases, each filled with motivational programs in tape cassettes. He uses them and he urges his staff to use them. All do at some time or other during the season, though admittedly not with the same fervent belief as their boss.

"One of the reasons I got into the Dale Carnegie program," Ralston adds, "is that it helps a coach a great deal with in-depth personal interviews with players. Gosh, football has changed a heckuva lot. When I was a player, you could tell a boy to run through a brick wall and he would. Today, you're coaching individuals; you don't coach an athlete, you coach a mind."

Ralston said it has taken some players as many as 10 games to accept his ideas. "The big thing is consistency," he says. "You don't swing around in different directions every time you talk to different players or when different situations arise. A major element is that we learn when to say 'we' and when to say 'I'. Another is to keep the pressure off the players, something I learned a long time ago from Lynn Waldorf. He said it is the coach's responsibility to accept the pressure and keep it off the players. Granted that's a fine line. You do it, for example, when the performance is lousy by saying, 'It's my fault.' I'm a great believer that if you make a mistake, admit it quickly and emphatically and don't dwell on it. I've made a lot of mistakes in coaching and if they come up, I can refer to them. But when we lose I usually feel that it's my fault."

Turner says it still is that way at Denver. Ralston absorbs all the pressure himself and never publicly blames a player. It's not a bad way to run things, Turner adds, because it cuts down a lot of discussion and still places the responsibility for anything that's gone wrong where it should go.

"If a guy makes a mistake, he'll still get together with him but never to embarrass him," says Turner. "He'll chew out a guy in the privacy of his office but only for a mental mistake. He accepts the physical ones but if a guy continues to screw up because he doesn't think or won't pay attention, then John simply gets rid of him."

Another observer noted that Ralston has discipline on the field, where it matters, but he never closes his mind to anything. Even when a player quit his team, he never rapped the fellow. He'd find a nice way to say he was leaving the program.

The obvious question is whether or not this gives the player a tendency to shrug off responsibility for any mistakes. Ralston says no, pointing out that athletes "don't think this way. They want fame and fortune and ninety-nine percent of them know the way to get it is to win, to excel. That requires work.

"In a game it's a bit different because they cannot totally escape responsibility for what happens. If a man fumbles three times or a quarterback throws four interceptions, then whether or not I say it's my fault, it's pretty obvious that everyone shares in it. And if you had players who wanted to shrug off the responsibility, they wouldn't stay around too long just because of that attitude."

Ralston carries his motivational principles on both a personal and unit level. Not only does he gather around his kicking team before a game but he sees to it that the entire team watches the special teams film. Every member of that often unsung unit is given recognition for whatever "positive contribution" he makes in a game. Ralston emphasizes those positives because it's a very good way to reach the guys on the bottom of the roster. "We're constantly doing things to involve the total team," he adds.

The on-the-field involvement with the Broncos' kicking team is Ralston's way of making a final check to see whether or not the players are ready. While he stands in the huddle or moves around it, he is constantly checking eyes, looking for an intensity that will tell him whether or not a player has the proper emotional readiness.

"It's an individual thing," he maintains. "By 'getting ready' the player should be building up an emotional process that would allow him to strike somebody, almost like allowing him to get into a street fight. I go out there knowing I don't have to worry about six or seven of those players but there might be one or two I can help at the last minute.

"It really is a superficial thing because if a player hasn't gotten himself ready through the week and peaked himself to a point at one o'clock on a Sunday afternoon where someone is going to blow a whistle for the damndest street fight you ever saw . . . well, he better be ready. I can look in a man's eyes and see what I'm looking for. If I don't see it, I'll really jump on the guy. Maybe I can make him realize that every street fight in the world has been won by the guy who gets in the first punch."

And what if he doesn't find what he's looking for as he steps into that huddle or circles it?

"It depends on the individual," Ralston says. "A lot of times I'll hustle around the huddle so I can get over with him and put my arm around him. I'll ask him if he's ready to go, if he's going to get in that first lick . . . something to encourage him. If he's returning a kickoff, I'll tell him, 'All the way with this one,' or something of that nature. It's the words of encouragement that count."

Ralston and his players both admit his presence often is hardly noticed. There are leaders in each unit and they're generally talking to the younger players. Ralston works the outside of the huddle while the unit's leaders deal with those on the inside. The emphasis is generally on the newer players, seeing that they have their assignments and realize what must be done.

He gets together with offensive and defensive units on the sidelines and spends time with individual players during the game.

"You'll see him in front of you and that look he gives you is his way of challenging you," Dawkins says. "He'll look at you and say, 'Are you going to do the job?' and you had better look him right back in the eye and say, 'Yes, I'm going to do the job.' If he doesn't see what he wants, he'll give a guy a pep talk. It may sound a bit corny but if you hear it enough you begin to believe it."

Ralston assumes his role as cheerleader during the game. The talk is of successes or failures and it consumes a goodly part of his time during a game. It's one reason why he turns responsibility for running the offense and defense over to his assistants.

"I'll get with the guy who has made a mistake and who may be hanging low and try to bring him back," Ralston says. "I tell him to forget it and get him ready to handle the bigger opportunity. The big thing is not to allow a positive attitude to become negative. It's an ongoing process that begins the moment the team begins preparing for a game until it is over. It is a necessary ingredient in all of our motivational processes."

Throughout Ralston's philosophy one word emerges—attitude. He's constantly seeking those who share his attitude on becoming the best. It was the keynote of his first talk to his first high school team. He talks about it in every conceivable situation, from going on the field to win to approaching a learning experience.

"The great ones set a standard for themselves to be the best at what they're doing," Ralston says. "That's attitude. I've always been that way and I'll always be looking for people who subscribe to the same idea. You never worry about outside pressure. The pressure of satisfying yourself to be number one is the only one that counts. If you can do that you've taken care of everything."

No coach—himself included—ever will have a team with the same high attitudinal pitch that Ralston strives to achieve, but he says it still must be an objective.

"You've got to be around a guy for a period of time before you can change attitudes, even attitudes of those kinds of players," Ralston admits. "If he doesn't change, he won't last long any place in professional football.

"The optimum may be a guy like Floyd Little, who lived in positive expectancy. Though he experienced a lot of losing years at Denver, there was no problem with his attitude."

"Positive expectancy" is another of the terms that Ralston uses to make his point. He says it means a player expects to be successful everytime he steps on the field; that his team will be successful and he works to make it happen. His attitude is totally positive.

"On your team," says Ralston, "there always will be a lot of guys who go on the field saying, 'I know we're going to win,' but the subconscious is saying otherwise. And the subconscious usually wins out. It's the old comfort zone type of thing and I'm a strong believer in that. It's like a pro golfer who's on top after thirty-six holes and not used to being there. Chances are he'll be back down in the pack when the tournament is over.

"You've got to expand that zone. You've got to say, 'By God, everything we're going to do will be successful. We're going to win!' You've got to see the scoreboard as a successful experience and this takes time. Force out the negative . . . put in the positives . . . change the subconscious."

"Comfort zone" is another Ralston-ism—and he readily gives an illustration of what it means. Some people leaving a ghetto will move into new housing units and soon the new ones look as bad as the old because the people just are not used to anything different. It's the same as going into a home worth a half million dollars and feeling you're not really supposed to be there.

"I recall my first season at Stanford and we were ahead of USC eleven to nothing at the half. We had no right being there because we did not have a good team. You can guess what happened in the second half. We lost twenty-five to eleven and, in a sense, we were comfortable because what finally happened was what was supposed to happen.

"That's the feeling you must contain," says Ralston. "You've got to get the feeling of stretching yourself, of jumping into a new group of people and constantly upgrading and stretching until you're not going to be comfortable unless you're on the top of the heap."

There have been some vivid examples of the "comfort zone" afflicting the Broncos during his tenure at Denver. In 1972, the team led the Minnesota Vikings 20-16 with 37 seconds to play and lost 23-20. All week the team had been reminded by the media of the Vikings' great defensive dominance and of the extraordinary offensive talent of quarterback Fran Tarkenton and in the final seconds it succumbed to what it felt would happen.

In 1974, the Broncos had a streak of three victories and in the next game led the Browns 21-9. They lost 23-21.

"This team hadn't won four in a row for twelve years," says Ralston. "That's a helluva thing to overcome. So was never having won at Kansas City before we finally licked that. You might not think those kind of barriers mean anything until you go out and play a game. The squad never had seen itself successful flying back from Kansas City. To go there with a positive feeling that you will win when you never have is tough."

"Comfort zone" experiences don't necessarily result in failure. Ralston remembers the Broncos leading the Jets 30-7 at halftime in New York a couple of years back and finally winning 40-28. At Oakland in 1972, they led the Raiders 23-6 at the half and held on to win 30-23.

"In both games we should have come out in the second half and doubled the score," he says. "But we got back where it was comfortable for awhile, seeing everything slip away. Players are conscious of this. The player always thinks he can win the big one but the trouble is back in the subconscious, filed away. Right at the end of the game the subconscious takes over and the 'sure enough' happens ... sure enough, we found a way to lose the game, to make the mistake that cost us.

"The PACE [Personal Accompanying Effectiveness] people call that the 'sure enough' experience. How many times have you seen a team ahead in the final minutes only to lose—and lament that poor team is unlucky, particularly if it has a string of such losses. In recounting the game, a person will get to the climactic moment and begin, 'Sure enough, so-and-so kicked a field goal and they lost.' There's the 'sure enough.'"

Conversely, it also can describe the successful team, the one that kicks the field goal to win. People have marveled at George Blanda's last-second heroics for years but he only caps a winning effort by the Oakland Raiders who never expect to lose—consciously or subconsciously—when they play a regular season game. In the post-season, it could be said the "sure enough" works the opposite way because they have yet to achieve the ultimate success.

Ralston feels he came close only once in his first four seasons at Denver in totally eliminating the comfort zone malaise. That was in 1973 when the Broncos went down to the final game of the season against Oakland with a chance to win the title and were beaten. Still, the team never had seen itself as a division champion, as winning the one game that would make it a champion, and sure enough, it didn't.

As Ralston describes these psychological impediments they seem akin to cracking the sonic barrier or the four-minute mile. Once achieved, there is the experience of having done it, then the confidence that it can be accomplished over and over. This explains, in part, the ability of some teams to win crucial games.

Ralston proved it to his own players a couple of seasons ago in a game against the Chiefs. The Broncos held a slim lead in the final seconds of the game when a pass by Chiefs' quarterback Mike Livingston bounced off tight end Gary Butler and into the hands of Denver safety Charley Greer. A completion could have set up the winning field goal but the Broncos escaped with a victory.

Had they known how close they had come to losing?

"We knew somehow we'd stop them," defensive end Lyle Alzado remembers.

This kind of attitude is tied directly to Ralston's motivational beliefs and teachings. He says the intensity, then the competence that a player assumes stems first from the coach and the latter's own competitive instincts. It is the coach's responsibility to channel the athlete's self esteem and confidence so the fear of failure will not inhibit his performance in a game of football—or in life, either.

The coach, Ralston insists, can turn on the key that will generate success in a player and he cites six prime competitive ingredients to make it happen:

(1) The desire to get better. The athlete himself must want to improve and to succeed in whatever else he does. He will not settle for mediocrity;

(2) He must satisfy himself and will not be happy being second best;

(3) He must develop concentration. The mind, Ralston contends, quits long before the body loses its efficiency. The mind must be disciplined to respond to the body;

(4) He must possess intensity;

(5) He must possess courage. The highest form he calls "two o'clock in the morning courage," that which is necessary on an unexpected occasion; and

(6) Above all, integrity and tough-mindedness are essential to perform well under adversity.

How successful a player is in assuming these qualities depends upon the coach's ability to transfer his own competitiveness to the player. And how he does it is just as important. You get a good idea of Ralston's basic approach in his declaration that "the tyrannical coach often is controlled by his own demands of ego and emotion." He sees nothing but ultimate failure in this approach, not only for himself should he ever try to assume it, but as a broad-based projection.

Plunkett feels that Ralston himself changed from the fringes of this association in the late sixties. He had been adamant on hair styles, clothing and other amenities which shifted radically in appearance. He finally realized that to get as much from his players at Stanford—which at that time was becoming as wild a looking crowd as ever played football—he would have to meet them part way. In 1969, Plunkett's junior year, the players returned to find Ralston's rules much more relaxed over previous seasons, though still with some parameters he clung to as a means of maintaining the ideas of a team concept.

"It was a bit of pragmatism on his part," Plunkett believes. "The alumni were on him pretty good because the team had not won a title or a Rose Bowl though he kept saying we would. I think he figured if he was going to do it—and he'd better to keep his job—then he would have to get the players on his side. It showed a lot for him to have the capacity to change and everyone responded."

Ralston agrees he changed right along with them. He also agrees with Plunkett in substance at least, that a coach must study what it takes to get his job done, then work *with* the players, not against them. It holds true, he adds, in professional football which is nothing more than an extension of a player's athletic and personal life.

Yet he has done this without destroying the competitiveness of his teams. In fact, he's raised their quotient—in college and in the NFL—several notches. The whole idea of competition remains a keystone in his approach to player relationships in professional football as well. Like Tom Landry of the Dallas Cowboys, he sees it as a bulwark in our democratic processes, a stanchion that can support our society.

"Competition is the mainspring of the American system," Ralston has declared on numerous occasions. "Youngsters who are imbued with the spirit of competitiveness seldom are swayed by insidious propaganda. We believe they withstand this technique because sports essentially are based on honesty, fair play, and by competing according to definitive rules. Athletes also are taught to think on their feet, make spot decisions, and are not fearful of competing against overwhelming odds. It aids them in making their families, their communities, and their countries. They have a very sound foundation on which to base their lives.

"Today's athlete reflects the feelings of millions of young people across the country. They want to have a creative input into the overall picture. They do not necessarily want to be led or to be told what to do. They want to be free to act creatively. That's precisely what I want my players to be able to do . . . to do their own thing. The way I see it, my job is to free their minds of the hangups that keep them from doing their own thing on the football field.

"A coach must be involved today," Ralston adds. "A player with a personal problem, regardless of what level he's playing on, cannot help but be distracted on the field. His concentration is broken and he will not play well. It's one reason why I don't hesitate to try to help my players with problems outside of football, if at all possible."

This has not been lost at Denver. Little, a sensitive and introspective person, says

Ralston's finest quality is his firm belief in people—sometimes to a fault.

"He helps with a man's problems in any phase of his life because he wants to help the guy enjoy playing football," Little says after playing for Ralston for the final four seasons of his career. "Personal contact is his style. Perhaps he is the last of a breed considering the breaches that are being driven between player and coach with so much unionizing.

"He's a firm believer in people and in mankind. There never is a day when he doesn't believe that if a person sacrifices and works for something, he'll win. And he'll go to almost any end to help a player achieve that.

"But John should realize that the leopard never changes his spots and there are people who just aren't going to respond to this. Sometimes, I thought he was too tolerant of those players, like taking the blame publicly for some of their mistakes. I think he's getting there in this regard, at least in view as to their ultimate value of the team."

That may be true but it would probably be unnatural for Ralston to totally abandon this method. To do so might make all that he has preached as false and thus brand himself as a phony. Players do not have gray shadings in making such distinctions so Ralston will continue to deal with the player who makes the mistake in his own way.

"An athlete needs to be pumped up after he makes a mistake," Ralston says. "At least the guy who makes the occasional error while trying to do his best. The kind that hurts—and hurts enough to make me consider removing the man from the game, if not from the team—is the selfish, mental error. I say selfish because he is thinking of himself, not the team; and mental because there is no excuse. In that group put such things as jumping offside, going in motion before the ball is snapped, things such as that.

"A guy who fumbles or drops a pass—well, no great athlete ever *tries* to drop a ball. You don't excuse them, you relate to them and establish a rapport, then you reassure the player. It's the same with a quarterback. No matter what a quarterback calls, he's never wrong as long as he adjusts at the line of scrimmage. I'll ask a quarterback why he did certain things, though only in the context of rehashing the game to find ways to improve.

"A player must be willing to face the second guess and some post-game analysis if he is to become efficient and totally involved. But always, this is done within the goal-oriented framework of moving upward. It's not a critical type of thing. You just relate to becoming better in the future by what may have been a mistake in the past."

Ralston has the same philosophy with a running back. He says he is not in the game carrying the ball, seeing what he sees as each play develops. He will tell him after looking at the films what he should have done "but at the moment he did it, he must be allowed to think he is correct. You cannot have a smooth-functioning team if a guy always is afraid to make a move, wondering whether every one he makes is a correct one."

That is only one means of establishing a strong relationship with his players. Though his motivational beliefs run throughout this area, he also executes certain mechanics in building and strengthening these relationships. The player, he says, must have a solid foundation of principles directed toward achievement, accomplishment, and excellence to be receptive to them. He has a nine-point set of "commandments" that a player must be committed to following. He got his list by taking each letter of the word "intensity" and making it stand for a key thought. It goes like this:

(I) "Intestinal fortitude, or more emphatically, just plain American guts. That is what made America what it is today and what can make your team and you the best in your endeavors.

(N) "Noise, not by mouth but through action. The name of the game is still 'knock' no matter how complex it gets with our new varied offenses and defenses. If you knock down the other team or the other guy more times than it or he does to you, you win.

(T) "Training. If you are going to participate in a team sport, live by it; if not, get out of it. This will be better for the sport, your team and you.

(E) "Energy, the amount correctly applied in an effort is directly proportionate to the result obtained. There is no dishonor in being blocked; the dishonor is in having such a deficiency of energy that you allow yourself to stay blocked.

(N) "Need. The greatest 'need' in football or in life itself is pride. Taking enough pride in your team and yourself so that you acquire the knowledge through your coach or through your own efforts and therefore can honestly say, 'Under the prevailing circumstances I, physically and mentally, offered my team and my coach one hundred percent of my talent.'

(S) "Sacrifice. If you are not willing to sacrifice enough of yourself to give your team your best effort, then strengthen your team by getting out and letting someone participate who will.

(I) "Intelligence. To play this game you must be smart—not smart aleck. There is a tremendous difference between these two.

(T) "Thoroughness. If you are thorough in execution no one can criticize you. If you are not, there is a teammate on the bench who should be where you are.

(Y) "You. If you don't have the desire to win and to practice to win, no coach or employer needs or wants you. Most of all, without this need for self-satisfaction your life will be a fruitless, unrewarding one. Nature endowed us with the mobility and brain to do with ourselves what we wish. If you do not use it to the best of your advantage you are not a very good athlete but even more disappointing, you are not much of a man."

It is wrong to think that Ralston lets his well-conceived ideas and philosophies do all the work. The fact that he even talks in terms of removing a player from a game or from the team for the "selfish mental error" is one clue that he demands a positive response to all that he teaches. Most of all, he is not just a nice guy trying to get along.

Indeed, a former Marine, he has been likened to a "drill sergeant with a smile," and there are some former Denver Broncos' players who can attest to that reputation. He is not slovenly in his approach toward attaining perfection in execution, insisting that a play or a defensive alignment be done right before a team leaves the practice field or goes on to something else. The difference often is that he does not bellow like Vince Lombardi or berate or pick like Don Shula.

"The belief that doing it till it is right is nothing more than the belief that excellence doesn't come easy," Ralston says. "You don't sit by a cold stove and ask for heat. You've got to put some wood in it. It's not hard to sell our squad on the idea that if good things are going to come, they'll come as the result of hard work. I don't know any other way and I'm no magician. If you want to achieve results you've got to work harder.

"And one way is repetition, doing something until it is correct and can be done over and over perfectly. At the same time it's gotta be fun but, often, that is up to the player. If he pays attention and does his job, he'll find that it's fun because he'll win. Nothing is more fun than winning."

This was a bit of a change to the Broncos because during Lou Saban's tenure, they had been expected to adjust to things without much explanation.

"John will take more time for everything," tackle Mike Current says. "He's very precise. We've been treated more like college players than pros. In many cases it's been good because we got back to some fundamentals. But a lot of the players resented some of the little things. The more I see of John Ralston, the more he reminds me of Woody Hayes. He's not as obstinate and overbearing but things are going to be done his way."

Plunkett adds that for all of Ralston's capacity for change at Stanford, one thing never changed—Ralston's insistence on things being done absolutely correctly on the practice field. While some of his "drill sergeant" reputation may have eroded from his first years there, his former players say he worked them very hard during drills in the spring and early fall. He never relented in his beliefs about conditioning.

"We hated some of it," Plunkett admits, "but it paid off in the end."

Ralston says nothing puts a man's body to the physical demands of football—and that includes Marine Corps training.

"Football is a street fight," he repeats. "You must capture the emotion, yet keep your mind free. We teach players how to get to that mental pitch, yet observe the rules, remember the assignment, hear the whistle. I tell them, 'Strike a blow, throw a fit for six seconds.' It's perpetual motion for six seconds."

Those on the Broncos know what he means. Their first introduction to Ralston was in training camp prior to the 1972 season. When that preseason ended, you knew that somewhere Lombardi was smiling because Ralston had run a camp that rivaled anything Vince had ever run at Green Bay or anything a Marine recruit ever underwent at Parris Island. It is almost impossible to believe that the same John Ralston who seems so placid in his approach to the sport ran that camp.

Ralston admits he demanded too much too soon from his players, failing to realize that the season is twice as long as he was used to in college.

"I also discovered you don't have to be in that good shape right away," he says. "College teams run about ninety plays a game while pro teams run anywhere from forty-five to seventy. Once I saw where adjustments had to be made, I didn't hesitate to make them."

Little refers to the difference in noting the Broncos had contact drills twice a day for three weeks in that first training camp, went to Washington and were bombed 41-0 by the Redskins in their first pre-season game. The players were so whipped, he recalls, they almost had to be lifted from their dressing cubicles and carried on the field. The next year, the Broncos' training camp "was a joy." The first practice was in the morning and if the afternoon was hot and muggy, Ralston shifted his second drill to the cooler evenings.

He has carried over this flexibility in all his dealings with players. Little, for one, professes amazement with the deft manner in which Ralston maintains such an even relationship with all types of individuals. But he works at it and one of his successful methods, talking to different players each day, has been copied successfully in Los Angeles by Rams' coach Chuck Knox.

"We try to get into some in-depth discussions with them," Ralston says. "I'll jump on one or two if I think they're having problems functioning within our system and try to get things ironed out. During training camp, I'll try to spend a lot of time with a couple each day so we can exchange ideas and get our goals on the same level."

The results have been as good as he expected because of a player's natural reaction to having someone interested in what he thinks and what he hopes to accomplish. The discussions are free-flowing and the player is encouraged to speak his mind about anything concerning himself and the team. He doesn't talk to the player from behind a desk—even if he calls in a man for a good chewing-out session—because he does not think players respond well to someone who is a total authoritative figure, the desk being the symbol of authority. Instead, he'll drag a couple of chairs into the middle of a room and talk to the man in an informal manner.

"If I can minimize the problems or the thought processes caused by the problems, it stands to reason they will perform better," Ralston adds. "It's just another case of coaching to your personality. I did it at Utah State and Stanford. Hell, I might like to be Bear Bryant or Vince Lombardi, the total authoritarian, but I know that would be a complete one-hundred and eighty-degree turn and the players would see right through it."

Plunkett and Vataha recall another Ralston innovation, the players' committee. Six or seven players will act as a committee to let their coach know the team's thoughts on matters ranging from training camp regulations to the kind of food served on charter flights. The players reflect the thinking and mood of the team to Ralston, and his thinking and mood when they report back to the team.

"The only time we had any problems," the two former Stanford players remember, "was before the 1971 Rose Bowl. Guys felt there should be more leeway in our practice schedule. John had made those sessions much more intense; we were spending much more time on the field than we had been used to during the season.

"So we met with him, got the curfew extended an hour, got the use of the cars but still continued to work just as hard. His lines of communication generally were always open but they never were used too much because we never had any serious problems."

Ralston uses more than the cerebral approach to improve player relations. Within two weeks of coming to Denver, he sought out Little to solicit his help in establishing a strong personal base with the team. He first convinced Floyd that he needed his assistance and persuaded him to forgo any thoughts of either retiring or seeking to be reunited with Saban at Buffalo. Until he retired in 1975, Little says Ralston followed every bit of advice he rendered in the realm of Broncos' player relations.

"The beautiful thing about the guy was that he came to Denver with an open mind," Little says. "He didn't say, 'Look, I'm the coach and this is the way it's going to be.' His door always was open and so was his mind. I could suggest something to him, or Charley Johnson could suggest something and he wouldn't say, 'No, we're doing it this way.' He'd say, 'Okay, let's try it and see what happens.' He had the common sense to draw upon some of the experiences of his veterans.

"Maybe the thing I remember best about him was that, though we were professionals and playing this game for money, he never treated us like paid employees. He talked to us like we were college kids and he was trying to find out what was going on in our heads."

Charley Johnson, who came to the Broncos from Houston in Ralston's first season, saw the difference in Ralston's emphasis on positives. Players, he said, reacted totally differently as people to the positive approach, the "do" rather than the "don't."

"In my years at St. Louis under Charley Winner," Johnson recalls, "It was all negative thinking: don't fumble . . . don't throw an interception . . . don't lose us the game. After a while, all I wanted to do was play it safe. I was more concerned with not doing anything bad out there than doing my job, which was to win. I was just getting my head back together at Houston when I came to Denver and really was ready for the positive approach.

"The word 'never' just isn't used by him. The word 'can't' isn't in his vocabulary. When I'd go over to the sidelines, he always had a word of encouragement. 'Now go out and show them how a pro does it,' he'd say. 'Show them that you are the best there is.'

"That emphasis on the positive rubbed off on all of us," Johnson adds. "We didn't think negatively; we'd think of doing something good. You can't be doing something bad if you're thinking about doing something good."

Ralston does it with more than words. You can believe that after the Broncos defeated Pittsburgh 23-13 in Three Rivers Stadium in 1973, Ralston won total favor with his team when he refused to leave that city until tackle Marv Montgomery, who had suffered a broken leg, was put aboard the team's charter. Not only that, Ralston rushed to the hospital and was present at the operation where doctors had to set both the tibia and the fibula in the player's leg.

At the hospital he called the airport, ordered a row of seats be removed so that Montgomery would have ample room to stretch out his leg and rest it comfortably. Something like that was worth 10,000 "positive expectancies" in the players' minds.

There still is not total acceptance—there may even have been some erosion in the years he's been at Denver—but he never really expected anything different. Nor do all of his well-conceived plans always go well. Once, at Stanford, he brought in a speaker to stress the positives before a season opener against Arkansas and found the man didn't even know Plunkett's first name.

"The players turned him off," he remembers. "They challenged him: 'What right do you have to talk down to us?' And you know what? They were absolutely right."

At Denver, his veterans have heard his positives and guarantees of championships and some have stopped listening and believing. Of course, a two-season spate of injuries that ruined its title hopes didn't help. But one player noted that accentuating the positives can have an affect only in direct relation to the accumulation of positives.

"We haven't gone anywhere," he added. "At first, we were happy to win because no one ever had been a winner here before. Then we were told we'd be Super Bowl champs and we haven't even made the playoffs."

Ralston's hardest work is in times like these, stressing his belief that "what the mind can conceive the body can achieve."

If he is discouraged he doesn't show it. He plunges right back to the task, firing away with his positive thinking approach, never allowing himself or his players an excuse for not doing better. In both 1974 and 1975, the team was listed as contender to Oakland's hold on the American Conference's Western Division and the grumbling became louder when it failed to happen.

Some said the pressure of being projected as a champion had an adverse effect, particularly in 1974. Ralston disagrees, noting that he set the standards to win the division.

"We don't care what other people think," he says. "When we set up a goal it's always a total commitment that we'll make. We'll stand up before television and say Denver will win our conference and go to the Super Bowl. It's inevitable that it will happen and we certainly thought it would happen in 1974 and 1975.

"But everything happened in reverse and the club showed a lot of mettle just to hang in and get a winning season in 1974 and do as well as it did in 1975, considering all the injuries to our front-line players. I have our goal written where I can see it. It says, 'Playoffs, playoffs . . .' see, we're talking about the playoffs and then it's going to be one game at a time.

"We talked about five and nine, seven-five, twelve and two but the numbers mean nothing. Look at the twelve and two teams that don't make the Super Bowl. I learned from Bud Grant that consistency is the key. No matter how consistent you get, someone is going to be better than you on a given day. You don't worry about it; you just concentrate on that consistency and then play one game at a time. In goal-setting for 1974, we even picked out the opponents we'd win and lose against and came up with a twelve-two season, including two victories in our first three games. What happened? We lost two and tied one and were out of it in the first three weeks."

Ralston says a team will react positively to that sort of goal and to the pressure that goes with it. But the Broncos never have been to the playoffs and can't see themselves winning the close games instead of losing them, which it takes to become a champion.

"Over the time I've been at Denver," he adds, "we haven't expanded that comfort zone to see ourselves in the playoffs. In 1973, we came down to the last game against Oakland and we didn't see ourselves as successful. That was a giant step forward getting that far but all the adversity we went through in 1974 and 1975 didn't allow us to make that one positive step to the playoffs."

"For all of the enthusiasm and positive thinking, Ralston still is on guard against his team getting an inflated opinion when it does become successful. It was a point he had planned to stress in training camp in 1974 only to see the players' strike eliminate much of what he had hoped to accomplish in all areas.

"Instead of being able to take them to training camp to shake off that inflated opinion, we [the team] sat in Denver and drank beer every afternoon," he says. "Oh, they thought they were working out every day at a high school field and they stayed together and no one broke the picket line.

"They had the unity, which is a nice quality to have, but it really involves a helluva lot of work to achieve that kind of unity. Certainly a lot more work and concentration than they were undergoing. There were other factors too, such as us not being able to make any changes in our personnel. We had a bad draft.

"We weren't in a position to say this guy is better than that guy and make the changes. We came right back to the idea that the only changes necessary were the three young guys (Claudie Minor, Randy Gradishar, and Jon Keyworth) coming onto the squad; that we could coach them better and make up for the points that were necessary to oust Oakland. But it didn't work out.

"The whole thing was compounded when we went up to Green Bay in our first preseason game, played well and the team got a little more fat-headed. It was almost utter chaos and everything seemed to come apart when we lost defensive tackle Paul Smith. He's the type of player you just don't replace from the bench."

There is a tinge of regret and some irritation when Ralston reviews such events. His team was one of two (Washington was the other) whose veterans did not cross the picket line during that ill-fated strike. There were reports at the time that he wanted his players to come as a team or not to come at all. He says that after urging them all to come to camp, he kept hands off on the advice of Jim Turner, the player representative whom he had known and coached as a collegian. Turner, whose judgment Ralston said he relied upon, had warned against creating any animosity between the players and was very adamant that the team stay out as a unit. It still rankles him that he heeded that advice and he believes Turner now agrees with him.

Still, Ralston believes relations with his players, even in the aftermath of the strike, were quite good.

"Human dignity is always respected," Ralston points out. "Once you gain that confidence I don't think they ask why so much as they have confidence in knowing yours is the best way to go. Certainly, players in certain positions like quarterback might ask why. That's why we give them the right to change the play at the line of scrimmage."

This also relates to what he calls the fine-tuning in a professional athlete's psyche, which often is balanced on two definite anxieties—fear of not making the team, and fear of being traded.

"You try to minimize those," Ralston says, "by attempting to get a hard core of people around you who feel they can become champions. Sometimes it's almost necessary to hide those fears while you gather this group because it will take time for them to get enough security to go out, do their thing in a game, enjoy playing, and reach the ultimate. If you can make their way easier for them while still maintaining the objective of achieving excellence, then you must do it.

"It's also important never to lose sight of the fact that football still is a game, and I bring it up to our players constantly. One definition of a game is that it be fun and that if something is fun, it indeed is a game. We've gotten the players at Denver to enjoy football as a game, to go out and participate in a relaxed way and not play with the fear of making mistakes."

The mechanics of that approach lay in the credibility through communication that he—or any coach—can project. Ralston says being trusted by the players is the top requirement of a manager, again making the distinction for himself as a coach. The players must know and totally believe that a coach/manager won't say something he doesn't mean.

"Communication is just one of the five skilled areas for a good manager in his relationship with a player," Ralston adds. "Motivation is another. Together they equal the creation of an atmosphere that will assist the self-motivated player. The other skills— delegation, decision making, and creative thinking—are more blackboard types of things that are important in staff relations. You've got to have the first two to get the total respect of your squad."

There is absolutely no doubt that Ralston is totally wrapped up in his job, so much so that his own emotional cover is paper-thin at times. Unlike most other coaches who relax as best they can after a game is finished, Ralston spends his evenings watching films of the game. When his team plays in Denver, a cab will arrive at his home around eight o'clock, drop off the films and he'll be immersed in them until after midnight. After a road game, he'll be in his office at 5:30 A.M. sometimes so he can view the movies before his staff arrives.

"My relaxation is going home with my wife, cracking open a can of beer, and sitting around for a couple of hours with either a feeling of exhilaration or in the depths of despair. The highs and lows of coaching are monumental.

"I like to get that film because if there are any injuries in there I'll know a little more about the injury. Sometimes a doctor will give a preliminary diagnosis and say he'll look at him the next day. But if I look at the film and the play where it happened I can tell something about what might be wrong. You get some kind of peace of mind because either the player will be okay or he may be lost for the year.

"The peace of mind factor is very important to me. I want answers, particularly if we lost. Was it a tipped ball, a fumble, bad coverage, or what that allowed the winning touchdown? Those things can ride pretty heavily in your mind unless you know for sure.

"The big thing for me as a head coach is, if we lost, then I must shake the loss, and there are times when I'll cry to do it. Hell, football is an emotional business and I'll go home and I'll cry to get it out of my system. I've got to find a way out from under that big gray cloud and get going first thing the next day. It takes assistant coaches maybe until Wednesday to shake it off but I don't have that much time.

"The only criticism I ever heard of Ara Parseghian is that he couldn't shake off a loss. But some way, with the film, an extra can of beer, and a little cry, by Monday morning I've got to be seeing something a little rosier. You can't dwell on the negative. If you do, you tend to be negative. You've got to get it back over to the positive side."

This emotional involvement spreads through Ralston's family. When the Broncos lost a wild game to the Kansas City Chiefs on Monday night a couple of years ago, his married daughter called from her home in San Diego to talk to her twin sister and before the conversation had gone far, both were in tears over the loss. At the same time, Ralston and his wife were crying and his son was so distraught that he didn't return to his fraternity house at the University of Colorado until the wee hours of the next morning when he could get in without getting a great deal of verbal abuse.

"There is a total, all-encompassing obsession to succeed in this business and it involves a lot of people, including every member of your family," Ralston says.

When Denver wins, Ralston becomes even more critical than after a victory. His feeling is, 'Great. Now let's go to work on next week.'

"After a loss, I've got to get the players thinking, 'Hey, forget the damn thing. Let's keep moving. It's over.' In the pro game, you can lose four or five times and still be a contender. In college, you can lose one time and be out the whole season and start talking about next year."

Ralston naturally carries these emotions down to the sidelines and into the locker room during a game. One of his most memorable moments in the NFL occurred at Yankee Stadium in 1972, his first season, when he kept stride-for-stride with Little as he raced 55 yards for a touchdown against the New York Giants.

"I could see him alongside me, clipboard in hand," Little recalls. "He was the first one to throw his arms around me when I got to the end zone. It was the same way with punt returns. If you got too close to our sideline when one of us was breaking a punt return, you'd better look out because John would blow you into the next county. I mean he throws his arms up and signals a touchdown before the referee can. I always called him our number one cheerleader."

That, of course, is one of his admitted functions during a game and the players don't mind a bit. Dawkins says the players responded to his enthusiasm because they know he doesn't have to keep control of the game with his assistant coaches handling offense and defense.

"At Stanford," Plunkett recalls, "He did his work all week long, put the thing together for Saturday, and then had enough confidence in his staff to let them run the show. He was like our number one fan on the sidelines and sometimes I think he got so excited that he really lost control of things. But I think some of that was due to the tremendous amount of pressure he was under at Stanford and when he saw we were succeeding, he was so overjoyed that he let it all go."

Ralston is the same way in the locker room at halftime. Dawkins and several other Broncos recall a game when Denver trailed 21-3 at halftime.

"Okay," he told his players, "we're going to win because we have them right where we want them. We're going out there in the second half and turn this game around."

"Our heads were hanging pretty low at that time," Dawkins remembers, "but when we heard that, it snapped us back. And we went out and won it. He was unbelievable. He was the kind of guy who believed that a fourteen-point deficit with two minutes to play didn't mean anything. He just refused to allow a team to tell itself it couldn't win."

He pursues the same philosophy each year in training camp. Gambold says he gives every player—draftee, free agent, tradee, veteran—a chance, regardless of how they may be regarded by others. He believes every one can make the squad and he treats the seventeenth round draft pick the same as the first round pick.

"I think it goes back to when John was the ninety-ninth guy at California and started something like two games in three years," Gambold says. "John was a great recruiter at Stanford and now, even though he's in pro ball, I think he feels he's still recruiting. Only instead of going into a kid's home, he's going over the cuts, the free agents, the waiver lists. For a number of players, coming to Denver was like a new lease on life, a second chance to prove themselves and everyone of them got a solid shot."

Ralston has a voracious appetite for studying the NFL's personnel charts. He says the only way to succeed is to know more about the players in the league—including his own—than do his opponents.

"Football's first commandment, is know thyself" he says. "That takes time. But you must do it because the players in the game are your talent pool. Good drafts are essential, naturally, but every team fills in with a half-dozen deals each year, more or less, and this is your balance wheel. A good team is one that does it right."

This function gets into his duties as general manager. He has seen to it that every player in the NFL is graded and the grades kept current as his coaches and personnel people study film. He breaks down his list to the top 600 players, or approximately half those playing, then divides them into four categories—A, B, C, and D. A is a star (there are at least four per team on the average); Bs would definitely make his starting team; Cs would make the squad; and Ds are below par.

The key, he says, is to accumulate as many "B" players to complement the limited number of As. This has been an ongoing process at Denver and a reason why the team has shown improvement since 1972.

He has come to enjoy the personnel constants in pro football as opposed to having his good players graduate after two or three seasons in college. However, he does see a parallel between the two. In college football, the seniors are the backbone of a team and when they leave a coach knows just how many will be coming along to replace them. It's almost that way in professional football except that a superstar could stay eight or ten years.

"As you get to know your squad you see the ones who will be in it a longer period of time," Ralston points out. "But you should be changing five, six, or seven faces every year. New people coming in, older ones moving out is the nature of the business. But the longer the older hands stay with you, the better it is because they help pass on your philosophy."

Ralston is not like George Allen in his preference for veterans, though he sees as a good norm an experience factor between four and eight years. There should be exceptions at both ends, he agrees, but a team that can maintain the four-to-eight average will have the perfect blend of youth and experience.

Much of the Broncos' player development rests in the hands of Ralston's assistant coaches. He prefers they handle all the teaching aspects, insisting on the same amount of dedication that he possesses.

Ralston is the first to admit that "it never has been a strength of mine to get into Xs and Os, in college or professional football. You have the X and O side, and the people side of football, and I've always been on the people side. My strengths as a college coach were involved in recruiting, though that's not to say I didn't enjoy conducting a college football clinic. But there are others who can do it much better than I."

Ralston has a great knowledge of the sport's more technical aspects. He must evaluate a team and a player's worth because he makes all the final decisions involving trades and the draft. He simply does not see himself as a great teacher in his role of head coach, feeling it more important to delegate that area of responsibility.

"Doing that is nothing more than analyzing how effective you are yourself," he points out. "We all want to achieve success as a team and as a program. If I can't make the big decisions, other than kicking during a game, then I'll delegate them. I want all of our staff involved constantly in everything we do and I get very close to them in this area."

His coaches say that once the authority is delegated he does not look over their shoulders. He places great trust in each coach and grants almost total autonomy during the week in practice and in a game.

"There are some coaches who don't get that involved in practice," assistant coach Jerry Frei (now with Tampa Bay) notes, "but during a game they feel the compulsion to become involved in asserting their authority. That's not John's style because when he gives you authority, you know it's yours. It makes working a whole lot easier because the players know they must relate so strongly to their unit coach and will not have the head man changing everything once a game begins."

Max Coley, Denver's offensive coordinator, had a very thoughtful oversight into Ralston's relationships with his staff and his overall coaching acumen. Coley considers his boss to be "a great coach because he's a positive thinker; is well-organized in that everyone knows what is expected of them; and is a goal-setter. He does not get into all the technical aspects as Chuck Noll (for whom Coley worked) does in Pittsburgh. The two present contrasting styles, both of which are successful.

Within the staff, he outlines all he wants done in his coaches' meetings and then allows it all to happen. He acts as the overseer. On the practice field he will patrol each group to see what is going on. His prime responsibility then is to see that the practice, which he organized for time and content, goes off according to schedule.

Like all coaches, Ralston leads a pretty dogged life during the season, worse if his team is not going well. In his first season at Denver, he came to work 15 minutes earlier each time his team lost a game.

"Goddamn it!" he says, shaking his head, "I was getting up at four-thirty in the morning. If we had lost any more than nine games it hardly would have been worth leaving the office to go home!"

Ralston, like Don Shula, is an early morning person in that both say they do their best thinking at that time. John lives a half hour from work and uses much of his "drive time" to bone up on motivational tapes or inspirational talks by famous speakers so as to set the mood for his own day. While his coaches do their film and classroom work, he handles his general manager's duties, then joins the entire squad on the practice field.

The Broncos' staff works late on Tuesday night preparing the offensive game plan for the upcoming week; and late again on Wednesday putting the defensive plan into order. Even after his staff leaves for the night, Ralston stays in his office, before walking two blocks to a nearby motel. He'll be back in the office before his staff reports the next morning.

"It's a seven-day-a-week proposition during the season, though surprisingly Friday evening and all day Saturday are not too bad," he says. "In college football, you never had any time. You worked just as hard the day before a game as you did the first day of the practice week. We don't do that at Denver.

"It's also nice to get a chance to relax the day before a game, either at home or on the road. I'll watch the college games on television because I never want to get too far away from college football. It's our life's blood and we can't do enough for the college game.

"I also want to break down this barrier between college and professional football. After all, we're all playing eleven-man football so let's advance the game. I have a side goal of wanting to be the first pro coach ever to speak at the American Football Coaches Association meeting. I always attend their football all-star game in June and was once a member of their board of directors. I'd really like to find a way we could assist their program."

With the exception of a half-hour television show on Monday night before the game, Ralston cuts out all personal appearances during the season—quite a cutback considering that he may speak from five to eight times a week between January and July. And you'll never see him on the town during the season, that postgame can of beer or two is the only indulgence he allows himself once training camp begins.

Ralston no longer burdens his players with an eight-hour day that begins and ends with meetings, and has a long on-the-field session in between. His player committee approached him with a request for earlier starts and earlier finishes so they could beat the rush-hour traffic around Denver and he accommodated them. Players report at 9 A.M. and are finished by 2:30 P.M.

During these practice sessions, Ralston keeps a close check on whether or not plans for the upcoming game are progressing satisfactorily.

"We work some offense, some defense each day through the week so we can adjust if necessary," Ralston says. "If we go back and see that something is wrong, then I'll take full responsibility. I'll step before the whole squad and say, 'That play was my idea and it's lousy,' regardless of which assistant proffered the idea. It's my responsibility, so I have to assume it."

Plunkett remembers when Stanford won the Pacific-8 title, then lost two games after being 8-1. The team should have won both, he admits, but simply let up after clinching the conference title.

"He really jumped on us at a team dinner when the regular season had ended," Plunkett says. "And it took us by surprise. I thought it was a little unfair because it was his job to prepare us and I think everyone deserved a share of blame of those losses. It was one reason why he took such strong measures in preparing us for the Rose Bowl.

"Maybe it's lucky that he did because if we hadn't lost those two games, we might not have worked as hard and might not have been as prepared as we were for that game against Ohio State."

At Stanford, Ralston had gained the reputation as a coach with an "interesting" offense. It resembled that of the pros in that he threw the ball much more than college teams normally did and had great variety on offense. It was not an attempt to copy the professionals, he says, but something born of necessity to offset a disparity of talent in competition with other rivals within the Pacific-8 Conference.

"We had to do something to keep the defense off balance," he says. "We tried to go counter to the down-and-distance theory, which involved throwing half the time on first down and that often can lead to throwing again on second and third down. Or we'd run on first down and when it seemed we should be passing, we'd run again. We always tried to break it up, tried to keep a defense from ever getting a good reading on us."

Ralston also decided upon the efficacy of a drop-back quarterback at Stanford once Plunkett came along. Before that, he had a sprint-out, roll-out passing game, but Plunkett didn't fit that image. Ralston sought help from the 49ers and had offensive linemen Len Rohde and Howard Mudd work at spring drills to help familiarize his offense with the solid pass protection techniques needed to protect a pocket passer.

He also had former 49ers' head coach Jack Christiansen on his staff as first a defensive coordinator, then as offensive coordinator, as well as Bobby Waters, another former 49ers' quarterback. Christiansen succeeded Ralston as head coach when Ralston went to Denver.

"Much of his style of play has stayed with me," Plunkett says. "He was wide open and not afraid to throw. I carried that with me into the NFL in the sense that I still like to throw deep and try something different when someone least expects it."

Ralston's teaching, both in football and his emphasis on motivation, may be the answer many sought as to why Plunkett came into the NFL and had such a superlative rookie season. He led the Patriots to six victories, including upsets of Oakland, Baltimore, and Miami, played every offensive down and was named rookie of the year in the American Conference. He still carries some of that exposure with him, particularly a feeling that he never can be beaten when he steps behind a center.

"You got confidence from winning under John," Vataha adds. "You could see the results of how hard work can get you some place and that attitude was the main thing

I brought to pro football. It gave me confidence I could make it in the pros, though I wasn't highly sought. I figured if Stanford could get in the Rose Bowl, I could play in the pros. I think this was a cumulative affect that he had, attitude-wise, on anyone who played for him."

When Ralston came to the Broncos he knew that he wasn't going to dazzle anyone with his offensive theories, so he didn't try. He did what every other NFL coach does every season—analyzed his personnel.

"It all centers around how strong the defense is," he says. "If it is strong enough to get the ball back on three downs and your kicking game is sound, you play one style of football. If you feel you've got to outscore your opponent while the offense is coming along, you play another style."

He tried the second way and it didn't work the first season because Denver, though putting more punch in the offense, was outscored 350-325. Under Coley's influence, the Broncos used the same style offense as Pittsburgh but still had the wide-open look that Ralston had used at Denver. When the club is healthy, it still looks that way, though there is more emphasis on the running game now with Otis Armstrong in the backfield.

Most of Ralston's early work dealt with a way to upgrade the defense. Denver had seven number one draft picks on its team but none were on defense in 1972. In 1974 and 1975, both top choices were for the defense, linebacker Randy Gradishar and defensive back Louis Wright. In fact, a dozen of his first five picks in four drafts were for the defense, just seven for offense.

"We had to do a selling job on defense at the start," Ralston says. "Joel Collier stayed on as defensive coach and Bob Gambold, our defensive coordinator at Stanford, came in and he helped with our thinking. At one point we were starting three rookies on that unit and when it is healthy, with Lyle Alzado, Paul Smith, and Barney Chavous across the front, we're as strong as anyone."

All that remains for John Ralston is to make good his promise to go to the Super Bowl. First, he knows his team must win the division title or wild-card spot, go to the playoffs, win the conference championship, then play for everything. The comfort zones must be expanded, the positive expectancies absolute, and the blocking and tackling precise.

Don Shula

"The secret of success is getting
inside different personalities . . .
and getting the most out of them."

Most American heroes have been the players . . . the doers.

With few exceptions—Knute Rockne, Vince Lombardi, and Casey Stengel, for
examples—our heroes have not come from coaches and managers.

Don Shula is another exception to the rule. No coach in professional sports was more
highly publicized nor easily recognized during the first half of the seventies than he
was. He was his profession's glamour boy, an individual whose achievements with
the Miami Dolphins became instant legend.

Shula is a man of the people, a worker in the truest sense. Perhaps that is the measure of his appeal.

Mention Shula's name to other coaches in the NFL and the reaction usually is:
"Shula's secret is that he just rolls up his sleeves and goes to work."

Shula has a personal manner that seems to fit everything within his world into its
proper niche. You can sit at dinner with him in a crowded New York City restaurant
and be aware of the buzz that follows his presence. He can be aware of it, too, but his
attentions are directed to you. And if the privacy of his table is interrupted by auto-
graph seekers, he is obliging, gracious, and not the least self-effacing.

You can be with him immediately after a football game in which his team did not
play particularly well but still managed to win and never know the torment still going
on within him. He treats such games as losses, but he doesn't treat those he must
meet as losers.

He is a straight-from-the-shoulder guy who enjoys give-and-take but who won't
hesitate to snap, "What the hell kind of a question is that?" He also has withstood the
pressure of four Super Bowls, where everything from the color of his game-day shorts
to the legitimacy of his talent has been put under public scrutiny, and he still emerged
smiling and jocular.

Perhaps what really has made him one of us is that he has not always been a winner.

In Super Bowl III, his Baltimore team felt the upset wrath of Joe Namath and the New York Jets. And there were times when he was told "he couldn't win the big one," the ultimate tag of the loser. He beat that rap—more than beat it, annihilated it.

He has squabbled with his bosses, once leaving one at Baltimore to go to Miami; and at Miami, threatening to punch that one in the nose for humiliating him in front of his wife and friends. Who among us never has lain awake at night reveling in the joys of someday doing likewise, but when the moment of truth comes about, saying nothing?

You get the feeling after a while that Shula could indeed walk into a saloon, order a shot-and-beer (he's a scotch and soda man, actually), and feel totally at home with working men who will look you in the eye and tell you right out what they think of your program.

Shula is like that. It is one of the reasons why he has been able to harness the energies, talents, and personalities of players in Baltimore and Miami. He is, as one coaching rival said, "a man's man."

Such assets aren't guarantees to successful coaching careers in the National Football League. But they can be the foundation on which success is built when the other elements are present. Shula has used all those elements wisely and well in forging a record that made him the youngest coach in NFL history to win 100 games, the first coach ever to take a team to the Super Bowl three consecutive years, and the first coach in 30 years to lead a team through an NFL season with a perfect record.

In seven seasons with the Colts his teams won 71 of 98 games. The Colts won one NFL championship and two conference titles.

When he became head coach of the Miami Dolphins in 1970, he said, "I'm no miracle worker and don't make me out to be one." Yet in his first season, he rallied a team that for its first four years was a sorry loser, and made it to the playoffs after winning 10 games.

"I don't have a magic formula that I'm going to give to the world as soon as I can write a book," he said upon accepting the Dolphins' job. "I'm not a person with a great deal of finesse. I don't have peace of mind until I know I've given the game everything I can, because the whole idea is to somehow get an edge. Sometimes it takes just a little extra something to get that edge. But you must get it.

"I try to do it with mental preparation, and physical preparation, and in general, with overall preparation to accomplish the ultimate. Of course, I know that the people we play have the same goal—winning—so I try to put more effort in our preparation. You set a goal to be the best and then work hard every hour, every day to reach that goal. If you allow yourself to settle for anything less than being number one, then you're cheating yourself."

Don Shula never cheated himself nor anyone else. He holds back nothing—physical, mental, or emotional. His life ethic won't allow it. His father was an immigrant who grew up near Painesville, Ohio, and worked for $25 a week as a fisherman on Lake Erie. Don took his turn on that job and found seasickness harder to take than hauling in bulging nets or performing the other physically demanding aspects of the job.

Losing became anathema to him when he was 10 years old and he would sit under his front steps sobbing after his team lost. Perfection became important when he was a freshman in high school and felt he had done so poorly on the first two days of football tryouts that he turned in his uniform.

Don Martin, one of his physical education instructors, brought him back and helped him realize, he admits, that his life outside the sport even at that age had been miserable.

Though he was a good offensive player as a halfback in high school, he soon found at John Carroll University that he needed to develop other skills and learned to play defense as a cornerback as well. He had limitations in speed for that position but he learned to maximize his assets, principally knowing more about his job and his opponent than anyone else. Some say that this ability to rise above his limitations is why he can motivate players to play to the limit of their skills in the NFL.

"It has been my drive to do the best I could in whatever I did," Shula says.

The Browns drafted him and his college teammate, Carl Taseff, on the ninth round in 1950. When Shula didn't hear from the team for a time, he called and wondered if the Browns had plans to sign him.

"They told me to be patient, that I'd be contacted," he recalls. "When they called and told us to come down to their offices, we must have been there about the time they put the phone on the hook.

"It was the first time I ever met Paul Brown and he told me he would offer me a contract for five thousand dollars. I signed it before he could draw the next breath because I was afraid he might change his mind."

Shula had already decided to become a part of pro football but he had to prove his worth. The Browns of 1951 were an established, veteran team that had won the NFL title in its first try. Ninth-round draft choices generally were not much to look at but Shula literally made the Browns look at him.

He remembers a scrimmage one day in which he blasted Marion Motley with a head-on tackle.

"Nice tackle, Taseff," said Paul Brown.

"Shula—the name is Shula not Taseff," Don replied.

He made his point because he started 11 games that season after veteran Tommy James was injured. Both Brown and Blanton Collier, his defensive assistant, have vivid memories of the young rookie.

"He was smart and he was a hitter," Brown says. "Some guys are great players but you know they won't stay with it. Don gave you the feeling he was vitally interested."

"When he came to Cleveland he impressed every one of us with his desire to know more about football," Collier says. "He was a great student of the game and we became pretty good friends. It was not a player-coach relationship as much as it was a joint venture. He worked very hard at the job and I knew then he had a great desire to be a football coach."

Collier, who became a head coach in the NFL and handed Shula his first heart-wrenching defeat when Cleveland upset the Colts in the 1964 NFL title game, remembers Don's inquisitiveness.

"Don always wanted to know why we did what we did," Collier recalls.

"It is something I find quite natural," Shula says. Not only in football but in everything. I have a very inquisitive nature. When I was a player, I didn't only know what I was supposed to do but also what the people around me would be doing. I always was thinking how the offense would attack the defense, how they would try to beat the things we were trying to do.

"Very rarely was anything put on the blackboard that I didn't ask, 'Why do we do this?' or 'What do we do if they do this?' or 'If I do this, what does he do over there . . . ?' No one seemed to mind, though I'm sure there were times when they wished I would keep still.

"But being inquisitive like that broadened my scope and gave me a well-rounded football background. It also helped me to sense that if another player didn't know what was going on, it helped him if I would ask a question to be sure the coach would repeat what he was saying. Then everyone would know.

"I always felt it was better to get it out in the open, regardless of what anyone thought. When I became an assistant coach at Baltimore I wanted to make sure the players understood it as well as myself."

That hasn't changed. His players say he always gives the "why" to everything that is put into his playbook.

Though his association with Paul Brown lasted just two seasons, its effect never has diminished.

"Paul Brown was the greatest influence on me, especially in the teaching aspect of coaching," Shula says. "In football, it's not what you know but what your ball players know that counts. We make it as much like a classroom as possible, using all sorts of teaching aids, followed by practice on the field, followed by going over mistakes and improvements in the classroom.

"What we do now started with the Paul Brown playbook. I admired his organization. He didn't leave anything to chance. He was very basic. Each year we'd come back to camp and he'd make a guy like Otto Graham take a test that would have a question like, 'What is a running play?' Otto would have to write out the answer.

"Weeb [Ewbank] and Blanton were two of Brown's assistants and when they became head coaches, they took their own variations of Paul's playbook. I worked under all three and what we do now in Miami is what I have taken from all three and made into our playbook. Of course, I've added my own variations as well as some from my assistants. But what we are doing now is what Paul Brown started a long time ago."

Being traded to Baltimore, along with Taseff and eight other players for five Colts —the largest trade in modern NFL history—marked the first major step in Shula's coaching career.

Keith Molesworth was the Colts' coach when Don arrived in Baltimore and he had adopted the Browns' system. Adopting it was one thing; making it work another.

"It wasn't being taught on the field the way we had learned it at Cleveland," Shula remembers. "So there were times when I had to step in and see that it was done the right way. I got kidded a lot about being a coach on the field but it never fazed me."

It didn't bother Molesworth either as the Colts struggled through their first season. When Ewbank became head coach the following season, he remembered Shula from Cleveland and was grateful for one other disciple from Paul Brown.

"Don wasn't afraid to get up in meetings and explain what we were trying to do," Ewbank said. "He knew our defenses thoroughly and he'd get on guys who didn't keep up. He was a perfectionist even then and he wasn't shy about sounding off to those who didn't pay attention. I never had any second thoughts about giving him added responsibility.

"In fact, I took advantage of his leadership. We were a growing team and we needed someone like Don to keep us together on the field."

Shula felt that his unofficial coach-on-the-field job should mean more money. Back home in Cleveland, he read where some baseball players had returned contracts unsigned as a gesture of their displeasure with management's salary offers. When he received the Colts' contract, he returned it unsigned.

A week later a letter came from general manager Don Kellett, saying in effect he assumed the unsigned contract meant Shula was retiring and would he please return his playbook.

"I got on the phone right away," Don remembers with a laugh, "and said, 'Listen, you've made a terrible mistake. I'm not retiring.'"

As a player, Shula got the job done without flare or fuss.

"He got by with his head," says Charley Winner, an assistant coach with the Colts under both Ewbank and Shula. "He studied the opposition and always wanted to know 'why' if something wasn't working. When he dealt with a player, both as an assistant coach and later as a head coach, he'd always ask, 'Are we asking too much of a guy?' or 'Are we stepping right on this?' He never stopped asking questions."

Shula tread a fine line of survival with the Browns. He had trouble covering their receivers—Mac Speedie, Dante Lavelli, and Dub Jones—in practice but in a game, he benefited from those around him and from his knowledge of an opponent.

"Don would have stayed in pro football a little longer if he had a bit more speed," Collier says. "Today, I would make him a free safety. We had a three-deep secondary with a lot of one-on-one coverage and not a lot of zone. Don was a good hitter and he had pretty good speed but not the quickness that a cornerback needs. But through sheer determination and hard work he was a pretty good one."

Shula was a four-year starter as a cornerback with the Colts. But Ewbank cut Shula just before the 1957 season began. Failure was infuriating.

"I was so damned mad I didn't know what to do," he says. "I had sunglasses on and I was glad of that because the players were going out to practice and I had to pass by them. I got in my car and just drove, trying to straighten things out in my mind."

He later signed with the Washington Redskins and played one more year. He retired as a player after the 1957 season. Instead of driving aimlessly again, he headed to downtown Washington, where the NCAA football coaches were holding their annual convention and landed a job as an assistant coach at the University of Virginia. A year later, he joined Collier as an assistant at the University of Kentucky.

It was during his year at Kentucky that Shula first met Bill Arnsparger and Howard Schellenberger, who later would become his top two assistant coaches with the Colts and Dolphins. And it also gave him a chance to study under Collier.

After his first season at Kentucky, he had two or three coaching offers, including one from George Wilson of the Detroit Lions. He asked Collier's advice.

"What do you want from life from here on out?" Collier asked.

"I want to be a coach in professional football," Shula replied.

"Then you've got to take that job," Collier said.

"He was concerned because the coaching situation at Detroit at that time was a little shaky. He thought the thing might blow up and he was concerned what would happen to him.

"I told him, 'Don't worry about that. You're a friend of Paul Brown. Weeb would help. I would help. Besides, you need the exposure of pro football.'"

It was the best advice he ever received.

"I've tried to learn from all and copy none," Shula says. "Everyone I played or coached under were different types and I learned from them while still being myself. I've never gone out and tried to be Paul Brown or Blanton Collier or George Wilson.

"They satisfied my great thirst for knowledge, my searching and looking to find out the what, the how, and why. The most important thing though is to learn from the people you work for. I tried to take all the things I've been exposed to and if I can incorporate them into the framework of Don Shula, that's fine."

From Brown came the importance of teaching, of organization, of establishing a timetable and sticking to it. From Collier came the importance of detail work, the bare bones and fine points of football technique that result in crisp execution. From Wilson came much of the Chicago Bears' teaching methods as well as how to forge a good relationship with players.

"Wilson was an ex-player. So was I, but he knew how to approach them and make his playing experience work for him," Shula says. "There is a fine line there because ex-players are not automatically accepted as coaches. You've got to know how to use what is a definite edge."

Being a very organized person, Shula surrounds himself with organized people in all areas touching his football operation. He outlines what he wants from them and then keeps close tab on the results.

The organization concept, of course, stems from Paul Brown. An example is his practice plan. He and his staff sit down after the day's work on the field and from film, video tape, or personal recollection, jot down every mistake made by the players. Before the next day's workout, Shula personally goes over each mistake with that player. A log is kept on each player and Shula can measure the man's progress.

The same organization is reflected in his staff's work schedule. Every day is accounted for long before New Year's Day rolls around.

"After being with him a year," Schnellenberger says, "you'll know exactly what you do every day, by date and by time. He follows a plan based on his years of experience as a head coach.

"Don can look at the schedule, then at the progress we've made and tell exactly at a specific time of the year where we are. He can measure his team's progress and stay atop any situations that might develop."

Shula puts it in sharper focus.

"The important thing is not what Don Shula knows or what any of my assistant coaches know," Shula says. "The important thing is that we can transmit to the people we're responsible for. They're going to be tested on Sunday afternoon and the fact that we win on Sunday afternoon indicates that we're getting through to them. That's what coaching is . . . the ability to transmit information."

This process begins about 6:30 each morning. "I'm a morning person," he says. "I work much better at that time." A Roman Catholic, he attends daily Mass at the chapel on the campus of Biscayne College, where the Dolphins have their football training facilities. He's in his office shortly after 7:30 and ready for his assistants, who arrive within the next half hour.

The day after a game, everyone analyzes the film and begins preparing for the upcoming game. The players report Tuesday for a film review of the past game and one-hour loosening up session on the field. When they leave, Shula and his staff begin getting the next game plan in order. This is generally a 17- or 18-hour day for him and when the team undergoes its difficult practice routines the next three days, he'll spend 12 hours on the job.

The results are not measured by time. Monte Clark, his former offensive line coach, was amazed at the meticulous planning for each day.

"Everything is laid out to the minute," he says. "There are four and a half minutes here, eighteen minutes there. He has taken the coaches out on the field and put us through warmup exercises just the way he wanted the players to do them. He has an exact spot planned for each man to stand."

To some of his players, the endless details often seem boring—like the positioning of a player's head when he lines up on the punting team, the step-by-step movement of a lineman in a given situation. To Shula it is not when to block a man but who will do it and where it will go.

One player, who had played for two NFL teams prior to joining Miami, couldn't believe the attention given to detail. He said one of his former pro coaches was happy if contact was made with an opponent. At Miami, he learned his position in minute detail, the final detail being making contact with the man across the line of scrimmage.

"The team sees him work so hard and that feeling rubs off," tackle Norm Evans says. "You just can't help it. He's made all of us believers in his system, whether we like it or not."

"We never let an error go unchallenged," Shula says. "Uncorrected errors will multiply. Someone once asked me if there wasn't benefit in overlooking one small flaw.

"'What is a small flaw?' I asked him."

Players say Shula never overestimates an opponent and doesn't believe in giving the psychological needle about obviously weaker teams. That always has been a challenge because for almost 90 percent of his head coaching career in the NFL, Shula's teams have been superior to their opponents. But if a team was really tough, he'd tell his teams just how tough; if not, he'd tell them they should be able to win and then work to see that they did.

His players have come to trust his evaluations. When he has an opponent's film on the screen, he will emphasize their use of formations, tendencies, and individual abilities.

When he is at the blackboard putting together his own formations, he gives not only the Xs and Os, but the theory of why the play has been designed, why it is run and what it was designed to do with other plays to be used in a game. It's as if he were back in Cleveland or Baltimore and making his coaches explain the "why."

Shula is all-business at work, in an interview, even playing golf. But he does not subscribe to something Tom Landry reportedly once told his players, i.e., "Nothing funny ever happens on a football field."

When his team works, it works hard but Shula maintains a good rapport with his players. It is, many say, the real essence of the man that he gets so much out of them and in such a demanding way because he never lets up once the team hits the practice field. The famed Shula temper, the acerbic tongue, and the pat on the fanny all are part of a day's work as much a part as the endless attention to detail.

Practice lasts an hour and a half, perhaps an hour and three-quarters, but no more. During that time there is no nonsense. There is no ban on humor, either.

Miami players recall with some glee the day Csonka tossed a rubber snake in Shula's direction and watched his coach's reaction. Everyone roared and they said for a moment Shula was too scared to know what to do. But he enjoyed the moment and never said an angry word to Csonka about it.

"Don has the knack of laughing at the right time," Bill Arnsparger remembers. "He's never been afraid to enjoy a funny situation and there were times when he laughed at things that were happening on the practice field when you wondered whether you should laugh or not. And there were times when no one laughed."

When he came to Miami to try and get his new team together, he found some sort of immediate success in the off-season because a good nucleus of his players lived in the area. This enabled him at least to get the passing game installed and make his quarterbacks and receivers familiar with what they would be doing.

But when training camp was scheduled to open, he was confronted with a player's strike that lasted until a week before the first preseason game. When the players finally came to camp, they found a schedule of four on-the-field workouts per day for that week.

Many players barely can manage two sessions but Shula gave no quarter. At the end of that week, they won their first game with him as head coach and presented him with the game ball.

"We had to get it done some way," he says. "The only way I could find time was to try to make the day longer. When they'd come in for the nine o'clock meeting in the morning, I'd try to make a joke out of it. 'Didn't you guys just leave here?' I'd ask. I didn't get a lot of laughs but we did get a lot of work done and we accomplished what we set out to do . . . we won that football game."

That's when the players really learned what Shula was all about . . . "Merciless," tackle Norm Evans remembers.

"Winning early helped," Shula adds, "because I was asking them to do so much. It made them think the work was worthwhile. They saw it pay off. If we had lost early, there might have been some raised eyebrows."

"That first year under Shula," Evans says, "was a training year. He was saying to us, 'Do it my way.' Now we know not to buck him . . . to take him at his word. And don't forget the Dolphins have a lot of guys who are self-motivators. But they get it done the way he wants it."

Regardless of the coach involved, this approach is a necessity if a team is to win. The prime reason being that a season runs 20 games, including preseason games but excluding postseason. If a team makes the Super Bowl, it can play as many as 24 as the Dolphins did in 1973 when they won their second consecutive NFL title.

In college football, a team begins practice about two and a half or three weeks before its season opener, plays 10 or 11 games, perhaps a bowl game after a two-week or month-long respite and that's it. In the pros, Schnellenberger noted, a team can play its preseason schedule and about half its regular schedule and that's the equivalent of a full college season.

"That's why Don wants his team on an even keel, he doesn't want it sagging halfway through the schedule," Schnellenberger said. "Professional football must be a day-by-day proposition where there is total involvement and total achievement. Somebody's got to stand out there and see that it happens and Don Shula does not abdicate that responsibility."

There also are the unexpected things. Shula tries to head them off before they arise. It is his belief that his team should never go into a game with the feeling it will win because an opponent is predictable. He wants it on guard for something different, the unexpected.

He believes the Dolphins can never afford to harden into rigid patterns or ways of being, or styles of playing. To him, football is a game of game-day adjustments which come about when things don't go as expected. He wants his players to detach themselves from the game, after a fashion, and keep thinking about alternatives and adjustments.

If there are to be no permanent patterns, then it follows that each player, regardless of his position, must necessarily be taught to innovate and deal with situations he hasn't practiced against. That is accomplished only by hard work, a common sense approach in Shula's book.

He wants his team to accept a flexible stance in every game. He has done the same thing through his career. He has changed, his players—at Baltimore and Miami—say, perhaps a little less rigid now than when he joined the Dolphins; a little more consistent than during his years with the Colts.

In his last few seasons at Baltimore he developed a consistency toward the game. In his early years, he'd be lax one day in his attitude toward mistakes, then more critical the next, particularly toward little things. His Dolphins' players say that he also has changed, though none will admit that he's any softer, any less demanding nor less critical. Perhaps, they say, the change really is in the way they operate within their coach's limits. They are doing things totally his way and the lash that can be Shula's tongue does not flick at their sensitivities nearly as often as it did the first couple of years in Miami.

"People always are waiting for us to have a letdown," linebacker Nick Buoniconti says. "They waited after we finished 1972 undefeated, then again after we won our second Super Bowl. When we lost Csonka, Kiick, and Warfield to the World Football League, they said, 'They're down now.' Even when we began the 1975 season with four starters on the defense out with injuries everyone thought we were down and out, what with our offense still jelling.

"But letdowns are for losers. Besides, how can you have a letdown the way that guy keeps you working on an even keel."

Shula-watchers have marveled over what they term the "self confidence" of his teams when really what they see is a team totally stabilized. The real strength of this stabilization, Shula says, comes from the leadership within the team.

"At Baltimore, John Unitas was the man. He was quiet but he was a leader. Ray Berry was the same way," Shula says. "At Miami, Bob Griese is very business-like but also very efficient, totally dedicated, and the most unselfish player I ever met. That comes from inner leadership and it must come from the top too. I don't spend a lot of time patting people on the back nor do I downgrade everyone if a game is gone."

That is not the popular picture painted of Shula. He always has been known for his firebrand temper and he never had hidden the fact that he has fought to control it throughout his football career. But he does not think of himself as Attila the Hun or some raging maniac who goes around ripping up telephone books or knocking over lockers when he is displeased.

"I used to have a vicious temper," he admits, "but I've mellowed a bit, I've matured a bit, and I have much better control of my own emotions now. You've got to remember that I'm an emotional person, though sometimes I'm told it may not seem that way looking at me on the sidelines. But I get so involved in a game that I've gotten carried away."

He got carried away one day at Miami, to the point of shoving an official, that he had a penalty flag thrown at his feet and 15 yards assessed against his team. He never again has allowed himself to be carried that far though he will let an official know in no uncertain terms if he feels there has been an error of judgment.

His constant battles to keep his temper under control are another thing that makes Shula more human. Sometimes he wins; sometimes he doesn't. But when he loses, there never is anything personal in his blowup.

"One of the big things I've learned is to become more understanding of others in this regard," he says. "There might be a better way to reach a guy than to blow your stack on the sidelines, depending on the player's personality."

Often Shula didn't consider personality. Some of his former Colts' players remember him having no distinction between player and/or official; he'd chew them all. One of his veteran Baltimore players once went to him after a particularly rough going-over and told Shula he didn't appreciate it, though he never resented his coach's criticism or temper. But he flatly refused to put up with any lava-like dressing down.

"After that," the player said, "we got along real well. He'd get on me and I didn't mind because it was my nature that I could take a roasting. But Don worked after that to control his temper."

"You have to know the players individually," Shula says. "That's when I think coaching comes in, where you understand each player. And because you understand him, you try to get the most out of each and every man in a pressure situation."

The problem then has become one of personal recognition. Csonka said he treated everyone the same when it came to a temper burst . . ."if he chewed me out, he'd be just as liable to chew out Bob Griese. If a guy has tender feelings, he either got over them quickly or he didn't last too long with Shula."

Don remembers his days at Baltimore when he could whiplash a player like Tom Matte. The next minute, he admits, he could kid with him and both instances would be separate and distinct. The chewing out made its point; the light moment was reflective of no hard feelings on either part.

Bubba Smith, the former defensive end of the Colts, found Shula's tirades unbearable. John Unitas once reportedly turned to Shula after being screamed at, handed him the football and said, "Here, you wanta be the quarterback?"

Even now, he is defensive about his reputation. Told that he used to be abrupt (and that is a *mild* description), Shula bristled and denied the accusation.

"I was involved and emotional," he said in his own behalf. "When I work hard then I may be prone to showing my temper. I might have been snippy in some situations. I'm the kind of guy who may be biting but when the situation is over, that's it. I don't carry a grudge and I get back to a normal relationship right away."

"Sometimes," one of his old Baltimore players said, "Don didn't realize that when he got on a guy, that man might not get over it as fast as a Tom Matte could. But he really worked on this and tried to get a good reading on everyone."

Shula often picks his spots. He has come in to a Tuesday film session following a loss and with all of his players expecting a good chewing out, has been calm, totally rational, and understanding in his critiques. Then there are times when he's come to the film sessions following a big victory and the players wonder whether they really won the game.

"It was his way of handling a successful team," says former Baltimore guard Dan

Sullivan, who played for Shula through Shula's career with the Colts. "A basic part of his philosophy is to go with what he feels is the best approach to maintain the highest level of accomplishment."

If there is something that Shula often is short of it is patience . . . but only when he feels a player is not working to improve himself. In Shula's book that is a player who continually suffers mental lapses, hence does not care, hence deserves no patient treatment.

"His attitude always seemed to be," says Bob Vogel, who also began with Shula at Baltimore in 1963, 'Why should I care more about you than you do?' He could be a very patient guy as long as he felt the player he was working with wanted to improve."

Shula gave a lot to the game, as a player and a coach, and he feels those who work for him should be just as dedicated and reflect this dedication.

"It disgusted him to see a player waste his talent," Charlie Winner says. "He produces winning teams because he is able to get everyone to go along with this feeling. The ones who don't aren't there."

In this regard, his assistants say that he demands more of a young player than any other coach . . . and he gets it earlier than other coaches do from their young players. He'll often show impatience with his assistant coaches who may tend to coddle a player.

"That player has the ability and should be able to do it," he will tell them in no uncertain terms. "You're giving him a chance to use being a rookie as an excuse for not progressing."

There were many who chortled in 1975 about Shula's alleged short fuse and short supply of patience when it came time to reassemble the Dolphins without Csonka, Jim Kiick, and Paul Warfield. They saw Shula frustrated because he no longer had the ball control of Csonka or the instant long-strike capability of Warfield.

"He never changed a lick," Evans says. "I guess he surprised a lot of people, maybe even some on our team but he had everything under control. He took a very statistical approach in that the team would do more throwing than it had the previous five years.

"He was very patient as he went about putting this new style into action. He never felt his offense would suffer that much because he had his line still intact and that is what really made us go in the past.

"We still were trying to polish this new approach after the season began but Shula never got impatient that we weren't fully tuned up. We knew he's never been known for his patience but then that wasn't the big thing because he does the job and tells his players to do the same thing. He's not as volatile or angry as he is quiet."

Regardless of what he is, Shula has, for all of his temper and impatience, the faculty of reaching his players and getting the most from them. This motivation technique is a combination of many things tempered through the years as a player and a coach.

In his term under Wilson at Detroit, Shula gained his insight into the subject of motivation. He and Wilson both were former players and they used this experience in relating to those who worked for them. Everything a player did, thought about doing, or tried to get away with was something they had tried during their playing careers. They knew all the tricks and shortcuts. Shula and Wilson could not be fooled.

"Wilson's way of handling his team tied in more with my personality," Shula says. "There was no way either of us could have taken a straight-laced approach to our relationships with the players after having played the game. As a head coach, you just can't go into a job with the idea that you can ignore these things.

"I let them know that I knew what was going on, what they were thinking and all the little tricks that would be tried. I established a relationship with them based on that premise. Yet in the final analysis I made it damn clear that I would call the shots and make all the decisions."

That was after he became a head coach. In his first pro job as an assistant with the Lions, he was concerned at the start about his acceptance by players who, in some cases, were older than he was (30) and, in others, much more talented than he had been. The defensive backs were his responsibility. Shula admits the Lions' defensive backs gave him a complete check-out, sitting back rather smugly at the meetings and tossing some tricky questions to see if he knew what he was talking about.

He did. And from then on, he had no problems.

Shula still has no problems and not solely because he is the head coach. The players of the seventies are no different than those of the late fifties or early sixties in that all of them basically want to win and want to do the most with their ability. Length of hair, dress style, and even personal style do not shade that basic desire.

"One of the first lessons any head or assistant coach learns is to get rid of guys who don't feel that way," he says. "Get rid of him in a hurry because he's a loser. You learn the sooner you can differentiate between winners and losers the better off you'll be.

"A lot of coaches have a tendency to stay too long with people with potential. We call them coach killers. As soon as you find out who the coach killers are on your team, the better off you are. You go with the guys who may have lesser talent but more dedication, more singleness of purpose . . . guys like Howard Twilley and Ray Berry. You spot them and stick with them because in a big game they'll win it for you.

"Guys like Berry and Twilley will never cause you to make a wrong decision. On the other hand, there's a tendency to spot a guy with potential and think you can bring him along. You wind up getting rid of a player who may be good but not quite as spectacular. This is what hurts a coach. I've always tried to avoid that situation, to go with the proven guy and make the other guy prove to me he has what it takes."

This approach alleviates a lot of motivation problems. So does his approach of having his team totally prepared, a lesson he brought from his time with Paul Brown. That is the confidence-building technique because a game, he says, often hinges on four or five plays. If a team can make those plays go its way, it can win. The edge is total preparation.

A good example during the first half of the 1975 season was an interception by free safety Jake Scott in a Dolphins' game against the Buffalo Bills. The Bills were leading 30–28 in the final minutes when Scott stepped in front of receiver J. D. Hill and stole the ball at Buffalo's 22-yard line.

"I think Scott read the play," Hill said afterward. "I made my move and the ball was right where I figured it would be. But Scott was there, too, and that was it."

"We had worked on that pattern during the week," Scott replied. "We felt we knew what Buffalo would do when it got into a tight spot. It is Shula's way to totally prepare us so that when the time comes and you need to make a big play, you can do it."

A few plays later Don Nottingham scored a touchdown and Miami had a 35–30 victory.

Many remember punter Larry Seiple running for a crucial first down to help break open the 1972 playoff game against Pittsburgh. Shula had alerted him to be aware of the Steelers' desire to set up good returns and their sometimes short-shrift in pressuring a punter. A great play by Seiple, everyone said, but one he was prepared to make.

Shula has another way of motivating his players: reward. He finds a way to make his men feel appreciated. He did this at Baltimore by naming Alex Hawkins as a captain of the Colts' special teams. He remembered the number of kicks he had covered as a player and the importance of that element in determining a game.

"I put the same demands on the special teams that I put on the offense and defensive units," he says. "Making Hawkins a captain evolved from that by putting the importance on the people who really have no identities on a football field, getting them to feel just as important as the guy who caught the pass or the guy who threw it.

"We used to show the kicking reel to the entire squad and it meant a great deal to the last guy on the roster to have Unitas say, 'Hey, nice block, nice tackle,' or to have Marchetti say, 'Nice going kid.' This upgraded our whole team spirit and team effort."

In other motivation areas, Shula is not known for any stirring pep talks. Sometimes he won't say a thing before a game; other times he says exactly what is on his mind. If he's upset, his players find out. It's not always the "here-he-goes-again" routine.

"My motivation comes from portraying as honestly as I can what they're going to be faced with, what's happened to other teams in similar situations, whether they've succeeded or failed," he says. "I just make the players look at things around them—the obvious factors—and I use that as a tool."

The ultimate motivation is competition and he quite simply asks, "How can you prove you're not the best unless you have competition?" In other words, unless each player competes to his unmost, then he never really will know how good he is. And once Shula gets this idea working—as he has done in Baltimore and Miami—then winning breeds motivation.

Shula is the ultimate competitor. He knows that his players, like all NFL players, have been weaned in athletics the same way. His own leadership capacity has been successful in drawing that from his team, a capacity that those close to the Dolphins say is reflected in a strong masculine image he has with his players. "They may not all like him," one says, "but they certainly respect the hell out of him."

There are many who see a certain arrogance in his bearing that, blended with his record of success, breeds this respect. He adds to it a great desire, his demand for perfection, and his willingness to work to any end to achieve it. He is not a dictator in the harsh sense but in Miami there is but one way . . . the Shula way.

"Don't get me wrong," Shula says. "If I see something that can be successful and even if it's not my style, I'll investigate it a little further. If it looks worthwhile I might incorporate it. I'm not so hardheaded as to ignore something just because it might be a little different than what I'm doing."

That is the mark of Shula the individualist. He's the same coach who once brought writers up short by his unstinting praise of Van Brocklin. When one expressed disbelief that Shula could hold such a minority opinion, Don snapped, "I'm proud of my friendship and association with Norm. I don't follow mass opinions. I make my own judgments of people."

After a 1974 Miami victory in New York over the Jets, Shula was beginning his postgame press conference but found he could not be heard because a bricklayer was busily tapping stones into place.

The man sensed the general hostility around him and bristled, "I'm not going no place," he said quite emphatically. "I'm working here."

Shula merely shrugged and moved the press conference several hundred feet down a corridor. "I'm on that guy's side," he said. "That could be me mixing mud. I used to work as a hod carrier myself between high school terms."

Don Shula understands . . . himself and other people.

"You've got to be yourself," he says. "A player will sense immediately if you're trying to be someone else. But if he knows you're sincere he's a lot more apt to go along with the things you're asking him to do. That's motivation right there.

"I've always made it a practice that anytime one of my players has anything on his mind in the way of a coach-player relationship, or vice versa, we can sit down and talk about it. If we can get it ironed out, fine. If we can't, then I can present my side so he knows what I'm doing and why I'm doing it. That way you can at least keep open the lines of communication.

"The worst thing that can happen is to simply make a decision and throw it at the player. Then he goes back to the locker room and starts talking to the player next to him. That's where dissension starts and that's what you work to prevent."

He simply tries to treat players the way he would have liked being treated when he played. That means he doesn't get involved in styles . . . hair, clothing, or life (as long as the latter is compatible with the player's overall health and well-being).

"The key word is moderation," he says. "I don't mind long hair if it isn't so long that it might cause an infection from, say, being rubbed raw by a chin-strap. But I'll draw the line the minute a player begins to think more about the way he looks than the way he plays."

Schnellenberger says Shula can carry this off quite neatly because he deals from the position of success and a winning team has the inclination to want to keep winning. All his rules are observed; all of his tantrums accepted; all of his demands adhered to . . . because they have helped produce a winner.

"What is overlooked in all of Don's player relationships," Schnellenberger says, "is the great asset he has of coming on with a straight-forward approach with everyone. If he sees a veteran making a mistake, he doesn't hesitate to call the shot on him. And he'll do it before the entire squad. Something like that could cause agitation but he's so consistent in the way he handles these matters that could-be problems are short-circuited immediately.

"Players always know where they stand. He doesn't mince words and he doesn't try to make you feel good. He is honest with the players, his coaches, and himself and this has created a healthy situation. When his players have a gripe, they're not afraid to come to him and sound off about it. He encourages it and once that is done if they still don't agree and it comes out publicly, he'll acknowledge their privilege to speak out."

To Shula, this is the most natural relationship a coach and player can have. It all stems from his own playing days when he admits he "was somewhat of a hell-raiser so I understand hell-raisers."

He was that. Some of his old Baltimore teammates recall the night he was among a group that borrowed a vacant taxi in order to make it to training camp for bed check. They also remember he took second place to no one during a night on the town and how one night he put away a heckler in the parking lot of one of his favorite watering spots.

"On Sundays I lined up and did the job to the best of my ability," he says. "All I ask of my players is the same thing, that they work hard in meetings and at practice. Whatever else comes, that's fine. Whatever other fun they have, that's fine, too. The more spirit you have on your team the better it will be."

Shula learned from some early mistakes he made at Baltimore. There were instances when he tried to get too close to his players and it hurt him. He still remembers Matte with great affection, a lovable guy with a great personality. Don found him amusing and used to laugh and joke and make light of some of things he did. With others not of the same personality, he remained aloof and strict with his rules.

"It got back to me that I favored Matte," he recalls. "Looking back I probably did but with the personality he had, I related more to him than those other players. You can't get into situations like that. And if you find it happening, you've got to pull away. It is a rule that I've followed strictly since coming to the Dolphins."

That's more often easier said than done but it is one of the drawbacks to being the head coach. No coach, Shula included, ever has been perfect in this regard. Red Auerbach, the toughminded former coach of the Boston Celtics who worked with some of the greatest basketball players ever, admitted he had the reputation for being a dogged coach. But he found it impossible to treat everyone equally and retired from coaching "when I mellowed and found it tough for me to be an s.o.b. and still be a good coach." Shula can understand that.

"Although you have a set of rules and regulations that encompass everyone you're responsible for, within those rules and regulations you deal with forty-three or forty-seven different personalities," he says. "To me, the secret of coaching is getting inside everyone of those different personalities and being able to extract the utmost of their ability.

"You kick some in the butt, praise others, continue to harass a third group. They're all different and you've got to realize this. You must analyze it and be able to take the necessary steps to get it all out of them, by whatever means will work best.

"Kiddingly I say to our guys when I might do something lenient or unexpected, 'I better be careful because I don't want to destroy the reputation I have.' They laugh and tell me, 'Don't worry coach. You won't.'"

It was not exactly the same approach he used when he became head coach of the Colts. He did not portray himself as something he still was not . . . a sage coach with all the answers. For one reason, some of the Colts had been his teammates. For another, he simply did not know all the answers but decided to work with his new team in trying to find them.

He hired Marchetti and Bill Pellington as player-coaches. This established a good controlling element between himself and the team because they were two of its leaders. They also were top-flight players and wound up becoming good teachers.

Shula then decided to carry on the same football system instituted by Ewbank, making only minor changes he felt would better suit a combination of newer and older players. He often has said it was easier for one man—himself—to adapt to 40 others than to have it the other way around.

"The Colts still had the old Browns' system, the same one I was brought up on," Shula says. "Rather than go in and try to force them to accept the Lions' system, which really was the Chicago Bears' system and one which I really wasn't sold on, I went back and did things the way they did and the way I was brought up."

Players then at Baltimore remember him coming with solid support from the veteran players and establishing himself immediately as boss. He also began his own system of revitalizing a team that many had called too old. He called in some of the older players and told them they could play until someone took away their job.

"That helped him get some good years from those guys," one of his former Colts' players said. "It means a lot to know you have a job and not see it go automatically to some number one draft pick.

Shula underwent some superb training in player relations at Baltimore. On one side he had such people as Unitas, Marchetti, Pellington, Berry, and other veterans who had twice been on NFL championship teams. On the other, he had the younger players who were to form the nucleus of the Colts' championship teams in the late sixties.

He had a more relaxed attitude with his older players and didn't try the hard-nosed approach he used in later years because of his unique relationship of having played with or against them. At the same time, he let everyone know the difference between a player and a coach. He was approachable, his former players agree, but never to the point of becoming too familiar. He'd give an extra chance to the jokester but with the more serious person, he'd be very impatient.

His relations with Unitas never were overly warm. Both were from the same mold and both could be abrasive at times. Unitas wanted to run his own game and Shula bridled a bit because he could not exert the control he wished. Though Don accepted Unitas's ability and leadership, it bothered him to lease some of the power he felt belonged to the head coach.

"You don't see that in Miami," one of those Colts says. "Bob Griese is totally controlled by Shula in that Don calls the shots and Bob goes along with his program. They've got a great working relationship and the results are very apparent."

The Colts of those days recall Shula and Unitas taking occasional verbal and psychological shots at one another. There never was any outward turmoil but when the two were miffed at each other, everyone could sense it. Often, at film sessions, Shula might comment about such-and-such a play not really being right for the situation at the time. Then in a future film session, Unitas might make note of that same play not working and adding his reference "though some people really like it."

Shula showed Unitas no special treatment, though he did defer to him as a general rule. He seemed to sense that Unitas did not function well if he was put on a rigid plan or under a set of restrictions.

"It could have gotten into a contest of who is boss," one player notes, "but Don did what he felt was best for everyone."

Sometimes it got touchy. In a 1969 game against the 49ers, Shula replaced him during a particularly rough afternoon. Unitas was upset but Shula did not flinch.

"I can understand his feelings," he said at the time. "He's been great for so long. But I didn't think John was throwing anywhere near the way he should. It was my decision to make."

When the Colts played in Super Bowl III, Unitas also voiced the opinion that he should be returned to the starting job as quarterback, even though Earl Morrall had led the team to 13 victories and through two decisive playoff wins, while also being acclaimed the NFL's most valuable player. Shula said no.

"It was not a tough decision because John never did anything that season that would have justified my telling him 'yes,'" Shula says. "We had the same situation in Super Bowl VII, where Earl had replaced Griese early in the season and led us through most of our unbeaten season.

"But Griese was coming along as we got to the playoffs and it was evident that he was razor-sharp. When Earl did falter toward the end of the season, I had no hesitation going to Bob.

"Before Super Bowl III, John Unitas did nothing in practice to indicate that he was going to step in and throw the ball and become the Unitas of old. So I stuck with Earl, maybe a bit longer than I should have in that game. Still, when Unitas took over he had plenty of opportunity to win the ball game but he didn't. I felt I made the decision I had to make."

The next season, when both quarterbacks went to camp, there was speculation that Unitas still might be number two. But Shula let them fight it out in the preseason and Unitas won the job. Later that same season with the team alternately winning and losing, he went back to Morrall as his number one quarterback.

"But you'll notice he wasn't so rigid in his approach that with seven minutes to play in a game against the Bears, he didn't turn to Unitas and let him bail out the team," one of the Colts remembers.

One of Shula's strong points as a coach is his ability to make the tough decision and not care about the reaction. His Miami players saw that side of him during the 1970 season. The team had won four of its first five games, then lost three straight. In that third loss, against Philadelphia, Shula replaced Griese with John Stofa. The number two quarterback threw two touchdown passes and just missed pulling out a victory in a 21–14 loss.

"I knew right away the questions would come, 'Will Stofa be the quarterback next week?'" Shula remembers. "The fans were down on Griese, even though a lot of his problems were our fault what with a new system and not enough time to master it.

"To the fan, it seemed like a simple decision. But having watched Griese and Stofa right from training camp, there was no doubt in my mind that Bob had to be our leader and that it was just a temporary thing with Stofa. I had to face that right away and it came about on the plane coming home from Philadelphia.

"I went back in the players' section of the aircraft and talked to Stofa. I told him that a lot of people were going to be wondering who I would start in the next game and I told him I would start Griese.

"'You did a helluva job,' I told him, 'but Bob is a fine quarterback and our future rests more with him so I'm going back to him.'

"The result was that I stopped dissension or agitation before it happened by not letting the papers speculate all week and waiting until the last minute to make the decision, and then having Stofa upset. I'd much rather have an upset Stofa on Sunday night than I would before the next ball game."

Shula says a move like that is instinctive with him. If he had thought about what the newspapers would say and listened to other speculative conversation, then he would have had to assume a cunning, conniving stance which is outside his nature.

"I do what I think is right and accept the results," he says flatly. "If you try to plan too many things you wind up getting out-finessed. The leader must call the shots and he must accept whatever consequences result. A lot of times those shots aren't popular but the thing I've found is that you must sit down with a guy, eyeball-to-eyeball, tell him what you're doing and why you're doing it.

"Even though he doesn't accept it, even though it might affect him in a negative way, he'll wind up respecting you and even talking to you later on and praising you for doing it.

"That's how I do it . . . tell him face-to-face, tell him why, listen to anything he might have to say, and still make the decision that is best for the team."

Many coaches are unemployed because they couldn't make the tough decision, or say "no," or worried more about being popular with their players. Shula has no patience with this approach, primarily because it doesn't fit his nature. He says he is honest, "maybe to a fault." He absolutely cannot finesse anybody nor does he lie when dealing with his players.

"The moment I even tried such a thing I'd light up," he says. "People could tell right away that Shula wasn't being straight. I never worked to be that way. My approach is head-on, straightforward, honest, let the chips fall where they may. That's the only way I can do business. I simply don't have what it takes to be shrewd and calculating. It's not in me and people sense it. I know it's not me because as soon as I ever have started such an approach I get flustered."

That is one way Shula keeps command of his forces. He's not averse to using a little administrative muscle either, nor will he hesitate to bring down his will on anyone he feels is usurping privileges which hurt him and the team. Former Colts remember one of their starters challenging an assistant coach immediately after a road game, continuing the diatribe on the bus to the airport, and on the plane home. The coach in question was very upset and made Shula aware of the situation.

The next day, Shula got rid of the player though he was a starter. He told the team, "We must protect our coaches. I don't mind a guy having a temper so long as he can get over something. I don't like it being carried so long. I have a temper and I'm able to get over things."

Then there was the Mercury Morris incident following the Dolphins' loss in Super Bowl VI. Morris sounded off immediately after the game about not being used much and, he claimed, it was to the detriment of the team. Shula sat on him the next day, even before the Dolphins boarded their plane to return home.

"I thought Merc was out of line sounding off to the media before sounding off to me first," he says. "I let him know during a discussion in my hotel room how I felt about it and he had no illusions about my feelings when we were finished.

"The big thing here is that I don't object to any of my players saying what they feel, as long as they say it to me first and we try and get it ironed out. If we don't get it ironed out, then they can say it to anyone they want. At that time, I felt Merc was looking for sympathy by doing what he did. I didn't hold it against him and even though he objected to what I said and might have had a legitimate complaint, I still was going to give him the opportunity to win a starting job.

"I reminded him that he had missed our first two training camps and told him that if he got a full camp under his belt going head-to-head with Jim Kiick, I felt he could win the job. If he didn't win, then he'd continue to be a part-time guy. So he went head-to-head with Kiick the next summer and there wasn't any question that Merc won hands down.

"But I wasn't giving in to Morris. I was giving him the opportunity he deserved to win a job."

Shula later had other run-ins with Morris, suspending him once. But Shula never let those disciplinary encounters cloud his judgment. Morris always returned, did things Shula's way, and would reclaim his starting job because he was forced to earn it. The lesson was not lost on the other Dolphins.

The consensus at both Baltimore and Miami is that his treatment of players is top-grade. Vogel, for example, recalls when one of his children was born with a birth defect while training camp was in progress. Shula told him to get his family situation straightened out, then worry about football.

244

This is the side of Shula that those outside his football orbit rarely see. Buoniconti claims that Shula took that basic love of family and transmitted it to his players "and made us into a family." Shula prides himself on being able to relate this way, to see the "other side" of a player's being. Those around him say he strives to treat his players the way he wanted to be treated; that he still remembers how he felt being benched without explanation by Paul Brown; that he remembers how he felt being summarily traded and later being cut.

Bill Curry, who played center for him at Baltimore, and who also played for Vince Lombardi at Green Bay, says that unlike Lombardi, Shula "inspires" a player. He does not intimidate; he lives and dies with a player.

Garo Yepremian, the Cypriot-born placekicker of the Dolphins, says that Shula is "the kind of guy who knows when to pat you on the back and when to put you down. Even if I miss a kick he says, 'Keep your head up. You'll get the next one.'"

This sort of credibility was built from the first day Shula faced his Miami players just as he built it in Baltimore from the first day. At Miami, he sold his team on the notion that hard work paid off in success and when the Dolphins won four games in the pre-season, they bought the idea.

"Our theme has been that hard work equals success," Shula says. "We haven't done it with magic or with better plays or anything like that. It's been team involvement, the team concept of offense and defense, and the willingness to do the work to get the club ready to play."

All of this has caused some to observe that Shula's relationship with his players is more like friend-to-friend rather than coach-to-player. Both sides make their points, either through humor or other human subtleties, or in Shula's case, through his own form of control. But there is a fragile balance here, one almost eggshell thin and both are particularly careful not to say or do anything that would fracture it.

One of the closest times it came to being fractured was after publication of a book written by Csonka and Kiick. Csonka had accused Shula of acting from spite in playing Morris ahead of Kiick because Jim had not finished the mandatory 12-minute, two-mile run at the beginning of training camp. Shula was hurt by the accusation but he followed his own rule and discussed the situation with Csonka.

"Larry told me that what he meant was that I made the decision that day [of the run] out of spite by bringing Mercury up with the first unit," Shula remembers. "That may or may not be true. I don't remember. But my decision to play Mercury during that [1972] season certainly wasn't made out of spite.

"I was very upset by that reference, especially coming from Csonka, who I had a great deal of respect for. His even thinking that of me, if he did . . . well, then there's no way he or I could even have a relationship. But we sat down and talked it out."

The heart of any coach's success is in his player relationships and it is interesting to look at how Shula's current Dolphins' team views him and the general impression he left at Baltimore. At Miami, the players who were with the Dolphins when he came seem to be forever grateful for him showing them the way to win.

"Before he came," Kiick now says, "I was just a football player. I ran here and caught passes there. I used to run right into the defensive coverage but he taught me how to read them. He helped me become a better player and to know what it takes to be a winner. When you've been a loser, that's a great thing."

Twilley sees Shula as a superb technician "but what makes him a great coach is his ability to size up a situation and get his players ready to handle it."

Arnsparger sees a different side of him.

"Don is great because of the decisions he has made," his former assistant says. "And the decisions he has made have been based on his religion. I know that everybody's religion affects them in everything they do. But it's much more true in Don Shula's case than most. His faith has made him the tremendous man he is. And although some people consider him very gruff and a hollerer, he is a warm man. I think it all goes back to the same thing with Don: his religion, his faith in God."

The Colts' players on the other hand, while speaking highly of him as a coach, felt he often allowed his ego to show through. One of them remembers the team's only loss in 1968 against Cleveland, and then a rebound victory the following week. After the win, the players made mention of a player meeting after the loss to the Browns and the media played it as the reason for the big victory. Shula called in his team captains and was upset. He said it was the best game the Colts had played and asked what right did they have to say that it was a meeting that was responsible for the win.

He also took a lot of credit for the Colts' success, some of his former players claim, and that bothered them, too. It also galled him to lose to the Packers during Lombardi's term in Green Bay (in seven of ten games) because it indicated that Lombardi was the better coach.

All of which goes to show that Shula, like all of us, is human. It is the mark of all successful coaches that they flaunt a certain ego, perhaps a deserved foible considering the price they must pay for their success and the pressures they must endure while achieving it.

They—and this certainly includes Shula—also must have other qualities to complement their human relationships. The least of these must be organizing their work and their workers and accumulating the best possible people to suit their philosophy.

It is one of those areas, talent appraisal, where Shula is particularly strong. Not only has he been careful to weed out the "coach-killers" but he has evolved the proper solutions to what were his potential problems. Take Csonka, for example.

A top draft pick from Syracuse in 1968, Csonka had not done much in his first two seasons at Miami. Three months after becoming head coach, Shula told Csonka to lose 15 pounds, down to 235.

"But I haven't been that light since high school," Csonka protested.

"You'll function better at that weight," Shula told him.

Shula then told guard Larry Little to drop 20 pounds to 265. Both Csonka and Little followed orders and within two seasons, both were tops at their positions.

Then there is Griese. Maybe it is the relationship that Shula was able to command from the start but the coach is unstinting in his praise of the Dolphins' quarterback, being careful at the same time not to bruise the reputations of either Unitas or Morrall. What he really admired was Griese's willingness to sublimate his role as a passer to the Dolphins' philosophy of becoming a running team during Csonka's five seasons with Shula.

"Remember two things," an opposing coach says. "Csonka wasn't much until Shula went down to Miami, but Shula saw what Griese could do for his offense and he got him to do it. Next, he convinced Griese that this was how the team could win and Bob functioned superbly within this philosophy."

Shula agrees.

"I can honestly say that Bob doesn't care whether he completes one of two passes for twelve yards or twenty-four of thirty-five for three hundred and fifty. All that matters is whether we have won. A lot of guys say that, but with Griese it is a fact."

Griese also works hard. This is another quality that has encouraged Shula's admiration. The quarterback goes about his preparation with the same organized approach as his coach, allowing a certain amount to be assimilated each day until he has covered everything the Dolphins will employ in a game. He is an inveterate film watcher, stopping by Shula's office every day to get different reels of an upcoming opponent.

"I seldom have to suggest anything to Griese," Shula says. "He usually has already thought of it himself. That's why on Sunday afternoon he always knows what we should do. Since he's human, he doesn't always execute it. But I like his percentage of chance."

What Shula has helped develop is a quarterback he considers "the best-rounded of all quarterbacks." Shula watched Griese work hard to develop a long passing game after coming to the NFL with an exceptional short passing game. Griese has total understanding of both the running and passing philosophy, something that surfaced in 1975 when the Dolphins were immediately successful without Csonka.

What Shula quickly saw with Griese was a total unselfishness to succeed, coupled with great overall knowledge of his position. It was the first time Shula ever had to help a quarterback develop, since he worked with the established Unitas and Morrall at Baltimore. The results only have strengthened his reputation as a coach who can extract the most from a talented player.

Those who work for him say that once he is sure of someone like Csonka and Griese, he will work them into his own particular knowledge of the game and, once proven successful, will not defer to anyone when it comes to theory or practical application. He may not be the absolute technician but he knows where everyone should be and what they should be doing.

Shula is a bit like Griese in that he did not know that much about offense when he became a head coach at Baltimore, wasn't afraid to admit it, then worked hard to overcome that obstacle. It wasn't too long, his former Colts' players say, before he knew the offense better than anyone and he would stand in the middle of the practice field and pick up mistakes when the offense and defense were working at opposite ends.

"I played under some of the best coaches in pro football," Stofa says, "people like

George Wilson, Paul Brown, and John Ralston. But none of them knows as much about *both* sides of the game as Shula does."

Morrall says Shula's mind is a neat storehouse of football knowledge. He doesn't muddle a quarterback's mind with unnecessary information, gives him a sound game plan and stays with it. When he does make changes, they are solid and workable.

Ted Hendricks, the linebacker who began his NFL career under Shula at Baltimore, calls him "a football genius . . . absolutely brilliant. He knows weaknesses and strengths. He can look over a team and tell you in a split second what will work against a certain defense and what will stop that team's attack."

With this knowledge goes demands on his players—in the off-season and in training camp. He demands that his players be ready for contact immediately in camp. It is not unusual for the second day of practice in a Shula training camp to feature some live hitting. He believes in being aggressive; he was an aggressive player and he weeds out the players who are not.

"Everyone gets their shots," his players say. "He'll match up the defensive backs against the wide receivers, offensive linemen against defensive linemen, running backs against linebackers. No one is missed and he does it knowing that players, particularly veterans, could get injured early."

At the same time, he does not kill off his squad during the long series of preseason games by subjecting it to an all-out, win-at-any-cost attitude. He goes into these games with a predetermined time for playing each man and holds to it . . . even if he happens to be losing and the temptation to win presents itself.

Experience has helped Shula develop the delicate balance of playing everyone, getting his team in shape, evaluating his talent, and still developing a winning momentum that has enabled his teams to make impressive openings to regular season competition. His system of preparation accounts for a good part of this; so, of course, does his playing talent.

His training camps, while demanding, are not excruciating. He doesn't make a bed check every night and when he does, it is not always at the same time. His players say he always seems to know when to check and when not to; in other words, there are never checks when Shula feels they need a little break. It stems, they say, from his own time as a player when he used to make occasional forays after bed check.

This relationship with the players carries over to his relationships with his assistant coaches. He treats them all as head coaches of their own particular specialty. When Arnsparger was in charge of his defense at Miami, Shula gave him the unique title of "assistant head coach."

Shula gives his assistants a great deal of voice in meetings and plenty of responsibility on the field. He does not put himself apart from them, enjoying their company professionally as well as socially. In the latter regard, there is not a heavy social relationship but everyone gets together a couple of times a year and often, after a Dolphins' home game, the coaches and their wives may have dinner together.

"I try to treat them the way I enjoy being treated, the way George Wilson treated us in Detroit," Shula says. "That's the way I am and how I treat people. Paul Brown was standoffish with his coaches but that was his way. I liked Wilson's way of working with coaches."

During a work day, Shula and his coaches are a cohesive team. He elicits their opinions and listens when they offer ideas. "If I'm not listening and you still think your idea is worthwhile," he will say, "then keep talking to me about it. Sell me. Don't quit because I'm not interested the first time you present something."

Shula spends most of his time on the field with the offense but in the weekly planning sessions, is together with his defensive coaches. There is nothing his teams do on offense or defense that does not carry his approval.

Arnsparger and Schnellenberger both say that Shula's talent in working with assistant coaches is that he gives them a job to do, does not look over their shoulder while they function and makes it known that the assistant has an understanding of the game and he wants him to use it. His ability to listen and to encourage ideas from his coaches, regardless of their tenure, makes the working relationship comfortable and productive.

"He attracts people by his success," Schnellenberger says, "and is able to select those he wants. There is no one mold to those he has coaching for him. The only prerequisite besides talent is that you must be a guy who works and who produces. You don't see him firing many people because he always gets the guy he wants."

It is not happenstance that many men who worked for Shula once were associated with him at Kentucky, such as Arnsparger and Schnellenberger; or at Cleveland and Baltimore, such as Carl Taseff and Winner; or came from a Cleveland Browns' background such as John Sandusky, Monte Clark, Vince Costello, Mo Scarry, and Chuck Noll.

It was this inter-relationship that helped produce Miami's famed "53 defense" a few years ago. Arnsparger had first come on the idea while he was an assistant coach for Blanton Collier at Kentucky. Its origins were with Bear Bryant when he coached at Kentucky a few years before. Bryant had used what is a three-two defense to beat Bud Wilkinson's famed split-T offense in the 1951 Sugar Bowl. Almost two decades later, it gained greater recognition when Bob Matheson was inserted in the Miami defense as either a down lineman or a linebacker. The move was forced by an injury to one of Miami's defensive ends and Arnsparger brought out the concept from the three-two defense that was used at Kentucky.

"Matheson had been trained as a linebacker in college, had worked at that position when he played for the Browns, and then played for a year as a defensive end at Cleveland," Arnsparger remembers. "We got him after the Browns gave up on him as a middle linebacker and when we had to improvise because of injury, one move led to another.

"I was given credit for that defense but it was a product of our whole staff in Miami. The offensive coaches noted the problems it would cause and the more they talked about those problems, the more we worked to create them. This was the sort of inter-action Don encouraged all the time."

Shula's basic defensive philosophy is to prevent the cheap touchdown by either a long run or deep pass. Fast scores like that can demoralize a team quickly.

"We try to take away what our opponent likes," he explains. "On the run, we want to contain the sweep or attack the inside play. On the pass, we want to force the quarterback to throw to areas where we can react and attack the receiver when the ball is in the area.

"The zone coverage we use enables us to have an extra man at the point of attack on the run while at the same time our secondary defenders are moving to areas that protect us from the long gain. The ultimate objective is to create long yardage situations and thus dictate the choice of plays the offense will be restricted to."

It sounds so simple when Shula explains it but the key, he says, is to "play the ball." That means the defense must get a jump to where the quarterback is directing his attack so Shula puts great stress on carrying out responsibilities and thorough knowledge of what each player is doing within this concept.

With his offensive concepts he strives to get an opposing defense to hesitate, to force it to wait and look, and then become unsure of exactly what it is seeing. To create this confusion, the Dolphins continually mix their approach. They run the basic fullback power slant used by many teams as well as other running plays designed to provide power for both running backs.

But Shula mixes this basic power football with a wide assortment of cross-blocking, traps, pulling sweeps, false key plays, and influence plays. Many have felt the Dolphins simply go out and overpower a defense with sheer strength.

"Not true," Shula says. "We respect our opponents too much to feel we can just go out and knock them off the ball play after play. There's a time to go with straight blocking but there's also a time to come with other things."

In 1975, he revitalized his offense with more balance but the same philosophy still prevailed. The Dolphins still had the strength in their offensive line to control the game and Shula made up for the loss of Csonka's running by varying the points of his attack and also opening up his passing game. But it still was the running that made Griese's passing effective, a long-proven theory that Paul Brown used to such success during his glory years at Cleveland and which has been followed by every coach ever exposed to this philosophy.

His football strategies have helped his teams to enormous success in two cities. The mark of a truly great coach is not to win once or twice but to do it consistently. Shula has had his teams in the playoffs or contending for them in all but three seasons (all of those at Baltimore).

"My big job in 1963 was to restore confidence in a lot of still-great football players," he recalls. "I wanted them thinking they could win the whole thing again. At the same time I brought in some young guys and the fusion of the two elements worked perfectly.

"But before I get sold on a young player, he's got to show me he can help. Those are the ones who have that great willingness to help you on your kicking team and make it reckless and aggressive. That tells you more than anything about a player. Sooner or later, if a player is great on the special teams, then you know he will be a heckuva player for you."

In breeding this individual success and harnessing it into team success, the problems multiply in maintaining much more than a competitive or winning edge. After the Dolphins finished their perfect 1972 season by winning Super Bowl VII, Shula the realist took over. He knew it would be virtually impossible to go 17–0 again and he knew, too, that every opponent would fire itself up in an attempt to become the first to beat the Dolphins.

"We felt we could be ready for that if we realized that it would take more work to stay up there than it did to get there," he says. "I was especially concerned about the players saying, 'Well, are we going to have to go through all this stuff again? We've proved we can win so why do we have to go back to the fundamentals? Why do we have to adhere to this or that?'

"But I sold them on my original approach and they continued to do the same things we did in our first season. We didn't go unbeaten but we won the Super Bowl again and then found out what it really meant to be successful. Everything seemed to cave in, what with the World Football League defections, player demands, increased outside interests, and just being a ripe, juicy target of opportunity. The players did not have the hunger for success they had before that 1972 season."

There are some, Al Davis of the Oakland Raiders being the most notable, who say that only a hungry team can take Shula's methods. Once his team begins a string of successes, then it breaks down. Shula disagrees.

"In Miami, we were a young team that needed leadership," he says. "As soon as my staff and I established a plan and got that leadership, our players accepted it and never have questioned it. Each year we've been more demanding than the year before. This has not caused any great problems because the players enjoy what goes along with hard work and success. They enjoy being talked about as the best team ever and I think they realize how much they'd miss hearing it if we ever fell down."

It probably will not happen as long as Shula has his way. For one thing, Shula treats poorly played games the Dolphins manage to win as though the game had been a loss. He does not wring his hands or lament but takes all the negative points and tells his players that if they play that badly the next week, they most certainly *will* lose.

This was one of the chief reasons the Dolphins were unbeaten in 1972, a feat Shula never thought impossible because he came within one game in the 1968 regular season at Baltimore and still feels his team should have won that Super Bowl (against the New York Jets).

"At the beginning of the season you don't say to yourself, 'We can't win every football game,'" Shula says. "I believe you go out every day trying to win and every week trying to win."

But Shula sees a softer meaning to Lombardi's saying that winning was "the only thing."

"You set a goal to be the best and then you work hard every hour of every day, striving to reach that goal," he explains. "If you allow yourself to settle for anything less than number one then you are cheating yourself.

"I'm that way. I loved to compete against Lombardi and the most frustrating time in my life was when he won five games in a row against teams that I coached. He had me climbing the wall. But when the win finally did come against his football team, it made me feel just that much better.

"You've got to have a burning desire to compete and that's something that's in me. A couple of years ago I went out to Colorado and intended to ski only a couple of days. But I was out there every day, competing against those slopes, daring them to get the best of me.

"Was I mad? Not at all. Did I feel cheated if I fell? Not as long as I was skiing to the best of my ability. It's the same in football. We're in this game to win and that is how we should target every day we work at our job. I think that's really what Vinnie meant when he said winning was the only thing."

Shula also disagreed with Lombardi's preaching that a team must "hate" its opponent. To him the more respect he has for an opponent as an individual and as a player, the harder he will try to win. It is his idea that if you put an opponent on a pedestal and say what a fine human being, what a fine athlete he is, and then go out and beat him, then victory puts you above him.

"I respect and admire the people we get a chance to compete against and get that much more joy in winning," he says. "By admiring and respecting an opponent, I think you get a tremendous desire to whip them. In my mind, that's completely different from what Vince said."

It is ironic that Shula is thought of only in terms of success after having to live under the public glare as the coach who "couldn't win the big one." This was most prevalent after his Miami team lost to Dallas in Super Bowl VI, following the loss to the Jets three years earlier as well as previous losses in NFL playoff games against Cleveland and Green Bay.

Perhaps it was the final test of his mettle before his unbridled success or, perhaps it was the ultimate catalyst that drove him to forge that success. Whatever, much of his feeling toward shrugging off that tag was personal. He simply was tired of being referred to as the "only coach ever to lose two Super Bowls."

What was even more galling was the obvious lack of recognition for his team, which had beaten Kansas City in double overtime, then stunned the favored Colts in the AFC championship game.

"All I heard about was our loss to Dallas in the Super Bowl," he says. "That in itself was a great challenge to me and the team. We may have been young but we felt the frustration of losing because we knew we were capable of bigger and better things."

Then came 1972 and the perfect season. The Dolphins simply gathered steam, even after Griese was hurt and Morrall took over as quarterback. The ironic part, Shula notes, is that everyone became aware that no matter how many games the Dolphins won, nothing would count unless they won the Super Bowl, too.

"We went into that game sixteen and oh and even if we had played a team that was seven-seven in the regular season and lost, no one would have talked about our perfect record; only that the other team was champion and that we still couldn't win the big one," Shula says.

"That was the weirdest sensation in my life, knowing that sixteen-one was not good enough, that it had to be seventeen-oh. The victory took me off the hook as a coach and it established the Dolphins as an excellent football team."

Throughout that final week of preparation Shula was nagged by the imponderables —the bounce of the ball, an official's decision going against his team at the wrong time, or even that his team could come out flat and get buried by the Washington Redskins. And his former boss in Baltimore, Carroll Rosenbloom, didn't help matters by telling everyone that Shula had "choked" in previous title games.

Many people who have had long associations with Shula remember not so much the perfect season or the back-to-back Super Bowl victories but how Shula never allowed the Super Bowl losses to steer him off his course.

"That saved us," Arnsparger says. "We didn't think about the game as we moved through the season unbeaten. Each day we all knew what to expect, what to think about. We never had time to dwell on the winning streak. When we began preparing for Super Bowl VII, he kept things as low key as possible. He didn't seem to let the personal challenge affect the team. He just blotted out any distractions and kept everything in its proper perspective.

"Yet we knew that he was living for the day when he could silence his critics. That's only natural. I know the criticism bothered me though I was just an assistant. Yet he kept those feelings to himself and kept everything under such control. To us, he was no different in preparing for that game than he was for any other game."

It really is hard to know what Shula is like after he loses because it happens so infrequently . . . only 39 times in his first dozen seasons compared to 138 victories. He broods a bit but does not take out his frustration on his coaches or his players—at least not until he finds out the causes for the loss. Then, on Tuesdays, he has films to back up his statements.

Some of his old Baltimore players still remember the way it was on the Monday morning following their loss to the Jets in Super Bowl III. Shula looked as if he had not slept as he walked through the lobby of the team's hotel and out onto the beach at Fort Lauderdale. For the next three hours he just stared at the sea, lost in his thoughts. He prayed for direction, he reevaluated his coaching program, and he sought inner strength to cope with what he knew would be a very trying and exasperating time as that game was replayed and discussed.

Shula strives to keep winning and losing in a keen perspective. It is the same perspective he transmits to his team as it prepares week-by-week, one that is business-like and without emotional peaks. That, he says, is how his team maintains its consistency and can accept winning and losing without feeling a rocket ride to the moon or that the world has collapsed.

"When we win, we know it's not final," he says. "We know we've got to line up next week and prove ourselves all over again. If we lose, we also know we're not dead and we must get off the floor and have a chance to change the score the next time we play."

That is not to say that he doesn't set up a losing team. He shocked some early arriving writers at his team's dressing room after the Dolphins lost their first game of the 1970 season to the Patriots. Every word was audible and one writer noted, "None of them were pleasant."

Later that season, when Miami went into a tailspin, the harsh words were put aside and Shula went looking for the causes. There was a great deal of soul-searching among all the Dolphins and Shula says now "we all decided that we believed in each other and in the things we were trying to accomplish.

"The real decision was to stick with the things we had done. The easiest thing to do at a time like that is to make wholesale changes. For example, if our shortcomings had been a lack of individual capacity on Griese's part, I would have benched him.

"But there also was this to consider: If I had benched him, it might have ruined his career. Faith is a two-way street. If I want faith from the players, it's up to me to show faith in them."

That faith and that week of soul-searching after the New England loss were the key elements that helped the Dolphins turn the corner to success. Arnsparger says the team finally realized that if it did what Shula coached it to do, it had a chance to win. That meant it had to be able to come from behind, to be able to stop someone on the goal line, to score from far out, to make long marches.

That breakthrough had been preceded by Shula's determination to give his team the same approach he had used at Baltimore, based on a great deal of teaching. At the same time, he did not forcibly install the Colts' offensive or defensive system based solely on its past success. He wanted the team to seek its own identity and it wasn't until half-way through the 1970 season that he established the run-dominated offense. That's when Csonka, Little, Norm Evans, Marv Fleming, and the rest of the offense proved it could best handle that approach.

"There was no question that some good talent was at Miami when I got there," he says. "But it needed help to be put together. It needed leadership. Some moves we made those first couple of years got our whole offensive line off the waiver lists with the exception of Norm Evans.

"But there still was a job that had to be done with this team, no matter what anyone says. It had been three-ten-and-one the year before and it never had been a winner. Whether somebody else could have come in and done the same job . . . who knows?"

The answer to that question could only be found in a coach who used the same approach as Shula. That man would have had to match the staff that Don put goether, then arrive at the same talent evaluations after hours of film watching, and finally be successful in convincing the players to make the changes.

"Many of our good players turned out to be better than we thought," Shula says. "People such as Manny Fernandez, Csonka, Kiick, Norm Evans, and others. We doubted, for example, whether Evans could do it at right tackle because he had gotten beaten too often the previous season to even play in the National Football League. Monte Clark, our offensive line coach, got him squared away. Now Norm is an all-pro."

"All-pro" means the best and that was the goal Shula set for his team right from the start.

"Getting in the playoffs was our first goal," he says. "And making it the first year might have been an achievement for most teams but for us it was a frustration because we didn't beat Oakland. But the players told me something about themselves because they were just as unhappy as I."

From 1970 to now, Shula has great pride in his team's accomplishments, particularly in his declaration that they have been done "the right way." That means he's won strictly by the rules of play, no shadings, no tricks.

"Some clubs want to win so much they'll do anything to get it," he says with a touch of disgust. "Our approach has been just the opposite. We've tried to do things the right way.

"And the right way are the rules and regulations and they are precisely what we go by. I may not like all of them . . . I certainly did not agree with the league making eight rules changes before the 1974 season . . . but once they are in, then we play by them."

That philosophy has been the essence of Shula's life, a life he says he's tried to work out in stages. Viewing it from where he now stands, Shula shakes his head in some form of amazement, noting that he could have been out of football long ago had he stayed just one more year in any of his three assistant coaching jobs.

The year after he left Virginia to join Blanton Collier at Kentucky, the entire Cavaliers' staff was fired. The year after he left Collier to go to the Lions, Blanton and his staff were fired. The year after he took the head job at Baltimore, George Wilson and his staff were let go at Detroit.

What he has achieved now, he says, "is everything I ever dreamed of, everything I ever wanted."

There is little doubt that the Xs and Os have fallen into place in fine style during Shula's NFL coaching career but to Shula there is not one particular element he ranks above another in fathoming that success. Rather, he sees it in a combination of things, foremost being credibility and communication throughout his organization.

"To have leadership, you must have both," he says. "Any time you shut off the avenues of communication you're going to lose the people you're responsible for. If your credibility is ever questioned or challenged or lost, you're going to lose your ability to lead.

"You've got to leave open the door so a player can come in and feel he can sit down and communicate. Occasionally I've gone along with what a player wants. Most of all, I'm not dictatorial. I don't say, 'This is the only way things can be done, period.' I'm willing to answer the 'why' question.

"The last point is important because it's the big difference in people today as opposed to when I first began coaching. The players of today ask more questions and I've found that answering the 'why' has made me a better coach, a better person, even a better father. It makes me think."